"*A God Named Josh* is a rich and compelling book, perfect for those both unfamiliar and overfamiliar with the story of Jesus."

—Mark Sayers, author of *Reappearing Church* and *A Non-Anxious Presence*

"*A God Named Josh* is absolutely fascinating. Modern, engaging, and relevant, even for those with little or no theological background."

—Jago Silver, illustrator of *The Jesus Storybook Bible*

"Wow! What a refreshing book! The same wonderful story, the same incredible Savior, the same good news . . . but written with such clarity that everything you thought you knew about Jesus will seem new and exciting. Read this book and give it to all your friends."

—Steve Brown, founder of *Key Life* and author of *Laughter and Lament*

"Too many people set aside the fact that Jesus was not only fully God but fully human. Jared Brock sets nothing aside! You will close this book with a far greater appreciation for who Jesus was and how He still impacts our lives today."

—Ken Davis, Christian comedian and author of *Fully Alive*

"This book feels fresh and different—it has something for those familiar with the idea of Jesus as well as those starting from zero. It will inform, challenge, and amuse those who read it; it will also invite you to come closer to its subject."

Clive Orchard, Team Leader at Ffald y Brenin Christian Retreat Center

"You know when you have a piece of art on the wall for years and then one day you actually notice it? *A God Named Josh* is like that, but for the life of Jesus. Even if you were raised in the church, you probably didn't learn 95 percent of what's in this book."

—Dave McSporran, producer of THIS IS ME TV

"Jared's attention-grabbing biography of Jesus is accessible, thoughtful, and fun. *A God Named Josh* will prove greatly engaging for those who know next to nothing about Jesus, and it might surprise lifelong Christians as well."

—Vicar Christopher Frost, Christian filmmaker and YouTuber

"Having worked for more than two decad
on earth, I believe with all my heart th

poor. In *A God Named Josh*, Jared Brock re-emphasizes this nearly lost theology and brings it vividly to life for the modern church."

—Simon Guillebaud, author of *Choose Life*

"In an age of abstraction and disillusion, Jared Brock brilliantly reveals something we all desperately need: an extremely real, human, flesh-and-blood God."

—Nathan Clarkson, actor and author of *Good Man*

"Jared Brock uses more than 1,000 Scripture references and an in-depth knowledge of historical details to deftly build a compelling case for Jesus as a revolutionary who changes our perspective on every aspect of life—political, financial, relational, philosophical, and spiritual. Reading *A God Named Josh* will deepen your desire to know Jesus more intimately."

—Harold Albrecht, former Canadian member of Parliament

"It's like meeting Jesus for the first time, all over again! Sometimes the best way to get a fresh new look at Jesus is to go backwards, and Jared Brock invites us on a journey to meet the Jesus with skin on. The one who lived as a Jew, rowed in wooden boats, wore sandals, and slept in the outdoors. The one with real siblings and friends and enemies. The one who cried as a baby, whose voice broke as a teen, and who cried again as his heart broke over the people he loved. Reading this book, I felt like I could smell ancient Israel—and see Jesus in all of his humanity. For those of you who have known Jesus for a long time, or have yet to meet Him, I'd like to invite you to meet a God named Josh."

—Sheila Wray Gregoire, author and host of the Bare Marriage podcast

"*A God Named Josh* is a wonderful book that shares new perspectives, insights, and practical applications drawing on the ancient Hebrew story. I loved it."

—Rabbi Evan Moffic, author of *What Every Christian Needs to Know about the Jewishness of Jesus*

"Jared Brock has written a biography on Jesus that is historical yet relevant, funny yet honest, intelligent yet simple, and timely yet timeless. I'll be using *A God Named Josh* as a reference for years to come."

—James Kelly, founder of FaithTech

A God Named Josh

A God Named Josh

Uncovering the Human Life of Jesus Christ

Jared Brock

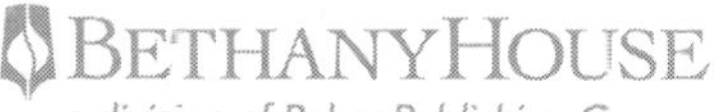

a division of Baker Publishing Group
Minneapolis, Minnesota

Published by Bethany House Publishers
Minneapolis, Minnesota
www.bethanyhouse.com

Bethany House Publishers is a division of
Baker Publishing Group, Grand Rapids, Michigan

Printed in the United States of America

ISBN 978-0-7642-3962-5 (paper)
ISBN 978-1-4934-4076-4 (ebook)

Cover design by Micah Kandros Design

Baker Publishing Group publications use paper produced from sustainable forestry practices and post-consumer waste whenever possible.

23 24 25 26 27 28 29 7 6 5 4 3 2 1

For my father, Gordon Alan Brock.
I want to be just like you because you want to be just like him.

Contents

Foreword

Talk about the Jesus I never knew! Jared Brock tells the old, old story with such zest, flare, and startling freshness that on almost every page I thought, and often said aloud, "I didn't know that."

Jared has mined deeply into the story and the history of Jesus—he seems all at once historian, journalist, investigator, theologian, adventurer-sleuth—and has written it all up as though he's breaking a story worthy of a Pulitzer Prize. And, well, he is.

Dorothy Sayers many years ago complained that preachers had committed the ultimate sin against Jesus: They had managed to make him boring—nothing more than a "household pet for pale curates and pious old ladies."

If that's been your experience, prepare yourself: Jesus is about to become thrillingly, subversively, dangerously, gloriously interesting again.

—Mark Buchanan, author of *God Walk: Moving at the Speed of Your Soul*

Introduction

"Thou hast made us for thyself, O Lord, and our heart is restless until it finds its rest in thee."

—Augustine of Hippo, *Confessions*

The other day I was tossing black beans in chili and cumin (with a squeeze of lime and a splash of jalapeño juice) when my wife, Michelle, looked down at the beans in disgust. She wrinkled her nose and asked, "How often do you think Jesus farted?"

We descended into a fit of giggles at the very thought.

But it got me thinking: Jesus farted. And burped. And did other human things. That's the insane wonder of the incarnation. The God of the universe, the all-powerful, all-knowing, all-present King of Kings and Lord of Lords, creator of heaven and earth, maker of oceans and galaxies and subatomic particles and kombucha—*The* Dude—humbled himself to become a helpless, voiceless, pooping baby, born to a teenager out of wedlock, in a filthy barn, in an overcrowded city, under the rule of corrupt religious officials and a murderous foreign dictator.

And he didn't stop there.

Jesus learns to crawl. And walk. And talk. And feed himself. He learns to read but never owns a single book. He goes through puberty. His voice cracks and croaks and eventually deepens. He gets body odor. He grows chest hair. He makes friends (and enemies). He learns to fish, and build things, and preach like nobody's ever heard.

At twelve, he ditches his parents on their annual family vacation. They freak. *Our preteen has gone off the handle.* They search the capital city and eventually find him in the temple. He's listening and learning, but he's also teaching. Everyone's amazed. He grows in stature, and in favor with God and man.

And then it happens. Around age thirty, he changes careers. He's a rabbi now. He collects a dozen young men—a rowdy and riotous lot, some zealous and others traitorous, all unbelieving to varying degrees—and invites them to follow him.

They're soon joined by others, including loads of epic women, and their merry band of seventy travelers walks at least 21,525 miles. They eat bread, fish, and figs, but not one tomato or potato or ear of corn. They hang out with a diverse cast of characters, including a grandpa named Heli, a desert-dwelling, river-dunking, grasshopper-chomping kinsman who gets beheaded, and a weird prophet-uncle who once lost his voice for nine months. Jesus laughs. He cries. He gets angry. He cracks jokes. He breaks up fights. He engages in economic sabotage. He mourns, he dances, he fasts, he feasts. He works, rests, commands, stresses, prays. He faces every temptation, bears every burden, experiences every emotion that we've experienced. And why shouldn't he? He's human.

And yet . . . there are miracles. Everywhere, miracles. Water turns to wine, blindness turns to sight, death turns to life. He reads minds. He sees hearts. He speaks with authority. He preaches a highly controversial theology with massive socioeconomic and political implications: the kingdom of heaven.

The people start talking. Who is this man, this Galilean with his treasonous political agenda? Could he be the Christos, the Messiah-King chosen not only to overthrow the dictator, but also to be the spiritual savior of his people? Nazareth, you say? Nothing great has ever come from that redneck, backwater part of the world. What's his name? Joshua, son of Joseph? *Yehoshua ben Yehoseph*?

A God . . . named Josh?

For those who don't know the Jesus story, here is a wonderfully brief overview directly from Wikipedia: "Jesus was a Galilean Jew, who was baptized by John the Baptist and began his own ministry. Jesus debated with fellow Jews on how to best follow God, engaged in healings, taught in parables, and gathered followers. He was arrested and tried by the Jewish authorities, turned over to the Roman government, and crucified on the order of Pontius Pilate, the Roman prefect of Jerusalem. After his death, his followers believed he rose from the dead, and the community they formed eventually became the early Church."

That's about as much as we can know for certain about the historical Jesus, give or take one murderous Jewish mafia boss we will meet in chapter 5. Jesus lived, ministered, was crucified, and then people believed he was God. This is the man we'll discover in the pages ahead, including how in the world a Jew named Yehoshua ended up with the English name *Jesus*. From naked infant to naked martyr, from crying in a cradle to crying out on a cross. From a fetus fearfully and wonderfully knit together in his mother's womb to his ascension and that coronation where he's crowned with glory and honor forever. For those of us who call ourselves Christians, he is fully God and fully man.

It's the latter I'd like us to discover in these pages. Is Joan Osborne's song "One of Us" ringing in your ears yet? "What if God was one of us, just a slob like one of us?"

What did Jesus look like? What did he eat? What did he wear? Did he keep a schedule? How did he pay his bills? Who were his closest friends? Was he married? Why was he was murdered? Was he really born on December 25? Who was the fake, Jewish crime family who covertly engineered his assassination and almost got away with not being named in Scripture? How did Jesus muster up so much love for his enemies? Basically, how in the world did God pull it off?

Over the next few hundred pages, we're going to dig into more than a thousand Scripture passages to find out. In the person of Jesus, we'll get a glimpse of how much God must love us. We'll never be able to fully fathom the depth of love it took to incarnate, but we know this for certain: Being a human is hard. Life, even the very best life, is full of pain and misery, heartbreak, loss. Even on the best of days, human life requires effort, struggle, sweat.

Being God is so much better. You don't have the constraints of a body or gravity or time. You don't have to feel pain or experience loss if you don't want to. Disappointment disappears when you know the future. You have total freedom and autonomy and unlimited resources. Why in the world would you set that all aside and come to earth as a helpless human baby—in wretched, Roman-ruled, first-century Palestine, no less?

You'd need to love something—or someone—an awful lot.

A Quick Word to Agnostics, Atheists, and Anti-Theists

Thank you for coming on this journey with me.

Everyone on earth familiar with Josh must place him somewhere on a sliding scale. Perhaps he was a deranged lunatic, a religious crank, or a dynastic warlord who got what he deserved for upsetting the Jewish elite and the Roman Empire. Perhaps he was a kindhearted sage who was innocently murdered. Perhaps he was a Greek-style philosopher who escaped crucifixion and lived out his days on the Med. Maybe he wasn't real at all, but rather a mythical hero.

Or perhaps he was God incarnate, sent down from heaven to reconcile us with his trinitarian self. That's what the gospel writers and the seventy-odd first-century Jews who spent three to five years in close contact with him believed.

Whether he is God or not, Josh is significantly more radical than most pastors and denominations will have you believe. His thoughts on money, politics, philosophy, and religion are downright disturbing. At the very least, he was the most influential man who ever lived—which should make us wonder why most of humanity refuses to seriously consider his message.

And then there is the crazy notion the gospel writers claim: that Josh is the son of God, but also one with God. It was a dangerous belief to hold in the first century. It is still a dangerous belief in our time.

What This Book Is Not

Josh's influence during his lifetime was minimal at best, leaving behind no great buildings like Alexander and Herod did, no great writings like from Cicero and Aristotle, and no great following save for a motley crew of seventy disciples led by a hotheaded fisherman named Rocky.

The greatest documentation of the life of Jesus is the eyewitness testimony of his followers as compiled by the writers of the four gospel accounts. It would be unreasonable to expect it to come to us in any other way. We would not expect Xi Jinping to commission a biography of an obscure Tibetan monk any more than we would expect a superpower like America to document the supposed godhood of a Puerto Rican cult leader with a following smaller than a university class. It is nearly always the fans and followers who leave behind details about their heroes. Proof of the authenticity and accuracy of the four gospels continues to grow as thousands of scholars—Christian and secular alike—pore over the text and unearth new evidence from the era.

Today, nearly every scholar agrees Jesus was a preacher from Galilee who got in some trouble with the temple elites and was executed by the Romans. Whether or not he resurrected and is God is not a historical question but a faith one. I will make little attempt to convince you that Jesus is God—that is what the gospels are for. We will focus on the human Josh, exploring history, archeology, philosophy, genealogy, and many other ologies, to fix in our minds a clearer image of the man many of us call Christ. Jesus is, frankly, brilliant. Even if you see yourself as a progressive secularist, a proper reading of Scripture will give you incredible insight into the human condition and the nature of reality. Yehoshua offers a sound moral code, time-tested wisdom for relationships and business, and counterintuitive perspectives on money, philosophy, politics, and virtue that can transform your way of being and living across any culture at any time. The Bible is the essential work for anyone seeking the good life.

The Truth Will Set Us Free

Who do you say Jesus is?

He asks his disciples this same question three different times. It's a powerful question, one he's still asking us today. Was he a con man, a spiritual snake-oil salesman, a rabbi gone off the theological rails? Was he a crazed fringe politician who thought he could take down the Jewish mafia and the Roman Empire? Is he the son of the living God, the supernatural made incarnate in human flesh? We don't know. Everything requires faith, and God loves us all so much that he lets us choose our orientation toward his son.

But you don't have to be a Christian or even believe in God to appreciate the life and legacy of Jesus of Nazareth. He is, undoubtedly, the most influential person in history, endowing a belief structure and way of life that led to a proliferation of churches, the invention of universities and hospitals, and the steady expansion of human rights. To be sure, horrible things have been said and done in his name—things he was decidedly against—but as you'll see in these pages, the man who Christians call Lord is a man worth knowing intimately and personally.

Let's meet Josh.

The Genealogical Josh

"History is the essence of innumerable biographies."
—Thomas Carlyle, *Essays*

What is the Bible, exactly? It is the story of one family discovering God. If you consider yourself a member of the Christian faith family, then this is your charter story, a library of books packed with various genres including poetry, mythology, wisdom, narrative, and YHWH-centered salvation history. As such, it is important to know your family tree. I am the ancestry nut in our family. I'm not nearly as committed as those in the Mormon Church, who try to trace their ancestry back to Adam and then squirrel away the data with two billion other names beneath seven hundred feet of granite in Utah's Wasatch Range, but I do my best.

I've taken multiple DNA tests and convinced my mother to nick the inside of her mouth and bleed into a test tube for a mitochondrial meandering, which grew our family tree to thousands of known cousins. Though I regret that several corporations (one of which is now owned by the government of Singapore) have my life sequence on file, the tests rather wonderfully explained why I sneeze in sunlight, prefer dark chocolate to milk, and have curly hair.*

It's weird to think that Jesus had ancestors.

It's even crazier to realize we know who they are. Josh's family tree contains a pantheon of wonderfully interesting and supremely sinful humans: warlords, kings, slaves, slave-owners, murderers, moon-worshipers, centenarians, ark-builders, prostituted women, prophets, priests, shepherds, and giant-killers, for example.

The Bible gives us two accounts of Josh's genealogy. Matthew starts with Abraham, while Luke starts with Adam. The lists are identical between Abraham and David but are radically different otherwise. That's because Matthew traces Mary's line through David's son, King Solomon, while Luke traces Joseph's line through one of David's lesser-known sons, Nathan. In the end, however, both lists end up at the same conclusion: Yehoshua ben Yehoseph is a double-bloodline king candidate.

Genealogy was a much bigger deal back in the day, especially if someone like Yehoshua wanted to make a legitimate claim to the Jewish throne. In the same way that I can't waltz up to Buckingham Palace and claim the crown, there were quite a few hoops one had to jump through to claim Israelite imperium. The first step, of course, was actually being Jewish. So before we meet Yehoshua's nuclear and extended family, it's definitely worth our time to dive into the historic family-nation-religion that would have defined Josh's life more than any other influence.

* Family lore suggests we were Huguenot Protestants named Le Broc, purged from France in the late seventeenth century by the Sun King Louis XIV. Thanks to DNA confirmation, I can boast I'm related to Napoleon Bonaparte (boo!), Marie Antoinette (double boo!), Nicolaus Copernicus, and the apostle Luke—the last of which I imagine looks great on a church elder application form.

The patriarch of Judaism was a super-wealthy, semi-nomadic, Hebrew-Aramean herdsman named Abram ben Terah. Abram was a tenth-generation descendant of Noah, and Noah could trace his lineage back to Adam, so why not just start at the beginning?

The Bible says Adam and Eve had at least five sons and two daughters (Genesis 5:4), while the Roman-Jewish historian Titus Flavius Josephus, in an *The Antiquities of the Jews* footnote, references a traditional claim that they bore as many as thirty-three sons and twenty-three daughters. This number might seem high to us, but in the days before entertainment, the necessity of work, resource scarcity, birth control, and other human beings, I can't think of much else better to do. The first family raised their brood somewhere outside of Eden, which itself could have been situated anywhere from eastern Africa to western Iraq, depending on who and what you believe.

We know the names of only two of Adam and Eve's sons, who lived long enough to expand the family tree. Cain and Seth and their wives start having kids and grandkids for several generations, most of whom are so incredibly corrupt and violent that the Genesis authors envision God being so disappointed with humanity that he decides to destroy the whole world—which is almost exactly what happens. Cain's descendants get wiped out by a massive flood, and if you do the math, so does oldest-man-ever Methuselah, who evidently grew so weary of life that he refuses to board his grandson Noah's 510-foot polymer-sealed boat (Genesis 6:14). For those interested, Methuselah's foreboding name means either "When he is dead, it shall be sent" (*Exhaustive Dictionary of Bible Names*) or "When he dies, judgment" (attributed to Dr. Henry Morris).

Forty days of flooding and nearly a year of drainage later, Noah's boat runs aground on a 17,000-foot dormant volcano just east of the current Turkey-Armenia border, where Noah exits onto dry ground with his three sons and their wives.

God commands Noah's sons to be fruitful and multiply, and they do so prodigiously: Their kids have kids who have kids, spawning families that turn into clans that turn into tribes that turn into nations. Japheth's kids head for the Aegean and eventually spread throughout Europe. Ham has a son named Egypt who heads for north Africa, while another son named Canaan seeds the Jebusite, Amorite, Hivite, Arkite, and Sinite tribes that fill the Middle East and Africa. Shem's family tree has so many branches that the Bible includes two lists of his descendants, many of whom scatter to the Far East and eventually into North and South America.

One piece of Shem's family, however, stays in the Middle East, and it's from that people group we derive the word *Semitic* today. One of Shem's great-great-great-great-great-great-great-great-grandsons was named Abram, and he plays a pivotal role in the future life of Yehoshua of Nazareth. It's this man who we call the founder of Judaism.

Uncle Abe

The Bible doesn't say where Abram was born, but it does mention that his brother Haran was born while their father, Terah, lived in a city called Ur, which was a few miles from the banks of the Euphrates in Sumer, now southern Iraq, and best known for its massive, pyramidesque Ziggurat. That's one proposed location, anyway. The Ur in question may have been 680 miles away in the modern-day town of Urfa, Turkey, but there are at least four other potential sites of Abram's birth. It's just as likely he was born in a drover's tent somewhere in the Mesopotamian section of the Fertile Crescent of modern-day Iraq, eastern Syria, or southern Turkey.

At some point before reaching middle age, Abram has an encounter that will not only change his life but will transform the world in ways that affect us to this very moment. You see, Abram grew up in a polytheistic family. He worshiped many gods. Joshua 24:2 states that Terah was an idol worshiper. Jewish records say Terah was an idol craftsman, and according to ancient Jewish authorities, Abram worked in Terah's idol shop as a teenager. In Genesis 31:19, we'll read about how Terah's great-great-granddaughter, Rachel, steals her father's collection of household idols called *Tera*phim.

For some reason, polytheism doesn't sit well with Abram. He believes in *one* god, not dozens or hundreds. He is, classically speaking, the world's most famous early monotheist.

Abram's god of choice calls himself *Ehyeh* (meaning "I will be") and later, through Moses, says we can call him *Yahweh* ("he will be"). The God of Abram is *Being itself*. We don't know the exact name origins of Yahweh, but he appears in the written record around three thousand years ago, in the late Bronze Age. In Abram's day, Yahweh was known (or misconceived) as a weather god and warrior deity, and he was just one of many gods and goddesses worshiped throughout Canaan. In time, however, Abram's all-knowing, all-powerful, all-present being will displace all the rest, proving himself to be God Almighty, King of Kings, Lord of Lords, ruler of heaven and earth, and the world's first widespread creator of the cosmos.

Within five hundred years, religionist scribes so idolized the name *Yahweh* they couldn't bring themselves to say it out loud, and went with *Adonai* ("lord") instead. Eventually, Jewish scribes got so religious about not saying God's name that they created a visual device to remind readers to say Adonai and not Yahweh. They snatched the four consonant letters from Yahweh (YHWH) and blended them with the three vowels in Adonay (AOA) and came up with the word YAHOVAH, to trigger people into saying Adonai. Centuries later, Christian scribes (who didn't know Yahovah was a made-up word) accidentally translated the name of God as *Jehovah*. In the meantime, the temple in Jerusalem is destroyed in 70 AD and the actual pronunciation of God's name is lost. Thankfully, God sent his son, Yehoshua ben Ehyeh—Josh, son of Being itself—through the human line of Abram, to redeem all of Adamkind to himself.

We will know God's name again.

At some point, YHWH had said to Abram, "Go from your country and your kindred and your father's house to the land that I will show you. And I will make of you a great nation, and I will bless you and make your name great, so that you will be a blessing. I will bless those who bless you, and him who dishonors you I will curse, and in you all the families of the earth shall be blessed" (Genesis 12:1–3).

That's it. No fireworks or earthquakes or trumpet blasts. *Let me lead you and the world will be blessed through you.* The Holy Spirit stirs something deep within Abram, and he converts from polytheism to monotheism, from a cultural-familial religion to a radical, unprecedented, world-changing personal faith.

Abram's life story invites us to do the same. Everyone believes in gods—ideas, spirits, ideologies, essences—in which we place our hope, trust, and faith. Even atheism is just a spread bet on a thousand little gods like self, capitalism, consumerism, progress, the rule of law, and a heavy dose of happiness-hunting individualism. When we place our ultimate faith in anyone or anything less than *Being himself,* we fall short of the glory of God. We exchange the truth for a lie, foolishly believing our patchwork pantheon of faiths and trusts can reward us with life to the full. In our blind pursuit of blessing, we miss the Blesser himself. The great truth Abram discovers is that nothing can save us except the One who made us.

Abram bets on YHWH. After the death of his father, Abram, age seventy-five, sets out from Haran. He takes his sister-wife Sarai and nephew Lot with him, along with all his possessions and herds and—unfortunately, like many of the elites in his time and ours—slaves. They make the five-hundred-plus-mile journey through Canaan and stop around modern-day Nablus in the

West Bank, about thirty miles north of Jerusalem. When Abram is ninety-nine, YHWH appears to him and says,

> "Behold, my covenant is with you, and you shall be the father of a multitude of nations. No longer shall your name be called Abram, but your name shall be Abraham, for I have made you the father of a multitude of nations. . . . I will establish my covenant between me and you and your offspring after you throughout their generations for an everlasting covenant, to be God to you and to your offspring after you. . . . As for you, you shall keep my covenant, you and your offspring after you throughout their generations. This is my covenant, which you shall keep, between me and you and your offspring after you: Every male among you shall be circumcised."
>
> Genesis 17:4–5, 7, 9–10

Circum-*what*?

The removal of the foreskin from the human penis by means of a flint was likely unheard of by most of their Canaanite neighbors, but Egyptian tomb artwork from Abraham's time suggests the practice was used for the sake of cleanliness and to mark the passage from childhood to manhood. Did he pick up the idea on his southern sojourn? In any case, it was a small sacrifice that sealed a massive promise, a stark reminder on the very organ used to create life, that YHWH's covenant was everlasting.

Later that same day, Abraham takes his thirteen-year-old son, Ishmael, and the hundreds of men in his household and does the deed without modern anesthesia. Talk about a bonding father-son experience. Has the old man lost his mind?

Within a few months, ninety-year-old Sarai, who YHWH renames Sarah, becomes pregnant for the first time. Abraham moves back to the Negev Desert and eventually lodges south of Gaza in the water-rich Philistine wadi of Gerar. When Abraham is one hundred, he and Sarah become the parents of a little boy named Isaac. The Jewish nation has begun.

Isaac, Jacob, Joseph, Moses

Abraham lives peaceably in the territory of the Philistines for years and years, until YHWH decides to test Abraham's commitment to the one true God. *Prove your love for me by sacrificing your only begotten son.* This probably doesn't come as a huge surprise to Abraham—all the gods require human sacrifice.

Imagine Abraham's surprise when, right at the last moment before he's about to kill Isaac, YHWH stops him and provides a substitute offering in the form of a thicket-trapped ram—a lamb of God, if you will. A God who doesn't require child sacrifice? This is a *big* deal. This whole mountain trek wasn't just to test Abraham's faithfulness to God—it was to prove YHWH's faithfulness to humanity.

So where did this first substitutionary atonement take place? Genesis says Abraham and Isaac were on a mountain called Moriah. Today, Jews and Christians revere the supposed spot in question as the Temple Mount in Jerusalem. The Temple Mount is pretty important to Judaism for a host of other reasons too: At the center of the mountain is the Foundation Stone of the world (not mentioned in the Bible), where it is said Adam came into being (geographically dubious), where the Ark of the Covenant rested (likely), where the two temples were built (by Solomon and Herod), and where the altar rested inside the Holy of Holies. Muslims believe it's also the spot to which Muhammad miraculously traveled over 750 miles from Mecca in one night, where he stood on a rock, was lifted to heaven, and received his teachings. *On the same rock where Abraham almost sacrificed Isaac.* The rock is now covered by a dome that is called, rather uncreatively, the Dome of the Rock. What are the chances that of all 1.59629 quadrillion square feet of physical land on earth, three major world religions—containing billions of ancient cousins—are all warring over one single stone? No wonder Yehoshua will later seem unconcerned if the whole thing gets torn down.

Abraham returns to what is now Be'er Sheva in the Negev Desert. He sends his chief of staff back up the Fertile Crescent to Nahor's town near Haran to find his son Isaac a wife from among his kin. The woman of choice is his brother Nahor's granddaughter Rebekah, who is straight-up lovely. When Abraham dies, he leaves everything he owns to Isaac. Isaac and his half-brother Ishmael bury their father in the cave with Sarah. Ishmael, unlike his father, has no problem siring sons, and produces twelve. They settle east of Egypt and eventually spread into all of Arabia, living in violent hostility toward all the tribes related to them. Those twelve tribes of Ishmael become the nation of Islam, a religion of works over faith.

After nineteen years of struggling with infertility—evidently something that runs in Yehoshua's family tree for generations—Rebekah gives birth to twin sons. Esau is daddy's wild child who loves to hunt, while Jacob is a mama's boy who prefers to cook.

Eventually Jacob heads back to Haran to find a wife and ends up marrying two of his first cousins, Rachel and Leah. For the next fourteen years, he's forced to work for his devious, grasping, polytheistic uncle. After twenty years of being financially exploited, Jacob decides to head back down the Fertile Crescent to the land promised by YHWH to his grandfather. (It's here that Rachel steals her father's Teraphim idols, suggesting she hasn't been won over to the monotheistic worldview.)

All told—and not without a long struggle with infertility on Rachel's part—Jacob has twelve sons by four women. These dozen will become the heads of the twelve tribes of Jacob, who himself receives a new name: Israel, meaning "one who struggles with God."

Rachel's eldest, Joseph, like his great-grandfather, is a semi-nomadic shepherd and stargazer with a penchant for getting himself in trouble. The seventeen-year-old is also a bit of a tattletale against his brothers and is his father's favorite son, adorned in multicolor haute couture. While Joseph delivers supplies to his brothers about twenty miles south of modern-day Nazareth, they seize him and sell him to their Ishmaelite cousins, who in turn sell him to the captain of the guard for the Egyptian Pharaoh.

This, as it turns out, is a boon for all involved. When a third famine rocks Canaan, the brothers head to Egypt to find food, just like their ancestors. They're shocked beyond words to see that their kid brother has ascended to VP of Egypt. Jacob decides to move his entire household—at least sixty-six people—back to Egypt.

This, as it turns out, is a horrible decision for all involved. Abraham's nightmare in which his descendants will be enslaved in a foreign land for four hundred years is about to come to pass. But first, Jacob, on his deathbed, blesses and/or curses his twelve sons, depending on their deeds and misdeeds, and says of Judah, "Your brothers shall praise you; . . . your father's sons shall bow down before you. . . . The scepter shall not depart from Judah, nor the ruler's staff from between his feet, until tribute comes to him, and to him shall be the obedience of the people" (Genesis 49:8, 10). With this remark, Jacob-Israel seals his family's destiny: Their future king will arise from the tribe of Judah.

Hundreds of years pass. The twelve sons of Israel die, Joseph included, but their offspring multiply into the millions. This, naturally, terrifies the Egyptians.

After an ill-fated attempt to get Hebrew midwives to murder all Jewish baby boys, the Pharaoh commands all his people to drown all Hebrew boys in the Nile. One descendant of Levi decides to hide her son in a bitumen-sealed basket along the bullrush banks of the great river. Pharaoh's daughter comes for a bath and rescues the crying baby. The baby's older sister, a girl approximately seven years old named Miriam, dupes the princess into hiring the baby's mother to breastfeed her own child.

Once weaned, the princess gives the boy a name that sounds like the Hebrew word for "to draw out" of the water: *Mosheh*. Moses, as we call him in English, will rescue his people from their four-hundred-year nightmare and finally get them on track to take possession of the Promised Land and become the holy nation they were ordained to become.

It has been said that Moses is a picture of the Christ to come, and readers of the Mosheh story and the Yehoshua story will quickly pick out the similarities: Newborn boys are killed by Pharaoh; newborn boys are killed by Herod. Who saves Moses in Egypt? A girl named Miriam. Who saves Yehoshua by fleeing to Egypt? his mother, Miriam. From whom does Moses descend? Joseph. Who is Yehoshua's earthly father? Joseph. Both Mosheh and Yehoshua fast for forty days and forty nights in the wilderness at the beginning of their public ministries. Moses turns water into blood. Yehoshua turns water into wine and later says wine represents his blood. Moses frees his people from slavery but can't bring them into the Promised Land. Yehoshua saves his people from the slavery of sin and eternal death and takes them all the way to heaven.

Four hundred and thirty years after the arrival of Jacob's twelve sons, several million Israelites—the text says 600,000 men plus women and children and the bones of Joseph—exit Egypt in a massive *exodus,* escaping through a warren of salt lagoons now known as the Bitter Lakes and home to the Suez Canal.

Promised Land, here they come!

Alas, it's not to be, not that day, anyway. After centuries of slavery, the twelve tribes of Israel don't yet know how to live as free people.

The northeast journey back to Canaan is less than 250 miles, but Moses feels called to lead his people south to the Sinai Peninsula for a time of purification and training, a hard reset that will see his generation die in the wilderness over the next forty years. This might seem like a brutal move on Moses's part, but the long-term effect is that it strengthens the Israelite nation, trains its army, develops an economy, coalesces a common culture, purges them of their polytheism, elevates their faith in YHWH, and ensures they won't be completely annihilated in the many battles to come.

To be sure, Israel has its ups and downs. But even amidst their setbacks and failures and misstarts at becoming a holy nation, God is patient and gracious. For several centuries, YHWH sends a series of warrior-judges to protect the nation from external threats while arbitrating internal ones. He then reluctantly allows them to be self-ruled by dictatorial kings, though it rarely ends well for the people or the monarch. Through his priests, YHWH gives Israel a tent and later a huge temple, both physical symbols of the bigger reality that God wants to dwell with his people. Through his prophets, he warns the nation when they've fallen off the path and are about to land themselves in pits of destruction.

Israel is supposed to be a theocracy, ruled not by dictators, tyrant-kings, and corporate-sponsored politicians, but by a holy body of law and a supreme court that upholds justice. In the end, neither courts nor laws will be necessary when every heart is flooded with the presence of God. From the beginning, the Israelites know that this body of ceremonial law is supposed to be temporary and that God will make a new covenant with the people of Israel and Judah (Jeremiah 31:31). Clearly, YHWH will need to send someone in the flesh to embody what it means to have a self-sacrificial heart.

Grace is already fully present in the Old Testament. The grand theme of Scripture is God's will to bless . . . and man's will to be God. Abraham does almost nothing right in his life, with one major exception: He trusts in God's promise, and that is enough. The Old Testament is filled with people whose lives yield cautionary tales; they're not heroes to emulate. The Bible could just as well be called *Horrible People and the God Who Loves Them Anyway*. Did YHWH save Israel from the Egyptians because they were obedient to his law? Absolutely not. Their salvation was an unmerited gift. The Law of Moses—a better translation is *instruction*—is simply the standards by which this faith family chooses to live. Once they learn to live in obedience to the rule and reign of YHWH, he will send a Messiah to free his people (and the rest of the human race) from sin and death for all time.

Messiah means "anointed one," and this Messiah will need to thread four consecutive needles: He needs to come as a human (a descendant of Adam); he must be an Israelite (a descendant of Abraham via Jacob); he needs to be a card-carrying member of Judaism (from the tribe of Judah); and he needs to be a scion of the Davidic line (the kingly family of David). YHWH sends scores of prophets who foretell other characteristics of the coming Christos. Whoever this person proves to be, his coming will cause the end of Judaism as they've known it but open the entire world for inclusion in a universal faith family with one Father, one Son, and one Spirit.

The people can't wait. Day after day, week after week, year after year, lifetime after lifetime, they plead and pray for God to come and dwell among them.

After more than fourteen hundred years of Israelite on-again-off-again faithfulness to the Law of Moses, YHWH decides it's time to send his Son to dwell among men as a living temple. It's time to introduce the Christos-King-Savior-Messiah who will fulfill the law and usher in a new covenant of love and grace and truth and spirit instead of the religiously lettered law.

In a Roman-ruled world with a global population of less than 300 million, it's time for Mary and Joseph to add a very special baby boy to the family tree.

The Infant Josh

"A baby is God's opinion that the world should go on."
—Carl Sandburg, *Remembrance Rock*

Of all of God's incredible works of creation, from supernovae to electrons and galaxies to quarks, the bit that probably impresses me most is that life gives birth to life.

As a child, I accidentally swallowed an apple seed and was terrified that a tree would grow in my stomach and explode through my rib cage. As an adult, I've visited the Brogdale Collections in Kent, home of the British national fruit orchard. In addition to hundreds of varieties of pears, cherries, plums, and quinces, the farm has over *2,200* varieties of apple trees. A well-cared-for apple tree will produce at least a bushel each year. Those 125 apples will produce around five seeds apiece if they're well pollinated. (My apple this morning had seven.) This means that every harvest, the Brogdale collection alone creates the potential for more than 1.3 million trees. Every apple contains an orchard. Life gives birth to life.

This is even more impressive in humans. When my adorable little niece, Inez, was still in her mom's tummy, her twenty-week-old baby ovaries possessed all the eggs she'd ever have—over seven million. Men, on the hand—always the overachievers—can release anywhere from 40 million to 1.2 billion sperm cells *per ejaculation*. That's a lot of potential life.

All that to say, I find it fascinating that the God of the universe didn't just appear out of nowhere, as Gabriel to Daniel or a burning bush to Moses. Yehoshua decided to start at the very beginning of human life. He decided to come into the world via conception.

In the Beginning

To become flesh, God puts himself through the same process every human since the beginning of time has undergone: the awkward, dangerous, bloody mess that is childbirth. And it doesn't start with his birth. Adam and Eve must raise Seth, who must raise Enosh, who must raise Cainan, Maleleel, my namesake Jared, and so on, for at least seventy-seven generations to get to Mary's son. The human Yehoshua, like each of us, was not only knit together in his mother's womb but was part of an unbroken thread of life-begetting-life from the beginning of life itself.

The womb belonged to a young girl named Mary, who was betrothed to marry a carpenter named Joseph. Betrothal is a strange thing for us to imagine today. It was more than engaged but less than married. There would have been a formal, legally binding, witnessed agreement between the families. Joseph would have paid the bride's price to her family. Jewish rules kept them from having sex in the year ahead, but breaking up would require a legal divorce. Strange indeed.

When Mary is likely around sixteen and living in a Galilean city called Nazareth (about twenty miles east of modern-day

Haifa), a holy messenger named Gabriel pays her a visit, which we read about in Luke 1.

"Greetings, O favored one! The Lord is with you." Mary doesn't take this well. Depending on your translation, Luke says she was greatly troubled, confused, agitated, perplexed, or disturbed by the stranger's statement. Why?

Well, for one thing, she couldn't place his accent. Perhaps he was dressed as a prophet or a rabbi. Even if he looked like a sailor or a carpenter, the culture didn't smile upon an adult male addressing a betrothed girl in such a friendly manner. Luke, who scholars believe interviewed Mary to get her story for his good news (gospel) report to Theophilus, says she basically thought, *What kind of greeting is this?*

Evidently her agitation was visible—the angel tells her not to be afraid, because she has found favor with God. Then he drops the bomb: "Look, you will conceive in your womb and bear a son, and you shall name him Yehoshua."

Yehoshua.

Does she savor the name on her tongue?

Does she know its meaning?

Yahweh saves.

Does she sound it out?

Yeh-ho-shoo'-ah.

Yeh-o-shua. It's sort of like three names squished into one:

Yahweh for Jesus.

Elohim for God.

Ruah for Spirit.

Is his name . . . a trinity?

Before we continue with the story, let's iron out how, exactly, a boy named Yehoshua ben Yehoseph ended up with the name Jesus. It's actually quite straightforward: The Hebrew name *Yehoshua* gets transliterated into Aramaic as *Yeshua*, which gets transliterated into Greek as *Iesous*, which gets transliterated into Latin as *Iesus*, from which we get the English *Jesus*. Mary and Joseph's everyday tongue was Aramaic, so there's a good chance they called him Yeshua around the house—or some nickname derived thereof. Because his earthly father's name was Joseph, or in Hebrew, Yehoseph, he was Yehoshua ben Yehoseph. Joshua is the sixth-most popular male name among Palestinian Jews of the era, and twenty-one different Yeshuas appear in the histories of Josephus. We know that Joseph's father's name was Jacob. If Jesus were born today in the West, we'd probably call him Josh Jacobson.

Gabriel's words ring in Mary's stunned ears: "You will conceive in your womb." Because every human life, even God in human form, requires a womb. Does Mary even hear what Gabriel says next? "He will be great and will be called the Son of the Most High. And the Lord God will give to him the throne of his father David, and he will reign over the house of Jacob forever, and of his kingdom, there will be no end." *A God named Josh.*

Mary's head snaps up and she addresses the stranger full-on, maybe even with her arms crossed. "How will this be, since I am a virgin?"

"The Holy Spirit will come upon you, and the power of the Most High will overshadow you."

Mary probably shoots him a look. *That's impossible.*

Maybe Gabriel shrugs, or laughs, or both. "Look, even your relative Elizabeth has conceived a son in her old age! She who was called *barren* is now six months pregnant. For nothing is impossible with God" (vv. 36–37 paraphrase).

We should pause here momentarily to note that, contrary to popular belief, Yehoshua and Yohanan the Baptizer are *not necessarily* cousins. The King James Version calls Mary and Elizabeth cousins (Luke 1:36), which would make Yehoshua and Yohanan second cousins at the closest, but modern translations use the more accurate *relative*. The two expectant mothers were kinswomen, distantly related, their future children cousins only in a generous colloquial sense. We can continue to call him cousin John, though *kinsman Yohanan* is more on track.

Mary, God bless her, suspends her disbelief and opens her spirit to this utterly crazy possibility of a pregnancy. "Listen, I'm a servant of the Lord; let it be to me according to your words."

Gabriel departs. Mary probably paces the room. Does she freak out? Most likely, especially if she's a normal teenage girl. Betrothal is a big deal. Joseph has paid for her. The families and witnesses watched them make the agreement. And now she's *with child*. In the ancient Middle East, such a thing is a punishable offense. Like fundamentalist Muslim families today, Joseph's family can demand an honor killing.

Within days, Mary heads south, through the hill country, to a city in Judah. Mary is a dead girl walking. She desperately needs the protection of her cousins. They are good people, godly people. She hopes she can trust them. She hopes they will believe her.

Pregnant

Not much is known about the couple Mary visited, except that Zechariah and Elizabeth were old and barren—well past menopause and the ability to procreate—and yet they still prayed for a child. In case you're wondering where this story is going, just look at the name of Mary's cousin and her husband: *Zechariah* means "God has remembered," and *Eli-sheba* means "God's promise."

Six months earlier, Gabriel told Zechariah the same thing he told Mary: "Do not be afraid." Why not? "For your prayer has been heard," the holy messenger said. "Your wife, Elizabeth, will bear you a son, and you shall call him John."

Barrenness in first-century Israel wasn't an unfortunate break—it was an utter disgrace. Their neighbors would talk. *"Elizabeth and Zechariah live holy and blameless lives, and yet God withholds the perpetuation of life from their home."*

So Elizabeth goes into self-imposed lockdown. Social isolation. No going out. No visitors coming in. Just her and her husband and her baby and her God. It is more than enough.

Luke reports that Elizabeth kept herself hidden for five months. Then, at some point early in her sixth month of pregnancy, there's a knock at the door. It's Mary. She enters Zechariah's home and greets Elizabeth. At the sound of Mary's voice, John leaps in Elizabeth's belly. Was it the first time Elizabeth felt him kick? The timing's about right. Elizabeth, filled with the Holy Spirit, shouts, "Blessed are you among women, and blessed is the fruit of your womb!"

In this moment, Mary receives external confirmation that she is, indeed, pregnant. She realizes that a miracle has occurred in her body, and she breaks into song (Luke 1:46–55). Mary's song is based on a song in 1 Samuel, prayed by Hannah, the prophet Samuel's mother. Mary would have known Hannah's song well, perhaps since girlhood. Had Mary rewritten it on the road? It was certainly an appropriate greeting for a dear relative who, like Hannah, had been written off as barren decades ago.

The two women look at each other, all smiles. *We're pregnant!* Elizabeth, previously barren; Mary, spermless. In Elizabeth, life is giving birth to life. In Mary, life is giving birth to eternal life.

Is such a thing possible? Not with humans, no. But with the creator of the universe, surely nothing is impossible. In this case, God himself planted the seed. Is that so hard to accept? It seems to me that all life, whether man-fertilized or God-fertilized, is nothing short of miraculous.

We know how babies are made: A spermatozoon fertilizes an ovum and becomes a zygote. But what *sparks* life? *Why* do chemicals react the way they react? I believe in the causation of all things. Drill down deep enough, ask *why* long enough, and you quickly realize that science has very near-term limits on causation. Science simply cannot answer and must instead say "just because," or "we don't know." And that's okay.

The *Oxford English Dictionary* defines a miracle as an "event that is not explicable by natural or scientific laws and is therefore attributed to a divine agency." Yet the deepest reality is that science will *never* be able to explain why life exists and gives birth to more life. Life is based on science, yes, absolutely. But life is also magical, or rather, supernatural. Life is deeply spiritual.

I think Albert Einstein was on to something when he once said, "There are only two ways to live your life. One is as though nothing is a miracle. The other is as though everything is a miracle." The reality is that a God-seeded conception isn't really that much more miraculous than a "regular" conception. Life is a miracle, pure and simple.

So Mary conceives, and God busts out his needles and starts knitting. And he works fast. Cell division in the zygote gets underway rapidly, in a process with the rather biblical-sounding name of *embryogenesis*. What starts as a one-cell organism quickly turns into a thirty-trillion-celled human being. It's a boon for the baby, but not so much for his mama. A new cocktail of chemicals courses through Mary's body. In the weeks and months to come, she'll experience cramps, bloating, mood swings, headaches, nausea. Hormones will surge. Breasts will grow tender. Bones will ache.

But it will be worth it.

Within four weeks, arms begin to appear, even though Josh will only be the size of a poppy seed. At five weeks, the third-of-an-inch embryo has eye retinas and lenses, along with leg buds and a brain. At six weeks, there's an audible heartbeat inside the pea-sized body. The heart likely starts pumping far earlier—a team of Oxford scientists thinks it could be as early as day sixteen. We've been able to hear human heartbeats since 1854, and those little *thump-thumps* are the first of three billion pumps the average heart will yield before giving out.

By week seven, Mary's blueberry-sized baby has fingers and toes; his bones begin to harden; his eyelids form, and behind them, retinal pigment begins to color the eyes of a baby not yet an inch tall.

At week nine, we no longer call Josh an embryo. He's now a fetus and clearly looks like a human being—or perhaps more accurately, a human bean. He's the size of a cherry. In the next month, baby Josh will triple in height, grow a chin, nostrils, and genitals, and kickstart his sucking reflex.

All this while the baby's mother eats French fries. (Or, in Mary's case, maybe some fish and bread and lentils.)

Luke reports that Mary stays with Elizabeth for three months—through her first trimester and her cousin's third. Josh is now the size of a plum. Mary's blood pressure rises, as does her dizziness. Elizabeth, who scholars believe was at least sixty, is probably having an even rougher time. But at least they're in it together. Their relationship is symbiotic. Not only do they get to share the companionship of family, but Elizabeth gets a spry teenager's help around the house. In exchange, Mary gets protection from the potential wrath of Joseph, his family, and her community.

Did Mary stay for the birth of Elizabeth's baby? Did she help out with her labor? Was this the first birth she witnessed? Did it terrify her?

We don't know. Luke fast-forwards his story to the next scene, but it's not unreasonable to think Mary stayed to help out with the birth. It's not every day you get to witness a sexagenarian go into labor, not even these days. Elizabeth gives birth to a son, and Luke writes, "Her neighbors and relatives heard that the Lord had shown great mercy to her, and they rejoiced with her" (Luke 1:58).

A week later, the community gathers for baby John's circumcision. "His name is Yohanan," Elizabeth says. The family looks at this new mom, baffled. They look around at each other. "None of your relatives are called by this name." But Elizabeth knows better. Her son isn't like anyone else in her family line. A new man requires a new start. The family is having none of it. Elizabeth protests, but they ignore her. As a woman, it's not her call anyway.

Zechariah grabs a writing tablet—possibly a small wood or leaden tile with a thin coat of wax and an iron stylus—and scratches down his name of choice: *His name is Yohanan.*

"His name is Yohanan." *Is.* Not *will be.* Not *should be.* No room for discussion and negotiation with relatives who'll pressure him to keep the family names going. *Is.* Present tense. The name has been given already. "His name is Yohanan." Its meaning? *The grace of God.*

Did you catch it? After more than 23,000 verses under the law covenant of the Old Testament, the first recorded written word in the New Testament means grace.

Grace was already defined and at work in the Old Testament—they wouldn't have a word to use in the name otherwise—but now the fullness of grace is about to arrive in the flesh.

Back in Nazareth

Mary returns to her family's home and, like her cousin Elizabeth, probably goes into hiding. As she enters her second trimester, her lemon-sized baby has vocal cords, teeth, and fingerprints. Josh doubles in weight the following week, and aside from the ligament pains, Mary's feeling a bit more energetic and way hungrier. Her hair looks amazing.

Josh grows in size from peach to navel orange to avocado to pomegranate to mango. Stretch marks appear on Mary's tiny waist. Her feet are swollen. By twenty weeks, hair appears on Josh's little head, and Mary might feel movements.

It's around week twenty-four when, according to tradition, Joseph visits his fiancée and discovers she's pregnant. Luke, who presumably interviewed Mary, doesn't record Joseph's reaction. For that, we flip over to Matthew. Our Jewish tax collector friend writes from the paternal perspective, presumably based on interviews and/or accounts by Joseph's friends, four other sons, three or more daughters, or close relatives.

Joseph stares at Mary. She is six months along. Her breasts are probably bigger than he remembers, and the baby bump is impossible to hide. Josh is the size of a cantaloupe, after all. While Joseph's been working hard to build them a home, she's been sleeping with the milkman, or the post boy, or one of the countless local shepherds or soldiers. Is it a months-long affair, or is this baby the result of a one-night stand?

It doesn't matter. Mary has brought great shame and dishonor to his family. He stares at her, jaw clenched in fury. If they were in Egypt, he could cut off her nose. If they were in Persia, he could hack off her ears. But this is Judea, where the crime of adultery bears the ultimate penalty for a woman: He can demand her immediate execution.

But Matthew clearly states that Joseph is a godly man. A righteous man. A kingly man from the line of David.

Joseph is a man faithful to the Jewish law, certainly; but he, like Mary, is full of grace and mercy. He decides not to disgrace her publicly, not to make an example of her. He resolves to divorce her privately and send her away quietly. Unlike in a public divorce, he won't have to specify the cause, nor will he need to refund his dowry. He just needs two witnesses to make it legal. Her parents will do. No one else needs to know.

In this moment, we get a glimpse of the character of the man who will raise Yehoshua. He is tender. He is kind. He knows his legal rights—he could have Mary stoned this very day—but he sets aside the law in favor of love, or at least, grace.

Besides, the lives of a harlot and a bastard son are shameful enough. Mary can never own land. When her parents die, she'll have to live with friends or relatives, earning her keep as not much more than a maidservant. If no one will take her in, she'll end up like Hagar, servant of Sarah, who was forced to wander the desert with her son, Ishmael.

Sometime shortly after Joseph decides to divorce his betrothed, a holy messenger appears to him in a dream. Matthew doesn't say his name is Gabriel, but check out his opening line: "Joseph, son of David, do not be afraid . . ." Trademark angelspeak. The messenger continues, "What is conceived in [Mary] is from the Holy Spirit. She will give birth to a son, and you are to give him the name Jesus" (Matthew 1:20–21 NIV).

Joseph wakes with a gasp. It was a dream, but it felt so real. *He wants me to marry Mary. He wants me to name her son Yehoshua.* Naming a son was every Jewish father's right, but this wasn't his son. This was someone else's son. If the messenger in the dream was to be believed, this was *God's* son.

Joseph, faithful man that he is, makes a decision. He'll marry Mary and name her son Yehoshua. They'll have their weeklong wedding celebration, but she won't move in, and he won't sleep with her until this baby is born.

While he is in Nazareth, presumably visiting Mary or having recently moved there, inconvenient news arrives: The Romans are doing a census. Luke reports that "Joseph went up from the town of Nazareth in Galilee to Judea, to Bethlehem, the town of David, because he belonged to the house and line of David" (Luke 2:4 NIV). In Sunday school, I was taught that Joseph returns to Bethlehem because it's the village of his ancestors and that *everyone* in the known world returned to the hometown of their ancestors. Even as a kid, this seemed strange to me. Why not count tax people where they lived? What if you didn't know where your ancestors came from?

Luke never says that everyone traveled to the town of their ancestors, but simply that they returned to their "own town" (Luke 2:3). Joseph registered as a tax resident of Bethlehem. It may have been his hometown, but it also may have been his *own* town, in the same way that a Canadian snowbird may winter in Florida at a family timeshare but still pay taxes up north. Mary is from Nazareth; Joseph is from Bethlehem. Perhaps the couple's plan was to celebrate their wedding in Mary's hometown of Nazareth, have the baby, then move south to Bethlehem. Maybe Joseph does the math and, realizing he'll miss the birth if he's stuck in Bethlehem, decides to take Mary with him. He likely owns property there, maybe some farmland, and needs to protect the title by paying his tax. Or perhaps the whole thing is a tax dodge because suburban Bethlehem enjoyed better rates than backwoods Nazareth. All we know is that native Galileans weren't required to register—Judeans were—and Joseph considered himself the latter. One way or the other, he clearly felt he *had* to make the trip with a very top-heavy teen in tow.

Mary can't believe her bad luck. Her teenage body can barely stand, what with this watermelon inside, let alone make the walk back to the Jerusalem suburbs again. Worse still, Bethlehem is five miles farther and nearly a hundred feet higher.

It's unlikely Mary rode a donkey to get there. After Yehoshua is born and presented at the temple forty days later, Mary fulfills her Jewish pregnancy purification ritual by offering a pair of birds to the priest on duty. Leviticus 12:8 says that doves or pigeons are to be sacrificed only by those who can't afford to sacrifice a year-old lamb. If Mary and Joseph were too poor to buy a lamb, they probably didn't own a donkey.

The journey is slow. Nine months before, Mary could have walked this route in four days or so, but now it probably takes much longer. So much longer that by the time they arrive in Bethlehem, every inn and hostel and guesthouse has put up a *No Vacancy* sign. In a village of roughly three hundred people, there weren't many rentable beds available on the best of nights.

Joseph eventually finds a place. It isn't great. Nothing but one-star reviews. It's practically a barn.

Away from the Manger

While folks today are accustomed to the modern nativity scene, it's far more accurate to say that Yehoshua was actually born in a rural, small-town cave barn.

In all likelihood—this being Mary's first baby—many hours pass in painful labor. By now, Mary is deep into her contractions inside a poorly lit stable. Have the animals even been evicted? Did Joseph summon a midwife? If not, there's no time for that now. The physician Luke later reports, "She gave birth to her firstborn, a son. She wrapped him in cloths and placed him in a manger" (Luke 2:7 NIV).

The baby is safely out of the womb. Yet another miracle. Someone, perhaps Joseph, snips the umbilical cord. The baby takes big, gulping breaths of cold air and starts to whimper and cry.

Joseph and Mary check between the baby's legs to confirm what they already know.

It's a boy!

Mary probably does to Yehoshua what most Hebrew moms did with their newborns at the time: She washes the little nudie in water, rubs him down with salt, and wraps him tightly in a swaddling blanket. Unlike most mothers, she then places her four- to nine-pound bundle of joy in a livestock feeding trough.

The Royal Birthday

What date did this little boy decide to pop into the world? Was it really December 25, on the day most Christians now celebrate the Christos-mass (king feast) called Christmas?

As a child, I believed that Yehoshua was born on December 25, 0 AD. But this date is completely inaccurate because the Roman numeral system had no concept of the number zero. And this we know for certain: Most researchers no longer believe Yehoshua was born on December 25.

Unfortunately, researchers don't agree on an alternate date, and there are quite a few options out there. I'm almost ashamed to admit how many days I've happily gotten lost in theories and counter-theories, in historic timelines and prophecies and Jewish ceremonial calendars.

Early Christians didn't celebrate our Christ's birth on December 25. Neither Irenaeus nor Tertullian includes Christmas in their lists of Christian festivals. Origen suggests in his homily on Leviticus that the Acts 2 church didn't celebrate Christmas at all, because first-century Christians believed only pagans celebrated birthdays: "Of all the holy people in the Scriptures, no one is recorded to have kept a feast or held a great banquet on his birthday. It is only sinners who make great rejoicings over the day on which they were born into this world below." Why would Yehoshua be the exception?

We know that Christians in Rome were celebrating Christmas at some point between 336–354 AD, with the first official December 25 celebration likely being held in Rome in 353 or 354 AD, likely under the direction of Pope Liberius.

It was a wonderfully convenient date for the Catholic church—December 25 did, after all, have several pagan connections that needed stamping out.

The December 25 date gained more acceptance after Emperor Constantine declared Christmas a permanent celebration in 379 AD, and gained its biggest boost when Pope Sixtus III celebrated the first Christ Mass on December 25, 435 AD. But this still doesn't prove that Yehoshua was born on December 25.

Like many, I'm extremely skeptical that Yehoshua was born on December 25. For one thing, arguments have been made that shepherds and their flocks didn't hang around outdoors at that frigid time of year. No one watched their flocks by night in December. Harvest was well past—there would be nothing for the animals to eat—and people usually brought their flocks into barns by October. People also doubt that the Romans would have scheduled a tax census for the most inclement time of year. December temperatures in Bethlehem can drop below freezing, and arctic thermals and electric blankets weren't exactly available with one-day shipping. Scholars have also argued it would have been nearly impossible for super-pregnant Mary to travel seventy-something miles through hills averaging two thousand feet above sea level in the depth of winter, especially with precipitation making many roads impassable.

These are all interesting points, but the most intriguing has to do with Josh's cousin, John the baptizer. Luke says that John's father, Zacharias, served as a priest in the course of Abijah. In 1 Chronicles we learn that priests were split into twenty-four courses, and each course served in the temple for one week, twice each year, from sabbath to sabbath. It appears that John was conceived around June 24, 5 BC. If Mary visited six months later—in late December, 5 BC—and found out she was pregnant, there's no way she could give birth at Christmas unless she somehow held Josh in the womb for a full year.

However, what if Yehoshua was *conceived* around December 25, but was born on September 29 in 4 BC?

The practical and political math potentially makes sense. A September birth makes it more likely that the shepherds would still be tending their flocks by night. It definitely makes more sense for a Roman census and the possibility of a pregnancy pilgrimage. It doesn't conflict with the astrological data, and seems to jibe with the Jewish priestly traditions. It's downright delicious from a symbolic perspective: Yehoshua entered the world to atone for our sins, and September 29, 4 BC in the Jewish calendar may have been Yom Kippur, Judaism's holiest date—the day of atonement.

Let's suspend disbelief and pretend for a moment that Josh *was* conceived on December 25 and born on September 29. If this were truly the case, how in the world did we mix it up for so long?

Perhaps we just screwed up our theology of the Incarnation.

If that's the case, then perhaps our birthdate confusion is simply a clash between Roman and Jewish worldviews, of Eastern and Western thought. For Romans, the date of conception mattered more than the date of birth. In some parts of the East even to this day, birthdays are derived from the date of conception, not the date of birth. If we believe life begins at conception, then Yehoshua may have "appeared in the flesh" as a zygote on December 25, though he wouldn't take his first breath for another nine months.

This, of course, brings us to Michaelmas.

"Michael-what?" Evangelicals ask. In Luke 2:9, our doctor friend tells us that an "angel of the Lord" (commonly thought to be Michael the Archangel from Daniel and the Revelation) visits a bunch of shepherds and announces the birth of Yehoshua: "I bring you good news that will cause great joy for all the people. Today in the town of David a Savior has been born to you; he is the Messiah, the Lord" (vv. 10–11).

Take a guess at which day Catholics and Anglicans celebrate Michaelmas.

September 29. And here's the really strange thing: No one knows when or why Christians started celebrating Michael's announcement on this particular day. We do know that Christians have been celebrating it since at least the fourth century and that the word *Michaelmas* means "Michael sent." The feast of Michael may very well have started as a mass commemorating the heavenly host sending shepherds the announcement of Yehoshua's physical birth. At the very least, we can all agree it seems quite strange to celebrate the announcement of the day of Christ's birth at a completely different time of year than the day it happened.

Here's another interesting coincidence: According to one calculation, September 29, 4 BC, was the start of the weeklong Feast of Tabernacles, a kind of annual thanksgiving harvest celebration where all the pre-exile people of Israel dwelled in tent-like booths called tabernacles.

When the Apostle John pens his gospel, he starts with an evocative, esoteric eighteen-verse prologue that includes a fun Greek word: "And the Word became flesh and dwelt among us, and we have seen his glory, glory as of the only Son from the Father" (v. 14). What's weird is that John doesn't use the usual Greek word for *dwell* here. Instead, he uses the word for *tabernacle*. In the same way that Christians are temples of the Holy Spirit (1 Corinthians 6:19), God becomes human and takes up residence in a physical body.

What if Josh was begotten of the Holy Ghost (Matthew 1:18) and conceived in Mary on December 25, and was born and tabernacled with us (John 1:14) nine months later, on September 29? What if, on December 25, we celebrate not only Josh's birthday into the world, but more so his actual physical *incarnation*? What if Michaelmas is actually Christmas, and the two are one and the same?

Heaven only knows.

If I were a betting man, I'd put my money on September 29, 4 BC. But too much is unknown to gamble anything more than a poutine and root beer on this.

Thankfully, the birth date of Yehoshua was of zero concern to the authors of the New Testament. There are more important fish to beer-batter and deep-fry. The gospel writers place much higher importance on theology than chronology, and so should we. Whether Yehoshua was born or conceived on December 25, when we celebrate the Christ-mass, we celebrate the fact that the Light of life has entered the world.

And now that Josh has exited the womb, let's see what our baby Lord is up to.

The Child Josh

"The soul is healed by being with children."
—Fyodor Dostoevsky, *Poor Folk*

We know almost nothing about the infancy, childhood, and teenage years of most of the Roman Caesars. We know zero about the life of Pontius Pilate before he arrives in Judea. We know zilch about the upbringing of the wealthiest and most powerful Jew in Israel who will orchestrate Yehoshua's murder. When the backstories of emperors are mentioned, they are usually tales about how they were conceived by gods from the Roman pantheon. Their stories typically start with their ascension to the throne or their first major victory in battle. But generally, we don't know their birthing stories, which preschools they attended, or what girls they kissed first.

The same is true for the rural first-century Jewish preacher named Yehoshua ben Yehoseph. We will see at the end of this chapter why the gospel recorders pay so little attention to the child Josh, but for now, let us discuss what we do know. Perhaps this is a slice more detail than most modern Christians would care to picture about their Lord and Savior, but the biblical fact is that Yehoshua ben Yehoseph was circumcised.

The Genesis 17:12-commanded foreskin-snipping ceremony—likely picked up by Abraham during his time in Egypt and maintained by the Egyptian-raised Moses through the desert years—was a common custom by Yehoshua's day. The text doesn't say who circumcised little Yehoshua, but the custom at the time was for the head of the household to do it. That said, Exodus 4:25 records a woman circumcising her son, and with Yehoshua's parentage in such strange spiritual limbo, it could just as easily have been Mary as Joseph who nipped the tip. Despite the fact that a name has already been picked out for the wee lad, Luke 2:21 tells us he remains nameless for the first week of his little life.

The deed is done on the eighth day, and assuredly the wailing commences. Another Jewish boy is marked by the sign of YHWH's everlasting covenant with the descendants of Abraham. The symbol of man's power is symbolically submitted to a higher power. But Deuteronomy 10:16 commands Jews to not only circumcise their penises but also their hearts, and follows it up with a shortlist of economic rules, suggesting the ancient author has a keen understanding of the male proclivity to abuse both sex and money. It will be Mary and Joseph's job to raise a boy with a circumcised heart, one who is marked in his spirit to walk in God's ways, love him wholeheartedly, and keep his commandments. This, of course, he will do, regardless of their parenting.

Sunday-school-raised Christians may conjure up an image of "we three kings" on double-hump camels visiting Mary and Joseph within moments of Yehoshua's birth, but this is likely the product of curriculum creators taking artistic license to pad an otherwise drab nativity scene with jewels. Matthew makes it clear that the Magi don't arrive in Jerusalem until after Yehoshua is born, and no camels are mentioned. According to Luke, the only folks to see the baby *in situ* are some peasant shepherds.

Let us also note that neither Matthew nor Luke say there are *three* wise men—that notion is derived from the fact that they gift the new parents with gold, frankincense, and myrrh. Among the nearly ninety paintings of the magi in the catacombs of Rome, one image depicts two magi, another four, another eight. Regardless of their number, word quickly buzzes around the Judean capital that Zoroastrian priests from Persia or maybe even Oriental astrologer-magicians are searching for the newborn king of the Jews. Yehoshua's birth wasn't the first time Magi had visited luminaries they found important. One group attended Pilate's birth, while others sought out Herod, Caesar, and Augustus.

The news of a rival regent's birth freaks out client-king Herod the Great, the evil genius hired by Rome to play overlord of Judea, and he summons the chief priests and scribes to the palace for a grilling. Where will this Messiah be born? "In Bethlehem of Judea, for so it is written by the prophet: 'And you, O Bethlehem, in the land of Judah, are by no means least among the rulers of Judah; for from you shall come a ruler who will shepherd my people Israel'" (Matthew 2:5–6). Herod pulls the Magi aside, out of earshot of the assembled chief priests and legal experts, and asks them to spill the details on the star they've been tracking for nearly two years. He commands them to head to Bethlehem, find the infant, then report back so he too can go worship the little one. Let us note that even the Jewish Matthew admits that Gentiles are among the very first people to worship Yehoshua; in other words, this baby-king of the Jews is fit to rule all mankind.

These men, being no dummies, ignore Herod's orders. They make it to Bethlehem, with Matthew recording in 2:11 that they visited Mary and baby in a house, not a stable. The Magi bow down and worship the baby—an unbelievably strange experience for a teenage girl from Nazareth—then present their costly treasures before returning east instead of north back to Herod.

Forty days after Yehoshua's birth, and evidently still staying in Bethlehem, Mary is now considered ritually clean. The fledgling family makes their way to Jerusalem to fulfill the purification rites of Leviticus 12:6–8:

> When the days of her purifying are completed . . . she shall bring to the priest at the entrance of the tent of meeting a lamb a year old for a burnt offering, and a pigeon or a turtledove for a sin offering, and he shall offer it before the LORD and make atonement for her. Then she shall be clean from the flow of her blood. This is the law for her who bears a child, either male or female. And if she cannot afford a lamb, then she shall take two turtledoves or two pigeons.

Luke says the young family paid with poultry.

Stepfather Joseph continues to have powerful dreams. "Rise," a messenger tells him, "take the child and his mother, (notice the messenger does not say *"your wife and your son"*) and flee . . . for Herod is about to search for the child, to destroy him" (Matthew 2:13). The family leaves under cover of darkness and heads for the place all of Yehoshua's ancestors had fled in times of crisis: Egypt.

King Herod, meanwhile, realizes he's been duped by the wise guys. He needs to kill this would-be king before it's too late. He puts out the order to kill every boy under the age of two in Bethlehem and its vicinity. Scholars estimate between three and twelve infants would have been killed in what is now known as the Massacre of the Innocents. There aren't any extra-biblical records of this event, but considering Herod murdered one of his ten wives, one of his mothers-in-law, one of his brothers-in-law, and three of his own sons, plus lit two Jewish zealots on fire, drowned a man at a party, and—concerned no one would mourn at his funeral—locked a bunch of leading citizens in a hippodrome and asked his sister to execute them on his death day, the infant slaughter may have been too insignificant to record elsewhere.

The "Flight to Egypt," as this passage is labeled in most Bibles, always perplexed me as a boy. I pictured a toddler Josh with a Teenage Mutant Ninja Turtles carry-on, boarding a Pan Am flight (or maybe he was part of the Delta Fantastic Flyer's club), checking out the pyramids as the family landed at Cairo International. Again, if one sees parallels between Yehoshua and the Egyptian stories of Moses and Joseph, this is entirely purposeful on the part of the gospel author. Wise men visit Yehoshua, wise midwives visit Moses, and neither set obeys the commands of Herod/Pharaoh to destroy the infants. Joseph the dreamer's father is Jacob. Joseph the carpenter's father is also named Jacob. Joseph in the Old Testament and Yehoshua in the New both start their public ministry around the age of thirty. Joseph and Yehoshua both feed starving crowds. These parallels are purposeful waymarkers on the road to faith.

Notice also what Matthew is setting us up to understand: that Judah isn't functioning as God's kingdom anymore. The Judean king is now acting like Pharaoh and murdering infants. Egypt, the former place of slavery, is now a place of refuge. Something has gone terribly wrong in Israel.

Yehoshua's family had a history of fleeing to Egypt that would have been well-known to Mary and Joseph. Abraham and Sarah went to Egypt during a famine. Isaac did the same. Joseph's journey to Egypt was not by choice, but it ended up drawing his eleven brothers and father, Jacob, to visit, eventually leading to several centuries of Jewish enslavement in Egypt. With this in mind, Egypt may have been seen the way many refugees once saw America—as the land of hope and opportunity, or at least, a place to lay low and build wealth before returning home. In this sense, boy Yehoshua may be loosely deemed a refugee. It would be an understatement to say that the theme of migration is a minor one in Jewish Scripture; from Genesis, YHWH starts issuing laws and decrees for the welcome, protection, provision, acceptance, and love of migrants.

Herod dies in the spring of either 4 BC or 1 BC (likely the latter), in so much pain from worms, body rot, and ulcerated entrails (Josephus's words in *Antiquities XVII.6.5*) that he tries to stab himself to death. Down in Egypt, Joseph has another dream in which a messenger says, "Rise, take *the child and his mother* and go to the land of Israel, for those who sought the child's life are dead" (Matthew 2:20). Note the word *those*. A typo, perhaps? Scholars believe Herod's heir, Antipater, was just as evil as his father, but luckily for toddler Yehoshua, Herod offs the hyper-violent son just five days before expiring himself. Not that Herod's other son, Archelaus the Ethnarch, does a better job. Before Rome can confirm him as ruler, the people demand a tax reduction and a new high priest, and amidst the Passover mayhem of Jerusalem, he unleashes his army, murdering three thousand rioters. Joseph wisely steers the family past Bethlehem and around Jerusalem, and withdraws to the district of Galilee, to Mary's likely hometown of Nazareth. Archelaus will do such a poor job that Caesar Augustus will banish him to France two years later. He will be succeeded by his brother, Herod Antipas, who will execute Yehoshua ben Yehoseph three decades hence.

But for now, the Ben Yehoseph family is happily embedded in Nazareth, where Luke reports "the child grew and became strong, filled with wisdom. And the favor of God was upon him" (Luke 2:40).

What was Yehoshua's childhood like? Did he live in a multigenerational home like much of the ancient world? If so, who were his grandparents? Luke's reconstruction of Josh's maternal family tree names his maternal grandfather Heli. Matthew, who traces Joseph's paternal line, says Joseph's father's name is Jacob. If Yehoshua were born today, perhaps he'd call them Grandpa Jake and Grandpa Eli.

Did Yehoshua have cousins, not including his distant kinsman John the Baptizer? We know Mary had at least one sister because Yehoshua's aunt is present at his crucifixion (John 19:25). While there is no mention of others in Scripture, it is highly unlikely that in the age before birth control, both Mary's and Joseph's parents didn't have several other children per couple. If Mary and Joseph did have multiple siblings, it is likely those siblings also had multiple children. If Mary and Joseph each came from a sibling set of four to eight, this gives Yehoshua something in the range of twelve to twenty-eight aunts and uncles, and somewhere between two dozen cousins to well over a hundred playmates on their annual family Passover pilgrimage to Jerusalem.

We know Yehoshua had siblings. It may come as a surprise to some readers that Yehoshua was one of at least eight children in the Bar Jacob family. His four brothers are specifically named in Mark 6 and Matthew 13: James, Joseph (nicknamed Joses to set him apart from his dad), Judas (nicknamed Jude), and Simon, and Matthew 13:56 suggests Yehoshua has at least three sisters.

It is with a potentially huge extended family in mind that we turn to the only recorded story from Yehoshua's preteen years.

When Yehoshua is twelve and on the cusp of Jewish young adulthood, the whole extended family heads south from Nazareth on a sixty-five-mile uphill trek to Jerusalem. The caravan could have included Miriam, Yehoseph, Yehoshua, James, Joses, Jude, Simon, their three or more sisters, Grandma and Grandpa Heli, Grandma and Grandpa Jacob, an untold number of aunts, uncles, and cousins, along with Jewish kinsmen like Elizabeth and John the Baptizer, friends, neighbors, and acquaintances. Passover in Jerusalem was, after all, a party no one wanted to miss, like a sanctified Mardi Gras meets Burning Man (or rather, burning sacrifices). Kids would've loved it—the animals, the smoke, the slaughter, the merchants selling their wares, and especially the Passover meal itself. More an event and spectacle than anything else, the dinner was a thrilling reenactment of those dramatic final moments before boy Yehoshua's ancestors made a mad dash from Egypt.

It was also a dangerous time to be in the capital. Potentially several hundred thousand visitors descended upon the small city; the streets were packed, with thousands of families camping out on the Mount of Olives like a perennial Woodstock celebration. The Romans were on high alert: They always brought in extra troops for crowd control because zealots often stirred up riots.

When the Holy Week ends, the family heads back north. Mary and Joseph assume Yehoshua is somewhere among their huge caravan, and they go a full day's journey—at least to Ramallah or maybe even as far as Shiloh—before they begin looking for him "among their relatives and acquaintances" (Luke 2:44).

At some point it dawns on Mary and Joseph: *We forgot Josh!* A real first-century *Home Alone* situation if ever there was one.

The parents (and perhaps others) beat a hasty retreat to Jerusalem and scour the city for their presumably prepubescent boy. They wend their way through alley after alley in a city shaped more like a rabbit warren than a modern metropolis. Do they go door to door? Do they check in at the temple? Do they desperately enlist the help of the well-organized Romans? Luke only says that it takes them three days to find the lad.

One can only imagine Mary's sigh of relief at the sight of her beloved boy. There he is, this scrawny preteen with barely a hair on his upper lip, sitting in the temple "among the teachers, listening to them and asking them questions" (v. 46). Not content to simply inquire, he also pontificates, and apparently quite well. "All who heard him were amazed at his understanding and his answers" (v. 47). In other words, Yehoshua is a prodigy.

Yehoshua isn't the first young person in Jewish history to do something special as a child. Miriam may have been as young as seven when she bravely convinces the princess of Egypt to pay Moses's own mother to breastfeed him. Scholars estimate Samuel was just twelve when he hears the voice of God in Eli's house. King David is a boy when he downs Goliath. Solomon takes the throne at nineteen. Teenager Daniel, who is kidnapped and renamed Belteshazzar, survives the propagandizing education system of Babylon. Josiah becomes king at age eight.

These stories may have filled boy Josh with wonder at the possibilities of being a Jewish superhero. As an adult, as we will see later, Yehoshua recruits a number of young disciples and will prioritize kids and babies amidst large crowds. Inspired by his master, Paul of Tarsus will later tell Timothy, a protégé who came to faith as a teenager, to not "let anyone look down on you because you are young, but set an example for the believers in speech, in conduct, in love, in faith and in purity" (1 Timothy 4:12 NIV).

Joseph and Mary are both astonished at the sight of their rabbi-surrounded son, but it's Mary who attempts to scold the boy wonder. "Son, why have you treated us so? Behold, your father and I have been searching for you in great distress."

Is the tone of Yehoshua's reply teasing or delivered with the matter-of-fact deadpan of a spiritual savant? "Why were you looking for me? Did you not know that I must be in my Father's house?" (Luke 2:48–49). His parents simply don't understand what he's talking about. They take him back home to Nazareth, and Mary tucks the memory away in her heart.

This is a fascinating story packed with meaning and implication, but I want to focus on the sentence that opens the vignette: "His parents went to Jerusalem every year at the Feast of the Passover. And when he was twelve years old, they went up according to custom" (Luke 2:41–42). The Greek word for "custom" here is *ethos*. The Bar Jacob family has an ethos that involves an annual weeklong family pilgrimage to worship God.

One July when I was six years old, my father loaded our family into the minivan and took us on an excruciating four-hour road trip to Joy Bible Camp in Bancroft, Ontario, for a weeklong family camp with a hundred or so other Christian families. But it was worth it. It became the highlight of our year and the start of an annual tradition that left an indelible spiritual mark on our hearts as we all dug into the Bible in such a special environment.

My family's annual weeklong pilgrimage wasn't our only spiritual tradition, and it was probably similar for Yehoshua's upbringing. What were the routines, patterns, habits, traditions, and rhythms of life that ruled the Bar Jacob family? Beyond their annual pilgrimage, the text doesn't say. But we know Mary and Joseph were devout Jews based on their actions in the gospels—they travel annually for Passover, they have Yehoshua circumcised, they perform the postpartum purification rites, they pay their son's redemption price. Because these were faithful Jewish parents who raised a future rabbi, based on what we do know of the period, we can take an educated stab at how Yehoshua was parented through childhood and youth.

What follows are eight of the likely spiritual disciplines Mary and Joseph employed in the discipleship of their boy into the Jewish faith. This collection is by no means certain, nor is it by any means exhaustive.

1. Prayer

It goes without saying that the backbone of most religions is a fervent commitment to prayer, but few did it with more dedication than the Jews of Yehoshua's day. Prayer was at minimum a thrice-daily activity—morning, noon, and night—though extra-zealous Jews would have emulated King David and his seven prayers per day.

The main prayer in Yehoshua's childhood would have been the Shema starting in Deuteronomy 6:4: "Hear, O Israel! The LORD our God, the LORD is One!" Three times a day, Yehoshua and his family remind themselves to listen to YHWH. The next line will become a favorite refrain of Yehoshua's: "You shall love the LORD your God with all your heart and with all your soul and with all your might."

As per the command in Deuteronomy 6:9, the Bar Jacob home may have had a small box on its doorstep, called a mezuzah, containing a copy of this prayer on a rolled-up piece of parchment, which young Yehoshua and his siblings would have touched as they dashed in and out of the house.

2. Torah

If prayer is how a Jew speaks to God, then Torah is how he or she hears from him. Rabbis believe that the Torah has seventy faces, and that a student can spend their whole lives looking into the diamond of Scripture and still not fathom all its facets.

In an early third-century Jewish source, Mishnah Avot 5:21, rabbis lay out the ideal life plan for male Jews:

At five years old for the Scripture,
at ten years for the Mishnah,
at thirteen for [the fulfilling of] the commandments,
at fifteen for the Talmud,
at eighteen for the bride-chamber,
at twenty for pursuing [a calling],
at thirty for authority,
at forty for discernment,
at fifty for counsel,
at sixty to be an elder,
at seventy for gray hairs,

at eighty for special strength,
at ninety for bowed back,
and at a hundred a man is as one that has died and passed away and ceased from the world.

Yehoshua seems to have followed the first three rungs on this life ladder, plus the early adult bits—bearing in mind that most scholars agree he was executed before forty. Everything past sixty seems quite depressing in our medically advanced times, but a Roman-pressed peasant really would have been little more than a husk of a human at a hundred. We will discuss in chapter 5 if Yehoshua successfully married at eighteen, and in chapter 8 we will discover his career exploits. Luke 3:23 says Yehoshua was "about thirty years of age" when he began his ministry.

While some secularist-leaning scholars cannot hide their glee at prematurely announcing Yehoshua was nothing more than an illiterate peasant preacher, this is unlikely, and not only because John 8 says twice that he writes. As a boy, Josh likely started hearing, reading, and memorizing the first five books of the Bible according to the timeline above, and as an adult, Yehoshua will quote from twenty-four books in the Old Testament. In fact, over a tenth of all his teachings are lifted from the law and prophets on which he was raised. The Illiterate Jesus Theory also conveniently skips over one of the 613 Mosaic commands found in Deuteronomy 31:19—that each and every male must write out the Song of Moses. Could an illiterate boy write out a song? Yehoshua affirms his commitment to obeying the whole Torah, and note how he does so in specifically literary terms (emphasis added): "Do not think that I have come to abolish the Law or the Prophets; I have not come to abolish them but to fulfill them. For truly, I say to you, until heaven and earth pass away, *not an iota, not a dot* will pass from the Law until all is accomplished" (Matthew 5:17–18). On top of all of this, Galilee was known for its relatively high proportion of scholars, as evinced by the large number of famous sages the region produced.

3. Shabbat

Saturdays were YHWH's day. No work would be done by Mary or Joseph or any of their parents or children. It was one of the top ten rules, carved on ancestor Mosheh's stone tablets: "Remember the Sabbath day by keeping it holy."

What is the Sabbath? It is the seventh day of creation, that sweet Saturday on which even YHWH sits back and celebrates the work he has done.

How does one remember this radical act of rest? By setting Saturdays apart as special. From sundown on Friday to sundown on Saturday, we bask in YHWH's shalom.

The exact rules for how to do this are laid out across several passages in Exodus. They forbid activities such as working, fire-starting, making your kids do chores, making your employees come in on their day off, making your animals work, or enlisting the help of visiting guests. While this might seem a tad bossy to lax moderns, after four centuries of seven-day slavery in Egypt, a legally enforced day of rest was nothing short of revolutionary. Yehoshua clearly understood this, as he later tells a pack of religionists that "the Sabbath was made for man, not man for the Sabbath."

4. Pilgrimage

Spring Passover in Jerusalem wasn't the only festival the Bar Jacob family would have penciled into their annual calendar. Passover was often paired with First Fruits, a celebration of the spring barley harvest. Next came Pentecost in early summer, to offer the first fruits of wheat. Rosh Hashanah, Yom Kippur, and Sukkot—otherwise known as the Feast of Trumpets, the Day of Atonement, and the Feast of Tabernacles—fell in the early fall and were collectively known as the High Holy Days. John 7:2

says adult Yehoshua attends the Feast of Tabernacles, and John 10:22 says he attends the Festival of Dedication in winter, so we may guess these childhood trips became a regular part of his life's annual rhythms.

5. Synagogue

Young Josh attended synagogue, and all four of the gospel writers say he continued this foundational weekly practice throughout his adult life. Synagogues were far more than mere churches where parishioners checked in for an hour each week. They were centers of study and community—like a church, school, village hall, and community club all wrapped into one. We know Yehoshua attended a synagogue in Nazareth as a child because the parishioners all recognize him when he returns to preach there as an adult in Matthew 13:53.

In addition to synagogue sermons and temple teachings, boy Yehoshua would have been steeped in spiritual story. As a child in a predominantly oral culture without unlimited and highly addictive screen technology, he would have heard the stories of his people recounted again and again until he knew them by heart.

6. Tithing

If the Bar Jacob family prayed three times a day, devoted themselves to the Torah, regularly attended synagogue, and made their way to Jerusalem for Passover, it is unlikely that they skipped out on their financial responsibilities to the faith community. A tithe, which means "a tenth," was something of a misnomer. There were actually three tithes.

The Levitical tithe required all non-Levite tribes to give 10 percent of their crops and livestock to the Levites so they could focus on church and governance work.

The Festival tithe was likely everyone's favorite tithe. Deuteronomy 14 required the people to set aside a tenth of their yield *so they could have a huge party*. Essentially, the tithe was a built-in savings mechanism to finance the many annual fall festivals.

At the festivals, revelers were instructed to "Eat the tithe of your grain, of your wine, and of your oil, and the firstborn of your herd and flock, that you may learn to fear the LORD your God always" (v. 23). If the journey to the festival location was too far to transport all your goods, the law even had a provision for selling them for cash before heading down to the party. Upon arrival at the festivals, partygoers were instructed to "spend the money for whatever you desire—oxen or sheep or wine or strong drink, whatever your appetite craves. And you shall eat there before the LORD your God and rejoice, you and your household" (v. 26).

The Poor Tithe, the least-funded then as now, was used to feed refugees, widows, and orphans, and was only collected every three years.

Added together, the triple tithe worked out to 23.3 percent annually, not including freewill offerings, the half-shekel temple tax that Yehoshua will later mint from a fish's mouth, and leaving the corners of your fields unharvested so the landless could gather a share. In other words, the tithe was the taxation system of the Jewish nation and, all told, it's roughly what a middle-class American now pays in federal taxes. It is also worth noting that it was an extremely progressive tax system—only landowners and herd owners were required to pay, not hired employees. Even within the herd-owning class, the first nine animals were tax-free, with the tithe only kicking in on the tenth. Tithes were also not required of the landless who earned their keep by air, sea, or hand. To wit, the future carpenter-preacher Yehoshua picked a pair of tax-exempt professions.

7. Kashrut

Of the 613 Old Testament commandments, modern readers will be pleased to know that we are so steeped in the world of Judaism that we easily keep most of these laws, food-related or otherwise, without even knowing it. When was the last time you laid siege to a city and chopped down all its fruit trees (Deuteronomy 20:19)? Or had sex with a woman and her granddaughter (Leviticus 18:17)? Or roasted one of your children over open flames for Molech (Leviticus 18:21)? Such were the shocking acts that Moses had to wean out of humanity.

There is no evidence that Yehoshua ever broke the dietary laws of his ancestors. The seemingly strict food rules were a loving set of guidelines that taught former slaves how to be free, how to become healthy, and thanks to its limitation but not elimination of animal proteins, how to eat sustainably.

8. Hospitality

In spite of immense poverty compared with our overwhelming riches, first-century Jewish hospitality puts twenty-first-century "entertaining" to shame. While Yehoshua and the New Testament writers will lift hospitality to apotheotic heights, the value of open-door generosity was already well developed by Jews in the age before radical individualism.

The precedent starts with Abraham in Genesis 18, when he hurriedly welcomes in three strangers for a meal and foot-washing. Reuel the Midianite is downright disappointed his daughters almost deprive him of dishing dinner to Moses, and he ends up giving the future leader of Israel his daughter Zipporah's hand in marriage.

Post-Yehoshua rabbis will try to protect hospitable Jews from being overrun with predacious guests, with the Midrash Tehillim quite hilariously stating, "On the day a guest arrives, a calf is slaughtered in his honor; the next day, a sheep; the third day, a fowl; and on the fourth day, he is served just beans."

Did Mary and Joseph invite people, including strangers and refugees, to eat and find shelter in the Bar Jacob home? If they were faithful Jews, yes. And if the recorded incident of adult Yehoshua washing people's feet in John 13 is any indication, he knew exactly how to welcome guests and make them feel at home.

There are parenting lessons for those of us who partake in the miraculous blessing of being fathers and mothers, though that is clearly not why Luke included Yehoshua's childhood account.

If there is one thing that enculturated Christians have lost, it is the basic understanding that being a Christian requires living as Christ lived. We seem to think that if we are a vanilla cake with chocolate sprinkles, this somehow makes us a chocolate cake, but nothing could be further from the truth. What makes a Jew a Jew is living like a Jew. What makes a Christian a Christian is, as Bible teacher John Mark Comer so often puts it in his preaching and teaching, "Being with Jesus, becoming like Jesus, and doing what Jesus did." Perhaps it's a fruit of how poorly we translated the word *pístis* as *faith* instead of *faithfulness*, as though faith is just a one-time payment not followed by a lifelong subscription. Historical Christendom has consistently taken the easy route, requiring a statement of faith instead of an embodiment of faithfulness.

Christ-centered parenting requires the discipline of discipleship. Mary and Joseph successfully raise Yehoshua in a faithful, discipled, discipleship-focused context. The result? Yehoshua "increased in wisdom and in stature and in favor with God and man" (Luke 2:52). In other words, Yehoshua went through the awkwardness of puberty and the heavy labor of character-building, and entered into virtuous manhood.

That is about all we know about the upbringing of Mary's first son. Why do the gospel recorders pay so little attention to Yehoshua the child? It is because his infancy, toddlerhood, and adolescence are not the story they are trying to tell.

Unbelievably, all four gospel writers start the story at the same place: with Yehoshua's baptism in the Jordan River. They *unanimously* agree that the gospel starts with Yehoshua's semi-cousin Yohanan the Baptizer.

Mark begins his gospel by stating that the story of Yehoshua, the Messiah Son of God, starts with his cousin John the Baptizer.

John, who does almost nothing like the rest, pens a poetic ode to the Light and Logos before jumping straight to the Baptizer by verse 19.

When Peter picks a disciple to replace Judas, he specifically chooses "one of the men who have accompanied us during all the time that the Lord Jesus went in and out among us, beginning from the baptism of John until the day when he was taken up from us" (Acts 1:21–22).

Matthew drops a stylized genealogy and blazes through the birthing backstory before getting to John by chapter three.

Even Luke, who tells us the most about Yehoshua's younger years thanks to his connection to Mary, starts with John's story, then flashes back to Yehoshua's childhood for a few chapters, then catches back up to John in the present by chapter three.

In other words, everything prior to Yehoshua's baptism is just a prologue to the *gospel* story.

And since we have now finished our third chapter, let us move on from the prologue and dive into that same story.

The Rabbi Josh

"The Jew is born as free as the wind, as indomitable as the Judean desert."
—Yasmina Khadra, *The Attack*

Yehoshua's Baptism

John the Baptizer did not invent baptism. The Jewish practice of ritual dunking, which they call *mikveh*, meaning "collection of water," was practiced well before Yehoshua was born. So how did Christians end up adopting the symbolic practice? It likely starts with a group of radical pre-Christian monks.

While not specifically named in the Bible, a group of ex-priests called the Essenes split from the corrupt temple elite and retreated to desert caves by the Dead Sea a few decades before Yehoshua comes on the scene. At Qumran, where nineteen centuries later we will find 972 Dead Sea scrolls, they essentially become hermit-monks who devote themselves to a purer form of Judaism as they eagerly await the Messiah. Josephus and Philo report they bathed in cold water twice a day and immersed up to four thousand members as a symbol of repentance. Many of their members lived as celibates, and Herod the Great granted them special privileges because he respected their severe lifestyle.

If a Messiah-awaiting, Herod-pleasing, ascetic desert-dweller preaching a baptism of repentance sounds familiar, it is because this is Yohanan bar Zkaryah's *modus operandi.*

Some scholars speculate John the Baptizer may have been an Essene, or perhaps was temporarily an Essene before going off on his own. The Essenes were known for adopting children, and we know that John lived in the wilderness prior to his public ministry (Luke 1:80). John's parents, Elizabeth and Zechariah, were quite old when John was born, and if Zechariah was indeed murdered for protecting John during the Massacre of the Innocents, perhaps John was taken in by these ultra-faithful Jews and raised in the safety of the wilderness.

Either way, nearly every scholar agrees John baptized Yehoshua in the Jordan River Essene-style, but they are split on whether or not Yehoshua was a disciple of his kinsman for a season. At the very least, the elder kinsman is a mentor to Yehoshua, and the distant cousins share a common vernacular that suggests they spent at least some time together. Josephus records that John has a huge following—over 60,000 Mandaeans still exist to this day—and that Herod Antipas eventually turns on John for fear he will incite a rebellion and overthrow his client kingship.

Yet John says that the person following after him is far mightier (Matthew 3:11). Whether or not he is the disciple who outshines his master, Yehoshua believes that among mere humans, "there has arisen no one greater" than his distant cousin (Matthew 11:11), that John is the fulfillment of prophecy (Matthew 11:13), and that he is the Elijah of their generation (Matthew 11:14). This last one would not have been a huge leap, considering John purposefully wore the same outfit as the famous prophet (2 Kings 1:8; Mark 1:6).

After his baptism by John, Yehoshua remains in the desert for a long time, and it's only when John is arrested that Yehoshua "withdrew into Galilee" (Matthew 4:12). What does he immediately start doing? "From that time Jesus began to preach, saying, 'Repent, for the kingdom of heaven is at hand'" (Matthew 4:17).

But we are getting ahead of ourselves.

Wilderness

After being baptized by John in the Jordan River, Yehoshua remains in the desert, perhaps with or near John's growing community of desert-dwellers. He stays for at least forty days and endures a series of temptations. Mark summarizes the whole forty-day fasting ordeal in three terse sentences, but Matthew gives the Joshua Tree-like experience a good half chapter. A spiritual being called *diabolou* in Greek (translated "the devil") and *HaSatan* in Hebrew (meaning "The Adversary"), tests Yehoshua with three temptations, the same three Moses experienced.

The first is to turn rocks into bread, reminiscent of Numbers 20:11 when Moses cracks a crag in a cliff and a spring bursts forth. Yehoshua resists the temptation to break his fast by quoting Moses's words in Deuteronomy 8:3: "Man does not live by bread alone, but man lives by every word that comes from the mouth of the LORD."

The second temptation sees Yehoshua standing on the pinnacle of the temple in Jerusalem, with HaSatan saying he should jump to his death to see if angels will catch him. Yehoshua again quotes Deuteronomy: "You shall not put the LORD your God to the test" (6:16). Jewish readers will immediately pick up on the allusion to the way the Israelites test Moses and YHWH in Exodus 17:2.

We head to the third temptation: "The devil took him to a very high mountain and showed him all the kingdoms of the world and their glory" (Matthew 4:8). Modern geographers know this is not physically possible, but so did ancient Jews. The tempter invites Yehoshua to become his disciple in exchange for political power, but the extremely hungry soon-to-be-rabbi is having none of it. "Be gone, Satan! For it is written, 'You shall worship the Lord your God and him only shall you serve'" (Matthew 4:10). This is a quote pulled from Deuteronomy 6:13 and an immediate picture of the end of Moses's life, where he's standing on a high mountain overlooking the land of Canaan.

But here's the whopping difference Matthew wants his readers to understand: Whereas Moses cannot lead his people into the Promised Land, Yehoshua can lead his people into the Kingdom of Heaven.

Rabbi

It is important to note at this juncture that Yehoshua was not a Christian in our sense of the word, nor was he a pastor.

Indeed, Christians weren't even called Christians until years after Yehoshua's assassination. Acts 24:5 suggests some were known as "Nazarenes." It was at Antioch in what is now Antakya in southern Turkey—then the Roman Empire's third most important city, and the second most mentioned city in the book of Acts—that followers of The Way were first called *Christianos*. As for *pastor*, the word and position as we now conceive it appears nowhere in the Bible, and local churches in the New Testament simply did not have full-time paid ministers.

So if Yehoshua wasn't a Christian or a pastor, then what was he?

The gospels make it clear: Yehoshua was born a Jew, raised as a Jew, lived as a Jew, preached to Jews, and died as a Jew. When asked to recite the greatest commandment, he quotes Jewish Scripture. Many of his utterances on the cross are from Jewish Scripture. His twelve closest disciples were all Jews. The only writer in the Bible who for sure wasn't a Jew is Luke. And one simply cannot be the Jewish Messiah if one does not keep Jewish law. Accordingly, everything Yehoshua says and does must be viewed through the lens of a first-century Jew. This is an extremely difficult task, considering the vast religious, cultural, political, philosophic, socioeconomic, cultural, and linguistic spans between us.

Yehoshua is not only Jewish, but he has a distinctly Jewish job: He is a rabbi. He is called "teacher" forty-five times in the gospels and "rabbi" fourteen times. *Rabbi* and *teacher* didn't mean then what they mean now. Before the age of commercialized credentialing, *rabbi* referred to anyone knowledgeable in Jewish law who could attract a following. Such was the case with John the Baptizer; John 3:26 says his disciples called him by the honorific. If the ideal Roman was a powerful soldier, the ideal Jew was a learned scholar. Yehoshua certainly falls into the latter category, with several people in the gospels calling him *rabbi*, including Mary Magdalene, Peter, Nathanael, Judas, Nicodemus, two of John the Baptizer's disciples, and a crowd in Capernaum.

Technically speaking, the rabbinic era of Judaism didn't get into full swing until after the destruction of the second temple in 70 AD, when it became a formalized professional distinction like *reverend*. Yehoshua is more of a *hasid*, a sort of forerunner to the rabbinical tradition. So it perhaps makes more sense to simply call him a *teacher* or *master*. John, who penned his gospel after 70 AD, calls him *teacher* twice (John 1:38; 20:16). Regardless, Yehoshua couldn't be bothered with titles and instructs his disciples to avoid the term (Matthew 23:8), seeing *rabbi* and *reverend* as yet another set of pride-puffing status symbols.

That said, the position was formalizing enough to require some bona fides. Many rabbis bragged about their ancestry, or who trained them (Paul does so in Acts 22:3). On one of his trips to the temple in Jerusalem, Yehoshua is cornered by some of the chief priests, who ask, "By what authority are you doing these things, or who gave you this authority to do them?" (Mark 11:28). In other words: *Show us your papers*. Yehoshua, of course, carries no earthly stamp of approval. He is an unauthorized rabbi with an unwelcome message, and it's only a matter of time before they seek to silence this rogue "blasphemer."

All rabbis have one core job: to attract and train disciples. Some rabbis are spectacularly bad at their job, and some are astoundingly good. Rabbi Tarfon marries three hundred women during a famine to make them eligible to receive tithes. Rabbi Akiva has more than twelve thousand disciples and is unsurprisingly executed by the Romans. Rabbi Yohanan ben Zakkai essentially creates the Mishnah that has since trained tens of millions of Jews.

The period in which Yehoshua ministered is now referred to as late Second Temple Judaism. Within a handful of decades, this second temple will be razed by the Romans, never to be rebuilt in the generations since. The Judaism of the late Second Temple period was about an inch short of anarchy. There was no Pope or lead denomination to instruct Jews on how to obey the Torah. Everyone jostled for power and lobbied for their personal interpretation to be the de facto temple stance.

Hillel and Shammai, both Pharisees, were two big-time rabbis in Yehoshua's day. Their Torah academies both sought an answer to the question "What does it mean to be a good Jew?" This is no easy question, especially when your nation lives under the boot of a tyrannical overlord like Rome. Within the Pharisaical party, these two rabbis battled for the hearts and minds of the Jewish people. One prioritized people, the other prioritized principles. One was liberal and graceful in his interpretations of the Torah, the other was a hardline literalist. One said anyone could study the Torah, the other allowed in only "worthy" disciples. In the words of one commentator, "Hillel was known for teaching the Spirit of the Law and Shammai was known for teaching the letter of the Law."

Unsurprisingly, the School of Shammai is the dominant religious party and will play a role in turning over Yehoshua to the Romans for execution (though not as big a role as most churchgoers think). They later sided with the Zealots in their war against the Romans, which ended disastrously for most everyone except the pacifist House of Hillel, which survived for fourteen generations and nearly four hundred years.

Hillel's grandson Gamaliel not only trains Saul of Tarsus as a Pharisee (Acts 22:3), but later defends John and Peter before the synedrion (Acts 5:34). Yehoshua is obviously familiar with Hillel's work, as their teachings align nearly perfectly. Their biggest point of disagreement is on divorce, where Yehoshua is even more strict than Shammai.

That Yehoshua is familiar with Hillel's beliefs is certain, especially considering Yehoshua builds on one of Hillel's most famous teachings. From the Talmud:

> On another occasion a certain Gentile came to Shammai and said to him, "Make me into a Jewish convert, but teach me the whole Torah while I stand on one foot." Immediately Shammai drove him away with the measuring stick which was in his hand. When the same Gentile went before Hillel with the same proposition, Hillel said to him, "What is hateful to you, do not do to your neighbor. That is the whole Torah, while the rest is the commentary on it. Now go and study it."

Note the heavy-handed response of Shammai, but also remember the Silver Rule: *Don't do what you don't want people to do to you.* Yehoshua takes Hillel's excellent (albeit negatively framed) advice and flips it to the positive in Matthew 7:12: "So whatever you wish that others would do to you, do also to them, for this is the Law and the Prophets." In saying so, Yehoshua marks his place in first-century rabbinical Judaism: He is a Hillel rabbi in a sea of Shammai Pharisees.

Hillel says *Do no harm,* Yehoshua says *Do good,* and Shammai beats strangers with a stick.

Recruiting and Attracting Disciples

Following his baptism, the desert season, and kinsman John's arrest, Yehoshua returns north to Galilee and begins his public ministry. Nowhere does it say that Yehoshua was exactly thirty years old when he comes out as a rabbi. Luke 3:23 says he was "about thirty," and considering one couldn't be a temple priest until at least the age of thirty, we can assume he was slightly older.

Having just recruited his first four disciples on his way up the Sea of Galilee—we will meet them formally in the next chapter—he enters the Capernaum synagogue and starts teaching. They're impressed by his sense of authority, but even more impressed when he drives an "unclean spirit" out of an outspoken attendee, sending him howling and convulsing to the floor. "What is this?" the crowds murmur. "'A new teaching with authority! He commands even the unclean spirits, and they obey him.' And *at once* his fame spread everywhere throughout all the surrounding region of Galilee" (Mark 1:27–28, emphasis added).

Yehoshua beats a hasty exit from the synagogue and ducks into the house of Simon and Andrew, where Simon's wife's mother is wracked with fever. Yehoshua lifts her up and the fever leaves, and she plays materfamilias and feeds the hungry men. By nightfall, word has spread, and Simon's house is besieged with sick people and the demon-oppressed. The gospel writer Mark, let us note, is historically considered the disciple of Simon Peter, and Mark/Simon report that the "whole city" gathers at Simon's door for healing.

Before dawn, Yehoshua ditches his new disciples and heads to the wilderness to pray. Simon and crew eventually wake up, scour the area, find him, and tell him everyone's looking for him. Yehoshua demurs. "Let us go on to the next towns, that I may preach there also, for that is why I came out" (Mark 1:38).

From there, they head out on a synagogue-storming tour of Galilee. Like many overnight successes, his is three decades in the making. By verse 43, he must instruct the healed to stop telling others about him, but it's no use. By verse 45, Yehoshua can no longer openly enter a town, but rather has to remain in the wilderness like his kinsman John.

The Ministry

Churchgoers may recoil thinking about B-list horror movies, but the reality is that Yehoshua is an exorcist; he performs at least nine exorcisms in the gospels. Some of his closest disciples were men and women he freed from torment.

In addition to his work as a teacher and exorcist, he is also a feeder of masses and a public healer. In this latter vocation, he is hardly out of time or place. Unlike the city rabbis who focused their time on studying the Torah and leaving behind a body of written work, the wonder-workers in rural Galilee focused on healing prayer and left little literature to show for it. The Galilean Hanina ben Dosa left almost nothing in writing but was massively famous for his miracles. Honi the Circle-Drawer was from northern Galilee, just like Yehoshua, and left no library of literature. Yehoshua himself leaves behind no writing at all, yet it was his healings that had crowds swarming him wherever he went.

The difference between these rural rabbis and their city counterparts was stark. The urbane rabbis usually set up permanent shops and let the people come to them. Healers like Yehoshua did paralytics a favor and went to them. While the cosmopolitans usually charged a hefty fee for their services, Yehoshua not only doesn't charge for his miracles, but he often throws in a free meal as well.

Yehoshua doesn't perform miracles to attract a crowd or earn himself some Benny Hinn-style healing riches. No, he does the opposite. The majority of his miracles happen in private, and they are an affirmation of his previous teachings. Without fail, he tells those he heals to keep quiet. Why would any rabbi bent on fame and a following do such things? The cynic inside each of us might say he was using reverse psychology, but that would lead to the admission that these miracles were real. Imagine, for instance, you are a woman who has been suffering from an eighteen-year hemorrhage. If you aren't healed and someone tries reverse psychology on you, it simply won't do anything because you weren't healed. But if you have indeed been healed, who could possibly shut you up?

By and large, Yehoshua's miracles are done in private. Only occasionally does he do something public and spectacular like feeding five thousand, but he never does tricks upon request. On three occasions (Mathew 12:38–41; Matthew 16:1–4; Luke 11:16, 29–32), religionists demand to see a miraculous sign that Yehoshua is the Messiah. He rebuffs each request, telling them the only sign they'll receive is "the sign of Jonah."

Jonah, as some will recall, is the hard-to-believe story of a fellow who gets eaten by a whale, prays for rescue from inside its belly, and three days later gets upchucked on a beach. At least that's the story I learned in Sunday school.

Whales come in two types: the baleen type, which eats plankton, and the toothed variety, which chomp their prey to death. A human would not fit through the esophagus and stomach of a baleen whale, nor would they survive the jaws and four acid-filled stomachs of a toothed whale. Further, whale stomachs do not contain oxygen, but rather gases such as methane, and would easily kill a human being far sooner than three days.

Some Bible defenders pivot and say that the word in Jonah 1:17 and Matthew 12:40 is actually "huge fish," which is true, but I think they're missing the point. Both Yehoshua and the Old Testament writers understand the miracle that we moderns seem to miss: Jonah didn't survive three days in the belly of the whale; he *died and was resurrected by God.*

Read the actual text of Jonah's prayer (emphases added):

> "I called out to the LORD, out of my distress,
> and he answered me;
> out of *the belly of Sheol* I cried,
> and you heard my voice.
> For you cast me into the deep,
> into the heart of the seas,
> and the flood surrounded me;

all your waves and your billows
    passed over me.
Then I said, 'I am driven away
    from your sight;
yet I shall again look
    upon your holy temple.'
The waters closed in over me to take my life;
    the deep surrounded me;
weeds were wrapped around my head
    at the roots of the mountains.
I went down to the land
    whose bars closed upon me forever;
Yet you brought up my life *from the pit,*
    O LORD my God.
When my life was fainting away,
    I remembered the LORD;
and my prayer came to you,
    into your holy temple.
Those who pay regard to vain idols
    forsake their hope of steadfast love.
But I with the voice of thanksgiving
    will sacrifice to you;
what I have vowed I will pay.
    Salvation belongs to the LORD!"

Jonah 2:1–9

"The belly of Sheol" (Job 7:9; Psalm 16:10; Psalm 49:14–15; Psalm 89:48) and "the pit" (Psalm 40:2; Job 33:18; Job 33:28) are clear Old Testament terms for "the realm of the dead." The "land whose bars closed upon me forever" is a reference to the gates of Hades (Matthew 16:18).

What if Jonah is half-drowned in a storm; he sinks to the bottom, dies, gets swallowed by a fish, and his spirit prays to God from the underworld?

What happens after the great fish spits Jonah's corpse back on dry land?

YHWH says, "Arise!"

It's the same thing Yehoshua says before raising the little girl in Mark 5:41.

What is the sign that Yehoshua will give the religionists to prove that he is God? The sign of Jonah. He will die, and three days later, God will raise him from the dead. What if the sign of Jonah is *resurrection*?

Yehoshua moves from place to place, doesn't accept money for healing services, is constantly telling people not to tell others about their healings or their speculations that he is the Messiah, and when people ask him to do miracles, he points them to an Old Testament sign of resurrection and redemption (Mark 8:30; Mark 7:36; Matthew 12:16; Luke 5:14; Matthew 8:4). Clearly, Yehoshua is not your average itinerate healer.

Nor is he your average teacher.

The Teacher of Teachers

The Socratic method of teaching and the kinesthetic learning model weren't developed in Yehoshua's day, but he did use the teaching methods available to him, most of which are still used in our children's classrooms.

1. Puns

Though it never shows up in our English Bibles, Yehoshua likes a good play on words. In Matthew 23:24, he calls the religionists blind guides who strain out a gnat but swallow a camel. Not very punny, unless you go with the Aramaic words for camel and gnat: You strain out a *galma* but swallow a *gamla*!

Or how about John 3:8? "The wind blows where it wishes, and you hear its sound, but you do not know where it comes from or where it goes. So it is with everyone who is born of the

Spirit." In Aramaic, the two words are the same: The *ruha* blows where it wills . . . so it is with everyone who is born of the *ruha*.

Yehoshua even uses a pun in nicknaming the presumably muscular fisherman Simon. Simon becomes Cephas or Peter. *Petros* in Greek means rock, as does the Aramaic word *kepha*. In other words, Yehoshua has a disciple named Rocky.

2. Similes and metaphors

We're heading back to grade school on this one. A simile is an explicit comparison between two unrelated things, joined by a connective word such as *like* or *as*. See Matthew 10:16: "I am sending you out as sheep in the midst of wolves." Luke 17:6 says we need to have "faith like a grain of mustard seed." Like similes, metaphors compare two unrelated things, but the comparison is implicit: "You are the salt of the earth" (Matthew 5:13) and, "You are the light of the world" (Matthew 5:14).

3. Exaggeration

The literalists among us (and those in Yehoshua's day) will be disgruntled to know he uses both overstatement and hyperbole to make his points. The trick, of course, is figuring out when he's serious and when he's seriously exaggerating, which is harder to do on paper than when he preached to a live audience. There are a few of which we can be sure: "If your right eye causes you to sin, tear it out and throw it away" (Matthew 5:29); "If your hand causes you to sin, cut it off" (Mark 9:43); "If anyone comes to me and does not hate his own father and mother and wife and children and brothers and sisters, yes, and even his own life, he cannot be my disciple" (Luke 14:26). Yehoshua does not want his disciples to be eyeless, handless, and family-less. He wants them to realize how serious sin is and how serious discipleship is.

Perhaps the easiest-to-spot example of Yehoshua's exaggerations occurs in Matthew 18. His disciples have been bickering about who the greatest person in heaven will be, so Yehoshua calls over a child and tells the adults to humble themselves and become a cultural nobody if they want to be great in heaven. He then drops three huge exaggerations on the adults *in front of the child*. If he acts them out, he no doubt elicits much mirth from the little one:

> "But whoever causes one of these little ones who believe in me to sin, it would be better for him to have a great millstone fastened around his neck and to be drowned in the depth of the sea.
>
> Woe to the world for temptations to sin! For it is necessary that temptations come, but woe to the one by whom the temptation comes! And if your hand or your foot causes you to sin, cut it off and throw it away. It is better for you to enter life crippled or lame than with two hands or two feet to be thrown into the eternal fire. And if your eye causes you to sin, tear it out and throw it away. It is better for you to enter life with one eye than with two eyes to be thrown into the hell of fire."
>
> Matthew 18:6–9

By making a purposefully exaggerative point in front of a child, Yehoshua gets across to the adults the severity of sin and its ability to separate us from God.

4. Poetry

Yehoshua employs at least five types of poetic parallelism. They don't rhyme, but they have rhythm.

Matthew 7:17
"Every healthy tree bears good fruit,
but the diseased tree bears bad fruit."

Mark 4:22
"Nothing is hidden except to be made manifest;
nor is anything secret except to come to light."

Matthew 10:40
"Whoever receives you receives me,
and whoever receives me receives him who sent me."

5. Proverbs

Proverbs, we must note, are not absolutes, but helpful generalities or truisms. When Yehoshua says in Matthew 26:52 that "Those who use the sword will die by the sword" (NLT), he does not mean that every single person who picks up a sword will be slashed to pieces in the end. He says in Matthew 10:24 that "A disciple is not above his teacher," but we know plenty of students who outshine their teachers and do them proud.

Yehoshua is about as proverbial as Benjamin Franklin, and he has a rich tradition of wisdom literature (Job, Psalms, Proverbs, Ecclesiastes, and Song of Solomon) from which to draw. Sages often recycled or innovated popular proverbs and sayings. For instance, a version of "Those who are well have no need of a physician, but those who are sick" (Mark 2:17) appears in Diogenes and Plutarch several centuries before Yehoshua speaks it.

6. Quotation

Many churchgoers will be surprised to learn that the Bible contains quite a few "secular" quotes. Paul of Tarsus, for instance, quotes Menander in 1 Corinthians, Aratus in Acts, and Epimenides's hilarious paradox in Titus. Yehoshua reframes at least one quote from Hillel the Elder, but more often than not, he can be found quoting the Torah. In fact, he quotes from twenty-four books in the Old Testament, suggesting he memorized huge swaths of Scripture. If he is not a scholarly savant, he has a mind like a steel trap.

7. Interpretation

Like Hillel and Shammai and many others, Rabbi Yehoshua gives his crowds and his disciples his unique perspective on passages from the Torah. Most of his teachings line up with graceful progressives like Hillel, but occasionally he says things that strike his audience as downright outrageous, as when he reads from Isaiah and then tells the crowd he has fulfilled the text in his person.

8. Questions

Unlike many of today's drone-at-students-ad-nauseam teachers, first-century rabbis had a teaching style that built on the Socratic method: They asked their disciples questions and then questioned their answers. Yehoshua picks up this technique early, as Luke 2:46 says that Mary and Joseph find their lost twelve-year-old in the temple, "sitting among the teachers, listening to them and *asking them questions*." By the time he is fully grown, this question-asking habit is fully developed. According to Martin B. Copenhaver's wonderful book *Jesus Is the Question*, Yehoshua is asked 183 questions in the gospels and he answers just *three*. More importantly, he asks 307 questions—more than a hundred questions asked for every one question answered.

When asked what must be done to inherit eternal life, he responds with two questions: "What is written in the Law? How do you read it?" (Luke 10:26). In Mark 3, the religionists are ready to pounce if Yehoshua heals a supplicant with a withered hand on the Sabbath. The rabbi stands the injured man in front of the cruel and callous crowd. It's one of the few times where the text says he is angry at their hard hearts. He asks this question: "Is it lawful on the Sabbath to do good or to do harm?" (v. 4). He then proceeds to heal the man's hand without waiting for a response.

9. Parables

A parable is a simple story that illustrates a spiritual lesson. Rabbinic literature contains well over three thousand parables, and Yehoshua contributes more than four dozen to that glorious pile. Parables like the Mustard Seed, the Sower, the Prodigal Son, and the Good Samaritan are legendary two thousand years later and must have set off a veritable firestorm of discussion (and disagreement) back in the day. Parables aren't Yehoshua's way to "dumb down" his sermons for the illiterate masses. If anything, they are the opposite—parables allow Yehoshua to speak clearly to real seekers while baffling unbelievers.

Matthew 13:34 says, "All these things Jesus said to the crowds in parables; indeed, he said nothing to them without a parable." Mark 4:34 adds that Yehoshua "did not speak to them without a parable, but privately to his own disciples he explained everything." This bugs the disciples so much that they ask him, "Why do you speak to them in parables?" (Matthew 13:10). He replies,

> Because the knowledge of the secrets of the kingdom of heaven has been given to you, but not to them. . . . This is why I speak to them in parables:
>
> "Though seeing they do not see;
> though hearing they do not hear or understand. . . .
> For this people's heart has become calloused;
> they hardly hear with their ears,
> and they have closed their eyes.
> Otherwise they might see with their eyes,
> hear with their ears,
> understand with their hearts
> and turn, and I would heal them."
>
> Matthew 13:11, 13, 15 NIV

In other words, Yehoshua didn't use parables to illustrate his points and make his message clear but to do the opposite: to hide the real meaning from those who couldn't be bothered to open their ears to hear. In Matthew 11:25, Yehoshua thanks God for religionist delusion: "I thank you, Father, Lord of heaven and earth, that you have hidden these things from the wise and understanding and revealed them to little children."

There is also a self-protective element in Yehoshua's parables. Because he regularly speaks in the presence of enemies, cloaked speech is a literary defense against trouble. Parables allow him to hide in plain sight. Matthew 21:45 says that the scribes and Pharisees eventually begin to pick up on this sneaky technique: "When the chief priests and the Pharisees heard his parables, they perceived that he was speaking about them."

In addition to all the practical reasons for using cloaked stories, Matthew 13:35 interprets Yehoshua's use of parables as a fulfillment of prophecy, allowing him to "utter things hidden since the creation of the world."

Puns, similes, metaphors, overstatements, hyperbole, poetry, proverbs, quotations, interpretations, questions, parables. As we can see, Yehoshua is an able teacher who employs as wide a range of tools in his oratory as he did in his carpentry, and we didn't even discuss his riddles (Matthew 21:23–27), irony (John 9:32–41), *a fortiori* arguments (Matthew 7:9), rhetorical devices (Matthew 7:16), or paradoxes (Mark 12:41–44). Added all together, any fair-minded person will concede that this teacher is almost certainly not illiterate.

But enough about the methods. What set Yehoshua apart from every other teacher in history was not his teaching style, but the message he conveyed.

Before one can understand what Yehoshua is saying, one must first understand what he is *not* saying. Many Christians believe he says that the Jewish law is henceforth abolished, but this is not his message at all. Not once in Scripture does Yehoshua break the Law of Moses, and there isn't a single verse in the entire Bible where he tells his disciples to do so. Quite the opposite, as Yehoshua upholds the law time and time again.

Matthew 5:17, 19: "Do not think that I have come to abolish the Law or the prophets. . . . Whoever relaxes one of the least of these commandments and teaches other to do the same will be called least in the kingdom of heaven, but whoever does and teaches them will be called great in the kingdom of heaven."

Luke 16:17: "It is easier for heaven and earth to pass away than for one dot of the Law to become void."

After healing a leper in Mark 1:44, Yehoshua says, "Show yourself to the priest and offer for your cleansing what Moses commanded."

The list goes on. Yehoshua is not here to abolish the law. Not even the Pharisees accuse him of breaking the Mosaic law—it's their rabbinical traditions that he violates (Mark 7:5).

The Pharisees believe Jews can win salvation by perfect obedience to God's laws through their man-made traditions. Yehoshua cares far more about our internal condition than our external behavior. Perfecting the latter never heals the former. Fix the inside, and the outside will fix itself. In Matthew 23:25–26 he says, "Woe to you, scribes and Pharisees, hypocrites! For you clean the outside of the cup and the plate, but inside they are full of greed and self-indulgence. You blind Pharisee! First clean the inside of the cup and the plate, that the outside also may be clean." Yehoshua uses another inside-out metaphor in Matthew 7:15: "Beware of false prophets, who come to you in sheep's clothing but inwardly they are ravenous wolves."

The religionists had become so fixated on rules that they had abandoned the rule-giver. Yehoshua says it is time to repent—it is time to return.

Rabbinical Innovations

> *"The works of monks and priests, however holy and arduous they be, do not differ one whit in the sight of God from the works of the rustic laborer in the field or the woman going about her household tasks."*
>
> —Martin Luther, *The Babylonian Captivity of the Church*

We will get to Yehoshua's core message, but it is worth dwelling for a moment on three major innovations he brings to his Jewish audience.

The first of his innovations is to strip away the religionist barnacles from the weighty hull of Judaism. One can best picture the teachings of Yehoshua as a power sprayer or sandblaster against the crusty temple elites of his day. His blistering attack on the religious establishment is so fierce and overwhelming that it disorients many of his entrenched hearers. To quote John MacArthur's *New Testament Commentary*, "Because Jesus swept away the traditions of washings, special tithes, extreme Sabbath observance, and such things, the people thought he was thereby overthrowing God's law."

Take, for instance, Saturdays. As a faithful Jew, Yehoshua obeys the *biblical* Sabbath mandates to the letter, but he openly flouts the religionist's burdensome rules and shoddy interpretations of what it means to keep Saturdays special. He ignores the Pharisaical cup washings, the use of separate cutlery, and the highly superstitious hand-washing routine, and he doesn't let the Sabbath keep him from healing a crippled woman (Luke 13:10), healing Simon's mother-in-law from a fever (Mark 1:29), healing a man's withered hand (Mark 3:1), healing a blind man (John 9:1), and healing a demon-possessed man (Mark 1:21).

Yehoshua tends to ignore their man-made rules and traditions, except for the times when he straight-up trolls them. Luke records one brutal and hilarious scene in chapter 14: "One Sabbath, when he went to dine *at the house of a ruler of the Pharisees*, they were watching him carefully. And behold, there was a man before him who had dropsy." (The painful condition is now better known as edema, a build-up of fluid that causes swelling in hands, arms, feet, and legs.) Yehoshua asked the Pharisees and experts in the law, "Is it lawful to heal on the Sabbath, or not?" (vv. 1–3). They remained silent. And no doubt squirmed in anger while Yehoshua takes hold of the man and rids his body of bloat.

After the healed man exits, Yehoshua presses his Sabbath-is-for-man case. "Which of you, having a son or an ox that has fallen into a well on a Sabbath day, will not immediately pull him out?" (v. 5). The religionists at this party remain awkwardly silent.

How could wonderful things such as healing possibly be seen as sin? Because religion crept in. Sabbath was a revolutionary innovation for the former Hebrew slaves—Isaiah 58:13 calls the Sabbath a total and utter delight—and the original guidelines for keeping Saturdays holy were extremely simple: "For six days, work is to be done, but the seventh day shall be your holy day, a day of Sabbath rest to the LORD. . . . Do not light a fire in any of your dwellings on the Sabbath day" (Exodus 35:2–3 NIV). "Remember the Sabbath day, to keep it holy. Six days you shall labor, and do all your work, but the seventh day is a sabbath to the LORD your God. On it you shall not do any work, you, or your son, or your daughter, your male servant, or your female servant, or your livestock, or the sojourner who is within your gates" (Exodus 20:8–11, with Deuteronomy 5:12–15 and Exodus 34:21 repeating the same).

That's it. There are no other biblical rules about how to keep the Sabbath holy. Don't work, and don't force others to work; don't even go through the arduous task of collecting firewood and rubbing two sticks together to light a fire; just rest and remember the Creator. That is how one keeps the Sabbath. But that didn't stop the religionists of Yehoshua's day from erecting a vast and rickety scaffolding of extra rules around the honorable edifice. Like all bureaucracies, they made it up as they went, metastasizing details until the bloat made Sabbaths significantly *more* work than the other six days and blotted out the meaning of Sabbath itself. *Remember the Saturday that God rested from his great and good work.* Yet the religionists want to *kill* Yehoshua for an activity as simple as eating raw grain (Luke 6:1) because they conflate it with commercial harvesting.

The actual rules of the Sabbath as outlined in Exodus are quite basic: Don't work or force others to work. Yet to this day, orthodox Jews follow a huge list of rules that includes no writing, no erasing, no tearing paper, no cooking, no baking, no driving or riding in cars, and no turning on or off anything that uses electricity. There are now thirty-nine *categories* of prohibited work; Jews are told that even their fridge light should be disconnected before Shabbat by unscrewing the bulb slightly, and a freezer whose fan is activated when the door is opened may not be used. Another crazed extrapolation? Turning Joshua 3:4 into a "Sabbath's day's journey" and ruling no one can walk more than 0.596 miles beyond their city limits. According to chabad.org, "The Shabbat laws are quite complex, requiring careful study and a qualified teacher." But Yehoshua says no, they aren't, and no, they don't. Go ahead and ignore the Talmud, the *6,200-page* interpretation of Jewish law. (But before we get too judgy, let's not forget that the United States has hundreds of thousands of criminally enforceable regulations. The Internal Revenue Code alone runs more than 6,800 pages.) Like all of YHWH's instructions, the Shabbat is meant to *free* us, not enslave us. He knows the Sabbath isn't supposed to be an arduous duty that humans owe to YHWH. In Mark 2:27, Yehoshua says Sabbath is YHWH's gift to *us*.

Yehoshua clashes with the religionist on all sorts of man-made rules and traditions, including the company they keep and don't keep, their ceremonial rituals, and the treatment of women. On each issue, he blasts away the barnacles to reveal the sparkling hull of his perfect law of liberty (James 1:25). In the same way Yehoshua heals the man with painful edema, he also wants to heal Jews from the excruciating bloat of religion.

Yehoshua's second rabbinical innovation is to never discredit or dismiss the Torah but to fulfill or further develop it by getting to the root of each instruction. Unlike the liberal Hillel types and the conservative Shammai types, Yehoshua isn't trying to interpret the Law—he's claiming authorial *intent*.

The Old Testament says "Do not kill"; Yehoshua says *don't even harbor unreconciled anger* (Matthew 5:22–25).

The Old Testament says "Do not commit adultery"; Yehoshua says *don't even look at a woman lustfully* (Matthew 5:28).

The Old Testament says "Do not divorce your wife without a certificate"; Yehoshua says *what God has joined together, let not man separate* (Mark 10:9).

The Old Testament says "Do not charge interest to fellow Jews"; Yehoshua says *loan even to your enemies without expecting anything back* (Luke 6:34–35).

The Old Testament says "The eyewitnesses must cast the first stone"; Yehoshua says *he who has no sin should cast the first stone* (John 8:7).

The Old Testament limits retribution to "an eye for an eye and a tooth for a tooth"; Yehoshua says to *turn the other cheek* (Matthew 5:39).

Why does he do this? Isn't the law strict enough? Well, that depends on your interpretation. Is it a law that binds, or a law that frees? It may be profitable to step back and ask ourselves: What was the law of Moses *for*?

Scholars generally believe it served four purposes:

1. To encourage people to return to their one true God, YHWH.
2. To protect them from harm.
3. To set them apart from other nations.
4. To teach them how to be free people.

Why would Rabbi Yehoshua want to do away with such a glorious body of law?

Matthew 5:17 says, "Do not think that I have come to abolish the Law or the Prophets; I have not come to abolish them but to fulfill them." *Fulfill* here means "to fill it up," like a half-empty glass. Yehoshua does not teach his disciples to ignore the Torah but to fill it up with mercy and grace and love.

Jews were to keep the Law for their protection and provision, but the reality is that they and we will never keep it perfectly because we are imperfect people. And that's okay because keeping the Law perfectly was *never* what made us right before YHWH. It was *always* faith (Hebrews 11:8–39). This is the realization that Law-trained Paul elucidates in Philippians 3:9: "Not having a righteousness of my own that comes from the law, but that which comes through faith in Christ, the righteousness from God that depends on faith."

Yehoshua unquestionably calls his disciples to an extremely high standard of morality, but he never says this is what wins them *salvation*. Faith alone can do the healing work that no work can do (Mark 5:34; Luke 7:50; Luke 17:19; Luke 18:42). We put our faith in YHWH and his son Yehoshua to seal our salvation, and we live it out through obedience to his Word. As Paul of Tarsus put it: Love *is* the fulfillment of the Law (Romans 13:8, 10).

If you're living under love, the law becomes irrelevant. If you aren't lusting, you don't need a law forbidding adultery. If you're committed to sober-mindedness (1 Peter 5:8; Titus 2:6–15; 1 Timothy 3:2), you don't need a law forbidding drunkenness. If you don't hate anyone, you don't need a law forbidding murder. Love fulfills the law's authorial intent.

Understanding Yehoshua's fulfillment of the law has profound implications for Christians today. If the Old Testament says, "Don't turn a profit off the poor," what is the loving action that deems this law unnecessary? If the Old Testament says, "Don't charge interest to your faith nation," what is the loving action that deems this law unnecessary?

The Old Testament laws were meant to provide, protect, and connect us to YHWH—but they were also a springboard to connect us to *what God wants to do in our hearts*. Instead of just following the rules in our head, love achieves the law's intent in a way that our hearts are transformed in the process. Anyone who loves God and others with all their heart, soul, mind, and strength will not only never break the law, but will fulfill its authorial intent by living a love-driven life.

If Yehoshua's first rabbinical innovation is to strip away the religionist barnacles, and his second is to fill up the Law, his third innovation is twice as uncomfortable for the religionists as the first two combined: He is disconcertingly un-Jewish in his attitude toward Gentiles. A Gentile was and is any person who is not Jewish, leaving the disciples with plenty of people to hate—Egyptians, Persians, Romans, Samaritans. Jews hated (and still hate) Samaritans in particular, and not without their reasons. Samaritans are half-Gentile; they worship God on Mount Gerizim instead of Jerusalem; they obey an ancient version of the Torah that Jews believe is fake; they opposed the rebuilding of Jerusalem; they aided Alexander the Great in his conquest of Judea. By Yehoshua's day, Jews had avoided Samaria for six centuries.

So what does Yehoshua do in John 4:4–42? He goes on a historical sight-seeing tour straight *through* Samaria. His presumed destination is the well of his ancestor Jacob, a deepwater borehole in the permeable limestone hills of this God-forsaken enemy territory. Knowing full well his disciples still hate the Samaritans of this particular ZIP code (Luke 9:51–53), he sends them into town to buy food while he takes a break from their moaning.

Here's where the story gets truly scandalous. As he is resting by his forebear's watering hole, someone approaches. A notorious someone. Who is the very first person to hear from Yehoshua's own lips that he is the Messiah?

A Samaritan . . . woman . . . living in adultery.

It is likely at this point that Yehoshua's disciples realize all bets are off. As if to hammer home the point to his disciples, Yehoshua does the unthinkable and agrees to stay in the Samaritan town for two days (John 4:40), winning himself a whackload of converts (John 4:41).

Yehoshua continues this reckless disregard for race hatred. In Luke 17:11–19, he heals ten lepers and the only one who thanks him is a Samaritan.

When he is accused of being a Samaritan and possessed by demons in John 8:48–49, he cheekily answers with, "I am not possessed by a demon."

I have feasted over Shabbat with Hasidic Jews in Brooklyn, but I have also experienced the scorn of religionist Jews in Jerusalem who would not come anywhere near the ten-foot communal table at a burger joint in the Jewish Quarter until I stood up. One imagines it similarly took the disciples a beat to get up to speed with the idea that Samaritans, Gentiles, and even Romans were people dearly beloved by their master, but it seems he gives them plenty of opportunities to acclimate. In Mark 3:7, crowds from Tyre and Sidon (Gentile towns) came to listen to him. In Mark 5, he passes through a Gentile-majority area and evicts a legion of demons from a human and casts them into a herd of two thousand decidedly unkosher pigs. In Matthew 15:21, he commends a Syrophoenician woman for her faith. In Luke 10 and Matthew 11, he shames the Jewish towns of Chorazin, Bethsaida, and Capernaum by saying the Gentile folks of Tyre and Sidon would've been more receptive to his message.

Right before entering Peter's home in Capernaum, Yehoshua heals a Roman centurion's servant and commends the soldier's faith, saying, "Many will come from east and west and recline at table with Abraham, Isaac, and Jacob in the kingdom of heaven" (Matthew 8:11).

He often hangs out with undesirables. In Matthew 8:1, he touches a man with leprosy. In Luke 9:40, it's a boy with epilepsy. In Luke 7:34, it's tax collectors and prostituted women.

While Yehoshua *says* he came to reach the Jews, unlike other rabbis in his time, this radical doesn't hesitate to heal and minister to Gentiles, women, prostitutes, tax collectors, children, beggars, lepers, and even a few Pharisees, and they love and follow him for it.

So what does Yehoshua the rabbi teach? Certainly not much compared with today's seminaries. Yehoshua offers no eight-year systematic theology degree. He doesn't even have an unpaid summer internship for gap-year disciples. He assumes his audience has a good base in the Jewish faith, and he builds from there. The gospels have around fifteen hundred of his sayings, totaling somewhere in the vicinity of 30,000 words—less than a third the size of this book. In so few words, Rabbi Yehoshua teaches a huge range of subjects, covering everything from forgiveness to divorce, and cup washing to murder. He teaches on love, hate, power, poverty, obedience, sacrifice, faith, marriage, and especially money, which we will discuss at length in chapter 8.

But all of Rabbi Yehoshua's teaching can be roughly boiled down to just one core theme: the kingdom of God.

The kingdom of God is Yehoshua's central teaching. There isn't a Christian theologian, secular scholar, or anti-theist historian who says otherwise.

What is Yehoshua's first public teaching in Mark 1:15? "The time is fulfilled, and the kingdom of God is at hand; repent and believe in the gospel."

What is Yehoshua's first public teaching in Matthew 4:17? "Repent, for the kingdom of heaven is at hand."

What does Yehoshua say in Luke 4:43 when his disciples ask him to stay in Capernaum? "I must preach the good news of the kingdom of God to the other towns as well; for I was sent for this purpose."

Yehoshua uses "kingdom of God" and "kingdom of heaven" interchangeably, as per the taste of the gospel writers, and the

Gospels are absolutely packed with these two phrases. In fact, *seventy-six* of Yehoshua's teachings are about this kingdom.

The first question that arises is: Who is this kingdom's king?

The answer depends on how one understands the concept of the Messiah. The Hebrew word *mashiach* originally meant "the anointed one." *Mashiach* applies to kings (2 Samuel 22:51), priests (Leviticus 4:3), and even the non-Jewish Cyrus II of Persia (Isaiah 45:1). One can even "anoint" wafers by spreading them with olive oil (Exodus 29:2). But like all words, *mashiach* evolves over time, starting from roughly "divine agent" to taking on mythical godlike status by Yehoshua's day.

For centuries, Jews had been bickering over who the Messiah would be and what he would accomplish. Some think he will be a priest. Others say he will be an angel. Most are pretty confident he will be a descendent of King David. For many, throwing off the oppressive yoke of the Romans is all that matters. Others are content just to be rid of the rules and regulations of the religionists. Others will settle for nothing less than total global domination by the Jewish race. The more devout hoped for a Messianic age—when shalom will flood the entire earth and all of mankind and nature will finally live at peace.

Looking back from our vantage point, it is now clear that the Old Testament is not simply a collection of the national literature of the Hebrew people. The entire library is an expression of Messianic hope, and you can feel this yearning from post-fall Genesis to the last gasp of Malachi.

Yehoshua is not the first or last so-called messiah to rock up to Judea. Hillel's grandson mentions two of them in Acts 5:36–37. Theudas attracted four hundred disciples before the Romans killed him and scattered his people. Judas the Galilean led a thousands-strong revolt and was also wiped out. The list of messiah claimants is so long that it is embarrassing. Athronges (a tall shepherd) and his four tall brothers led an insurrection against Herod Archelaus and lost badly. Simon of Peraea, a former slave of Herod the Great, also notably tall, declared himself king and burned down the royal palace at Jericho. A bit of a serial arsonist, he and his men burned down a number of Herod's houses before the Romans beheaded him. Rabbi Akiva thought Simon bar Kokhba was the Messiah—he did manage to create a somewhat independent Jewish state for a whole three years before it went back under the Roman heel, but not before 580,000 Jews were murdered and 985 villages were completely leveled.

The Jewish people cannot wait for their messiah. In addition to the crushing Roman taxation that funds their ongoing oppression, Jews are sick and tired of the violence perpetrated by Rome. When the Roman proconsul Pompey besieged Jerusalem, he not only murdered an untold number of Jews, but he entered the Holy of Holies, a truly unthinkable act. Crassus, the most money-hungry Roman of all time, later robbed the temple to finance one of his wars. Varus crucified two thousand Jews around Jerusalem. Archelaus murdered three thousand during Passover. No wonder the Zealots were on the rise and would eventually go to war with Rome.

The Hebrew word *mashiach* doesn't appear in our mostly-Greek New Testaments. The Greek word for *Messiah* is *Christos*, from whence we get the English *Christ*. True to Greek culture, *Christos* comes from *chrió*—to anoint with *olive* oil (extra virgin, no doubt). In other words, Yehoshua's English name isn't first-name-Jesus, last-name-Christ. His name and title are Jesus *the* Christ—Yehoshua the Rescuer/Priest/King/Messiah/God, depending on how you interpret *mashiach* and *Christos*.

The word *Christos* appears a whopping 538 times in the New Testament, and all are in reference to Yehoshua. All four gospel writers believe Yehoshua is the Christ-Messiah. All of Yehoshua's disciples believe he is the Christ-Messiah, though Judas Iscariot's understanding of the term differs more widely than the rest, mistakenly thinking his master is primarily a military revolutionary-in-waiting. Most important, Yehoshua ben Yehoseph knows he is the Christ-Messiah.

Because the term is loaded with much political charge, Yehoshua generally avoids voicing this belief. When disciples of his imprisoned kinsman, John the Baptizer, ask if he's the Christos or if they should expect someone else, Yehoshua gives a cloaked answer that will comfort his kinsman on death row. "Tell John what you have seen and heard: the blind receive their sight, the lame walk, lepers are cleansed, and the deaf hear, the dead are raised up, the poor have good news preached to them" (Luke 7:22).

However, Yehoshua occasionally cops to being the Christ-Messiah in private, when it's just him and his closest disciples (Mark 8:30; Matthew 16:17) or with blind dudes who've been rejected by their own parents and chucked out of the synagogue because they started seeing on the Sabbath (John 9:1–41). As noted earlier, the first person in whom he confides is the Samaritan woman of John 4:25–26. The only place he publicly admits he's the anointed one (aside from his Sanhedrin trial) is in his home synagogue in Nazareth—and they try to hurl him off a cliff for it (Luke 4:29).

But *mashiach* isn't the rabbi's go-to nomenclature. He's called all sorts of things by the gospel writers—Son of God, Son of David, King, Servant of the Lord, Prophet, Savior, Lamb of God, and The Word—but the title Yehoshua prefers to call himself is "The Son of Man." The cryptic phrase appears more than one hundred times in the text, and it baffles disciples and detractors alike. On the surface it might seem as though he's trying to communicate his humanness, that he's just one of the guys, but he's actually paying homage to a prophet's vision in Daniel 7:13–14 (which, incidentally, was written in Yehoshua's native Aramaic): "I saw in the night visions, and behold, with the clouds of heaven there came one like a son of man, and he came to the Ancient of Days and was presented before him. And to him was given dominion and glory and a kingdom, that all peoples, nations, and languages should serve him; his dominion is an everlasting dominion, which shall not pass away, and his kingdom one that shall not be destroyed."

If that isn't Messiah-speak, I don't know what is.

This title is brilliant. He can't openly call himself God because the religionists will stone him as a blasphemer. He can't openly call himself the Messiah or the Romans will execute him as a terrorist. So Yehoshua uses an insider's reference. He's the Son of Man. Who is the Son of Man? He is a spiritual being that looks like a *ben adam* (i.e., a human being) but can hover in the clouds and stand face-to-face with God himself. This man-looking being is given honor and a kingdom with a domain so large that it encompasses all of humanity—Gentiles, Samaritans, and Romans—and unlike earthly kingdoms, this one is indestructible and will last forever.

In other words, Yehoshua sees himself as the *christos-mashiach,* and a very specific version of that word: He's the end-times spiritual-king-of-a-universal-kingdom kind of Christ-Messiah.

The Son of Man is the king of this kingdom of God. If Yehoshua is not YHWH incarnate, then he is the most narcissistic rabbi in history, considering nearly all of his teachings are about himself and his kingdom. If we are to understand Yehoshua's life, we must make sure we are crystal clear about his central message. He believes no one can get into YHWH's kingdom except through himself (John 14:6).

What is this mysterious kingdom? Is it a new law to replace the Law of Moses? Is it the restoration of the Davidic kingship over Israel? Is it the total destruction of the Roman Empire and the beginning of YHWH's rule over the entire physical world? Or is it an empire of the mind, an eternal kingdom of spirit instead of flesh?

Let's not waste words: This kingdom is not an earthly kingdom. It is impossible for first-century Jewish listeners to separate politics from religion, but Yehoshua cannot make it clearer than he does in John 18:36: "My kingdom is not of this world." The word for *kingdom* here is *basileia,* connoting a sense of dominion and domain. Governors and kings and Roman emperors had *basileia*. The kingdom of God is Yehoshua's vision of YHWH's total rule and reign over all the world and universe. That will happen in the future. For now, the kingdom of God is wherever the rule and reign of God are present, be it one nation, one province, one city, one household, or one heart. It has no physical boundaries. It cannot be contained. It is in this world but it is not of this world.

The rabbi says the kingdom of God has already arrived (Matthew 11:12), but that it is also still on its way (Mark 9:1; Mark 14:25). To borrow from the Arthurian legends, it is the once and future kingdom. When the religionists ask him when the kingdom of God will come, he tells them it is already in their midst (Luke 17:21). Yet he teaches his disciples to pray, "Your kingdom come" (Matthew 6:10). Yehoshua is here to inaugurate the kingdom's arrival, but it won't be fully consummated until he returns. In other words, we readers are awaiting—to borrow Tolkien's fine phrase—the return of the king.

Where did Yehoshua come up with this idea? The phrase appears nowhere in the Old Testament, yet his audiences all seem to have some vague expectation of a coming kingdom. Eden was a kingdom. Abraham was promised a kingdom-sized family. Moses wandered the wilderness in search of a kingdom. Joshua carved out space for such a kingdom. The judges served "in those days where there was no king." David and his heirs ran a kingdom for a while. Perhaps the *mashiach* will restore the family-nation to its rightful place in the world? The vast majority of Yehoshua's hearers think his kingdom will be political and physical—but Yehoshua envisions a holy nation comprised of every tribe and tongue under the sun.

What Is This Kingdom Like?

Your average nation becomes a country by way of a document, such as the American Declaration of Independence or the British

Magna Carta. Yehoshua's kingdom, on the other hand, starts with a story. A series of stories, in fact. Mental images that paint a picture of what God's reign will look like when it is fully realized. These word pictures are the only way he describes his kingdom to the masses (Matthew 13:34).

The kingdom of God is like a mustard seed (Mark 4:30). Mustard is powerful and potent yet extremely divisive when people first encounter it. Mustard shrubs go viral, dropping seeds and spreading like weeds. In other words, the kingdom of God is a wild faith that runs roughshod over established religion.

In Yehoshua's vision of the kingdom of God, everything is upside down. There are no jousting knights in this kingdom. The well-dressed do not get the box seats. Consider his parable in Luke 18:

> Two men went up to the temple to pray, one a Pharisee and the other a tax collector. The Pharisee, standing by himself, prayed thus: "God, I thank you that I am not like other men, extortioners, unjust, adulterers, or even like this tax collector. I fast twice a week; I give tithes of all that I get." But the tax collector, standing far off, would not even lift up his eyes to heaven, but beat his breast, saying, "God, be merciful to me, a sinner!" I tell you, this man went down to his house justified, rather than the other. For everyone who exalts himself will be humbled, but the one who humbles himself will be exalted.
>
> vv. 10–14

Yehoshua startles his audience in Mark 10:15 by embracing some kids while telling the adults that "whoever does not receive the kingdom of God like a child shall not enter it." In first-century Jewish culture, this means that this is a kingdom for nobodies.

Not only that, but those accustomed to first-class will get reassigned to coach; those at the front of the line will find themselves in the rear. Yehoshua says the last will be first, and the first will be last. The gospel writers record him saying these words in four different contexts (Matthew 20:16; Matthew 19:30; Mark 10:31; Luke 13:30), suggesting this was a key teaching. What would such a teaching look like in our day? It means the Christian CEO doesn't accept a paycheck worth four hundred times their average worker's salary, but is instead the lowest-paid person in the company. It means the Christian pastor bends down to clean the toilets before ascending the pulpit. It means if a church has VIP seating for celebrities, it simply isn't a Christian church.

For the poor and abused, the kingdom of God is extremely good news. The kingdom of God is like hidden treasure and uncovered pearls, like a wedding feast where the poor and crippled are invited. It belongs to children and the childlike, the outcasts and the nobodies.

But for the rich and powerful, this new contender kingdom is terrifying. The first will be last and the last will be first. It is hard for rich people to enter the kingdom of God. The kingdom is like wheat and weeds—at the end of time, the wheat gets harvested and the weeds get burned.

Despite the immense amount of personal sacrifice and temporary discomfort this humbling new kingdom will require of us, isn't this what we instinctively desire in our heart of hearts? Romans 14:17 says the kingdom of God is all about right-way-of-livingness, shalom, and joy in the Holy Spirit. What could be better than a world flooded with justice and grace and truth and love and an infinity of shalom?

People respond differently when they learn about the kingdom of God (Mark 4). Some just never understand it. Some receive it with excitement but then walk away when times get tough. Many more hear about the kingdom, but money and social obligations and the desire for other things choke it out. But a few receive it gladly and multiply it into the lives of thirty, sixty, or a hundred others. It starts small, like a single grain of mustard or yeast—just one individual life—but it eventually spreads throughout society. But to be clear, this new covenantal kingdom is not a new religion, denomination, political party, or cultural revolution.

How does one experience said kingdom? By seeking it above all else. "Seek first the kingdom of God and his righteousness, and all these things will be added to you" (Matthew 6:33). Or, as I say to my Sunday school students: Seek first YHWH's kingdom and his right-way-of-livingness. Yehoshua's first public teaching in Mark 1:15 is this very invitation. "The time is fulfilled, and the kingdom of God is at hand; repent and believe in the gospel." The word for *repentance* means to turn around, or even better, to return. The literal definition in *Strong's Concordance* is "to change one's mind." Yehoshua invites would-be disciples to return their hearts and minds to YHWH, because his reign and rule have arrived.

So what is the rabbi's core message?

The time is now. The God-king is here. His heavenly kingdom has arrived. Return to the king and believe the good news.

A Stunning Success?

Yehoshua is not a successful rabbi-turned-messiah. The Egyptian had four thousand assassins (Acts 21:38). Judas the Galilean (Acts 5:37) had at least thousands, if not tens of thousands. Rabbi Akiva had more than 12,000 disciples, though some sources say 24,000 or even 48,000.

It appears as though Yehoshua's message is generally well received, especially by the poor and disenfranchised. (How little has changed in the twenty centuries since.) This radical rabbi's message incenses the religious establishment and will soon agitate the Romans enough to trigger his arrest, but for now, the crowds follow him in ever-growing numbers.

But Yehoshua's rabbinical "career" ends with fewer than six dozen disciples, many of whom are "mere" women.

And it makes sense. Who wants to turn the other cheek and serve without self-seeking? Who wants to give all their money to the poor and pray for their enemies? Who wants to pick up their own cross and march themselves to Golgotha so that others may live?

Yet is there any message more likely to bring about the kingdom of God and usher in heaven on earth?

Yehoshua knows his message is dangerous and divisive. He is not interested in unity for unity's sake. He is not interested in what we would crassly call "world peace." His message is deeply upsetting, unsettling, unnerving. He is desirous of unity among his disciples (Mark 9:50), but he correctly predicts the world will rage in opposition to this new family of faith. Using some of his most violent imagery in all the gospels, he foresees his message will slice like a sword (Matthew 10:34), shattering families (Matthew 10:35; Luke 12:52).

> "Blessed are you who are poor, for yours is the kingdom of God" (Luke 6:20). *Only the poorest of the poorest are anywhere close to innocent.*
>
> "Woe to you who are rich, for you have received your consolation" (Luke 6:24). *Enjoy your ill-gotten gain while it lasts.*
>
> "Woe to you who are full now, for you shall be hungry" (Luke 6:25). *You've starved out the poor and the tables are about to turn.*
>
> "Woe to you who laugh now, for you shall mourn and weep" (Luke 6:25). *You've mocked the poor and insulted their maker.*
>
> "Woe to you, when all people speak well of you" (Luke 6:26). *Friendship with the world is hostility with God.*

As we can see, his teachings are extremely upsetting to basically everyone with any semblance of wealth, power, or sense of entitlement. "I am owed" doesn't appear in Yehoshua's vocabulary, and he endlessly attacks entitlement regardless of socioeconomic status.

Though his public ministry gets off to a great start in Capernaum, his teaching just doesn't make much of a splash in his hometown. Mark 6, Matthew 13, and Luke 4 record the scene, with most Bibles tellingly labeling the passage "The Rejection at Nazareth." After a successful initial run in Capernaum and the surrounding villages of Galilee, and healing a few sick people upon arrival, he goes to the Nazareth synagogue on Saturday as was his custom. He decides to do a reading from Isaiah. They hand him the scroll, and he unspools the document. "The Spirit of the Sovereign LORD is on me, because the LORD has anointed me to proclaim good news to the poor. He has sent me to bind up the brokenhearted, to proclaim freedom for the captives and release from darkness for the prisoners" (Isaiah 61:1 NIV).

Then he rolls it up, hands it back to the usher, and sits down. Luke 4:20 says that "the eyes of all in the synagogue were fixed on him." What is going through their minds? *Is that it, your entire sermon? No commentary, no deep insight, no breathtaking prayer, no miraculous signs like the ones we heard happened in Capernaum?*

Yehoshua stares back at the home crowd and mic drops one sentence: "Today this Scripture has been fulfilled in your hearing" (v. 21).

Can you imagine if your son, or the son of someone you grew up in church with, had the audacity to say such a thing?

The crowd immediately starts chattering to each other. "Is not this Joseph's son?"

Yehoshua seems unsurprised by the tepid response.

> "Truly, I say to you, no prophet is acceptable in his hometown. But in truth, I tell you, there were many widows in Israel in the days of Elijah, when the heavens were shut up three years and six months, and a great famine came over all the land, and Elijah was sent to none of them but only to Zarephath, in the land of Sidon, to a woman who was a widow. And there were many lepers in Israel in the time of the prophet Elisha, and none of them was cleansed, but only Naaman the Syrian."
>
> vv. 24–27

In other words: When true prophets come to town, it's the Gentile outcasts who usually welcome them and the Jewish insiders who miss out.

This insinuation enrages the parishioners. "When they heard these things, all in the synagogue were filled with wrath. And they rose up and drove him out of the town and brought him to the brow of the hill on which their town was built, so that they could throw him down the cliff" (vv. 28–29). It's not exactly the warm welcome one would expect from a church crowd for a returning hero. He somehow gives them the slip and heads back to Capernaum.

This theme of rabbinical rejection is not an insignificant thread throughout his public ministry.

In Luke 9, a Samaritan village refuses to receive him.

In John 7, he narrowly escapes arrest.

In John 8, religionists try to stone him.

In Mark 12 and Matthew 21, he identifies with the Psalm 118 description of "the stone that the builders rejected."

In John 6, after one particularly tough sermon, "Many of his disciples turned back and no longer walked with him."

In Mark 5:17 and Matthew 8:34, a crowd of residents from the ten cities of Decapolis beg him "to depart from their region."

Despite the spectacular crowds in town after town, Yehoshua's healings and teachings don't seem to yield much in the way of converts and dedicated disciples. He chastises several Jewish towns, and then denounces the towns in which most of his miracles had been performed because they did not repent.

> "Woe to you, Chorazin! Woe to you, Bethsaida! For if the mighty works done in you had been done in Tyre and Sidon [Gentile cities], they would have repented long ago in sackcloth and ashes. But I tell you, it will be more bearable on the day of judgment for Tyre and Sidon than for you. And you, Capernaum, will you be

> exalted to heaven? You will be brought down to Hades. For if the mighty works done in you had been done in Sodom, it would have remained until this day. But I tell you that it will be more tolerable on the day of judgment for the land of Sodom than for you."
>
> Matthew 11:20–24

Then Yehoshua declared, "I thank you, Father, Lord of heaven and earth, that you have hidden these things from the wise and understanding and revealed them to little children" (v. 25).

As the day draws nearer to his Passover Week crucifixion, Yehoshua himself seems to be thinning the herd and winnowing the following. John 6 relates how Yehoshua scares away a huge number of followers and even a great many of his disciples. After feeding the five thousand near Tiberias, Yehoshua and his disciples cross the lake to Capernaum. The next morning, a bread-seeking crowd loads into boats and heads over. They find Yehoshua in the Capernaum synagogue and ask him what works of God they should do. He tells them to do just one work: "Believe in him whom he has sent" (John 6:29). They immediately ask him to perform another miracle, ideally something involving a free bottomless breakfast (John 6:30–34). Yehoshua claims that *he* is the eternal bread that came down from heaven. The crowd balks. Is not this Yehoshua, "the son of Joseph, whose father and mother we know? How does he now say, 'I have come down from heaven'?" (v. 42).

Yehoshua tells them to quit moaning, and then really freaks them out with a food-based metaphor they weren't expecting: "Whoever feeds on my flesh and drinks my blood has eternal life" (v. 54). This seemingly cannibalistic response repulses those who do not know the secret kingdom language. "When many of his disciples heard it, they said, 'This is a hard saying; who can listen to it?" (v. 60). After this, many of his disciples turned back and no longer walked with him.

It doesn't seem to faze Peter and the rest of the Twelve, for when Yehoshua asks if they want to abandon him as well, Simon speaks for the group: "Lord, to whom shall we go? You have the words of eternal life, and we have believed, and have come to know, that you are the Holy One of God" (vv. 68–69).

By the time of his crucifixion, Yehoshua will teach and feed tens of thousands of people but earn just seventy-odd disciples. But being a successful rabbi isn't Yehoshua's goal. He has far bigger ambitions.

Church Founder

There is a temptation in every culture to take the kingdom of God and try to stuff it into the culture. The Greek temptation is to make the kingdom of God a mere school of philosophy. The Roman temptation is to make it a legal framework. Our modern Western temptation is to turn the kingdom of God into a marketable, scalable, sellable brand. We are all guilty of trying to turn the kingdom of God into something it is not, be it a cult of identity, authenticity, political ideology, or tribal culture.

What was Yehoshua's ultimate plan? To reform Judaism? To start a new sect or denomination within Judaism? To start a new religion? To build a church?

The answer is yes. The rabbi's teachings do help reform Judaism; they do create a new Jewish sect; they do start a new religion; they do launch a new church.

But the answer is also no. Yehoshua never mentions the words *ordination, reverend, minister, presbytery, laity, liturgy*, or *clergy*. Being a titled church leader doesn't make one a Pharisee, of course, but all these titles tread on ground unfamiliar to the first-century rabbi who invites all disciples into a direct relationship with himself. Yehoshua definitely plans to build a church (Matthew 16:18) and assumes it already exists (Matthew 18:17). His church is a circular *ecclesia* with himself at the center, a called-out gathering of disciples from all ages, nations, cultures, and economic walks of life.

In other words, he is building a holy kingdom.

The Relational Josh

"Do I not destroy my enemies when I make them my friends?"
—Attributed to Abraham Lincoln

It is easy to forget that Yehoshua spends his life among real human beings. Yehoshua ben Yehoseph knows how to win friends and influence people, many of whom will later play eyewitnesses for the four gospel writers. He is a man rich in love, and his relationships can be roughly broken down into eight categories: family, the Twelve, the seventy, the women, the multitudes, friends, public enemies, and secret supporters.

The Nuclear Family

What do we know about Yehoshua's family?

His mother's name is Mary (*Miryam* in Hebrew, *Miriam* in Aramaic), and her name means "beloved" or "exalted one." She is a hardy woman who raises eight or more children, potentially without a husband during some of their teen years. The fact that Mary manages to raise at least eight children to adulthood is a feat not to be overlooked—the average life expectancy for Jews in Roman times was just *twenty-nine*. That said, as many as half the population died by age ten, and an untold number died in battle or by capital punishment. If you could avoid these three sad scenarios—and were lucky enough to not be born a slave, servant, or peasant—you stood a good chance of living a full life.

Yehoshua's earthly father is Joseph (*Yehoseph* or *Yosef* in Hebrew, *Yoseph* in Aramaic), and his name means "God will add." There is unconfirmed speculation that Joseph is significantly older than Mary, which wouldn't be unheard of in a time of arranged marriages. The rest of the family crops up throughout Yehoshua's public ministry, but Joseph drops from the biblical story when Yehoshua is just twelve, and considering Yehoshua assigns his mother's care to one of his disciples in John 19:27, it does not seem likely Joseph lived long enough to witness his stepson's execution.

We assume that Yehoshua is the eldest of the Mary-Joseph clan, but there are ardent believers who insist that Mary remains a lifelong virgin and that the seven or more mentioned siblings come from a completely undocumented first marriage of Joseph's prior to his wedding Mary. This is a tenuous bet at best, and for the purposes of this chapter we will assume Yehoshua is their firstborn. While the birth order is not clear, Yehoshua has at least seven siblings.

The first is James (*Ya'aqov, Yaaqob,* or *Ya'akov* in Hebrew and Aramaic), and his name means "to follow" or "supplant."

Up next is Joseph Junior, whom everyone calls Joses to differentiate him from his father (Mark 6:3; Matthew 13:55). Then Judas (*Yehudah* in Hebrew, *Yehuda* in Aramaic), whose name means "let God be praised." Judas is nicknamed Jude, presumably to set him apart from Judas the Betrayer and the other four Judases named in the New Testament.

The last of the five brothers is Simon (*Simeon* or *Shimon* in Hebrew and Aramaic), and his name means "he who hears."

In other words, Mary had five boys whose names started with the letter Y: Yosef, Yehoshua, Yaaqob, Yosef Junior, and Yehudah. Poor Shimon. At least he is listed in Scripture. Yehoshua's three or more sisters (Matthew 13:56) are not named in the text, which is unsurprising. We don't know what happened to them, but it is likely they married Jewish men and had prodigious families of their own.

Much has been made of the idea that Yehoshua has serious conflict with his nuclear family, perhaps that he is even estranged. John 7:5 says his own brothers don't believe him. Mark 3:21 says Yehoshua's family tries to take custody of him, believing he is "out of his mind." This suggests his family understandably takes a little longer to acclimate to their suddenly famous rabbi-possibly-Messiah relative. I have a brother, and even if he had been a seemingly perfect child, I would still have my doubts if he started calling himself the king of the universe.

That said, they may very well have believed in Yehoshua's miracles and message but simply disagreed with his methods. In John 7:3, Yehoshua's brothers invite him to travel to Jerusalem with them for the Feast of Tabernacles so he can show off his wonder-workings *in public*. While Yehoshua wants to quietly build a grass-roots movement—like mustard bushes and yeast in bread—brother James and the rest want a thunderbolt to the seat of Roman power.

Whether they're dubious of his godhood or his plan of attack, it is doubtful that this leads to lifelong estrangement. After all, Yehoshua continues to spend time with his family even after recruiting disciples and going public. John 2:12 says Yehoshua attends a wedding with his mother, then heads "down to Capernaum, with his mother and his brothers and his disciples, and they stayed there for a few days." Luke reports in Acts 1:14 that in addition to the eleven remaining disciples who gather in the upper room to devote themselves to prayer after the murder of

Yehoshua, there are others present, including "Mary the mother of Yehoshua, and his brothers."

Yehoshua's brother James evidently comes around to believing his brother is the Christos-Meschiach. James's Hebrew name means "to follow," and this he does by taking a major leadership role in the Jerusalem church after his brother's ascension. How does he start his biblical letter to the twelve tribes of the diaspora? "James, a servant of God and of the Lord Jesus Christ to the twelve tribes in the Dispersion: Greetings" (James 1:1). Galatians 2:9 describes Yehoshua's brother as an "esteemed pillar" of the church in Jerusalem; Paul says in 1 Corinthians 15:7 it's because Yehoshua appeared to James post-crucifixion—and it is James who makes the final rulings at the epic Council at Jerusalem in Acts 15. He even gets a nickname: James the Just.

Paul also intimates in 1 Corinthians 9:5 that at least two more of Yehoshua's brothers play a role in the church as well. Yehoshua's brother Jude makes a written contribution to Scripture, quilling the second-to-last book of the Bible that bears his name. In the letter, he calls his brother "Christ our Lord" (v. 25) and says he is his servant (v. 1).

While Yehoshua's siblings clearly had conflicting feelings about their brother near the beginning of his public ministry, they evidently found peace by the end.

The Family

When one thinks of the word *family* today, usually a nuclear image is conjured. But not so for a first-century Jew in a communal age. In addition to the nuclear family of Miriam, Yehoseph, James, Joses, Jude, Simon, and three or more sisters, Yehoshua likely grows up with or in close connection to Grandma and Grandpa Heli (Mary's parents), Grandma and Grandpa Jacob (Joseph's parents), plus an untold number of aunts, uncles, and cousins, and kinsmen like Elizabeth and John the Baptizer.

While the names of potentially a hundred or more family relations are now lost to history, Scripture does record the name of one of Yehoshua's aunts on his mother's side (John 19:25). Her name is Salome (Mark 15:40), meaning "peace," and she's married to Yehoshua's industrious fisherman uncle, Zebedee. She is also the mother of two of Yehoshua's inner twelve disciples, James and John. She is a woman of much pluck; later, she will ask Yehoshua to let her two sons sit on either side of the rabbi when his kingdom arrives (Matthew 20:21). While the other ten disciples are indignant, Yehoshua graciously responds that heaven's seating arrangement is up to his father, YHWH.

The Inner Twelve Disciples

If you ask the average churchgoer to name the inner twelve disciples, you are likely to hear "Matthew, Mark, Luke, John, Acts-ually, I don't think that's right. Wait a minute, let me see if I can remember."

Yehoshua preaches to literally tens of thousands of people and attracts and retains nearly six dozen disciples, but let's meet the inner twelve.

1. Simon bar Jonah (Peter)

Despite the fact that he is *not* the first disciple to join Yehoshua, Simon's name always appears first on lists of the twelve disciples. The reason is clear—he is the ringleader in faith, fun, and fury (John 18:10). Yehoshua's brother James calls Simon *Simeon* in Acts 15:14, likely to differentiate him from his own brother. The name Simon means "he who hears," and a perceptive reader of John 21:7 will realize the gospel writer is no literary slouch. "Then the disciple whom Jesus loved said to Peter, 'It is the Lord!' When Simon Peter *heard* that it was the Lord, he put on his outer garment, for he was stripped for work, and threw himself into the sea."

Simon is outspoken, brash, hotheaded, and unafraid of violence. We can assume his father's English name is Jonah because Yehoshua calls him "Simon bar Yonah" in Matthew 16:17. He is from Bethsaida (John 1:44) but lives in the fishing town of Capernaum. He trawls the Sea of Galilee with his brother Andrew and his business partners James and John (Luke 5:10). He is married (Mark 1:30), has a home (Luke 4:38), and his wife travels with him on mission trips (1 Corinthians 9:5).

Despite his self-protective instincts, in the end he will request of the diabolical Nero an upside-down crucifixion in Rome, seeing himself as unworthy to die in the same manner as his Lord.

Yehoshua rarely calls him Simon because he has another disciple named Simon and a brother named Simon. Instead, Yehoshua gives Simon an Aramaic nickname. "Jesus looked at him and said, 'You are Simon the son of John. You shall be called Cephas'" (John 1:42). As we learned in chapter 4, the Aramaic *Cephas* translates to the Greek *Petros/Petra,* which also means rock or boulder. Was Simon particularly muscular? Why else would you name someone Rocky?

Yehoshua uses this Petros-Petra combo for a tidy wordplay pun in Matthew 16:18, saying, "And I tell you, you are Peter, and on this rock I will build my church, and the gates of hell shall not prevail against it." The joke isn't any good in English, but it works in Greek. "You are *Petros* and on this *petra* I will build my church." Sadly, billions of Christians have not only missed the joke but also the meaning of the sentence. In fact, it might be the most widely misunderstood verse in the entire Bible. Read the text and context in Matthew 16:13–17. Nearly all the ancient greats from Augustine to Ambrose to Chrysostom to Jerome agree: Yehoshua is not building his eternal church on a hothead fisherman or the hard ground of Caesarea Philippi, but on the bedrock foundational truth that Peter has just expressed: Yehoshua is indeed the Christ, the Son of the living God.

2. Andrew bar Jonah

Though Simon is always listed first among the inner twelve, it is my strong hunch that his brother Andrew is the first of the disciples that Yehoshua recruits, having known him since their desert-dwelling days. (The Orthodox Church calls Andrew "The First-Called.") John 1:35–40 says Andrew starts off as a disciple of John the Baptizer but bids farewell to John after John labels his kinsman "the Lamb of God." In this sense, Andrew is the most experienced of the disciples.

He too is from Bethsaida and lives in the fishing town of Capernaum, working as a fisherman with his brother Simon. Andreas is a Greek name, and considering his brother's name is in Aramaic and Hebrew, either we've lost Andrew's real name or he mysteriously went by Andreas, which means "brave." According to tradition, Andrew refuses to be crucified by the Romans in the same manner as his rabbi, and is executed around 60 AD in Patras, Greece, on a *saltire* X-shaped cross. He now has a town and a golf course in Scotland named after him, and the St. Andrew's Cross is the emblem on the Scottish flag, believed to be the oldest flag in Europe.

3. Yohanan bar Zebedee

Yohanan is Yehoshua's maternal cousin. It is not unreasonable to speculate that the self-effacing John is the other disciple of John the Baptizer who joins Andrew in following Yehoshua in John 1:35. He evidently has a special connection with his cousin-rabbi, and when it comes time to pen his gospel as an old man, he calls himself "the disciple whom he loved."

John is Salome and Zebedee's son. He lives in the fishing town of Capernaum and works as a fisherman with his brother James and his father Zebedee (*Zebadyah* in Hebrew). John might be the wealthiest of the disciples, or at least the most politically connected, because as we will see later, John is a known quantity in the palace of Israel's high priest (John 18:15), perhaps as the high priest's official fish supplier. John's is an entrepreneurial family—his father is wealthy enough to have employees (Mark 1:19–20), and John and his brother James are business partners with Simon Peter (Luke 5:10). Not mentioning Simon's brother Andrew as a partner in the fishing business makes even more sense if he's been living as a disciple of John the Baptizer in the desert. John's name, meaning "YHWH provides protection," is particularly noteworthy when you recall John is the only one of the eleven disciples (neglecting Judas) to escape being murdered. It is to his cousin-disciple John that Yehoshua will assign the care of his mother, Mary (John 19:26–27).

4. James bar Zebedee

James is brother to John, son of Salome and Zebedee (Matthew 17:1), and Yehoshua's maternal cousin. Together, Yehoshua nicknames his cousins *Boanerges*: sons of rage or thunder. Was this because Yehoshua's uncle Zebedee was a bellowing blowhard, or because his sons were as feisty as their throne-seeking mother? Perhaps they inherited their father's anger. Luke 9:51–54 does seem to paint them as a tad hot-tempered: "When the days drew near for Jesus to be taken up, he set his face to go to Jerusalem. And he sent messengers ahead of him, who went and entered a village of the Samaritans, to make preparations for him. But the people did not receive him, because his face was set toward Jerusalem. And when his disciples James and John saw it, they said, 'Lord, do you want us to tell fire to come down from heaven and consume them?'" (He does not.)

While his brother John will be the last of the inner twelve to die, James, as reported in Acts 12:2, is the first of the group to be murdered.

Peter, James, and John form Yehoshua's innermost circle, which is convenient, considering two of them are his cousins, and the trio were already business partners prior to joining the wandering rabbi (Luke 5:10). We don't know why Yehoshua picked these men as his core followers, but posterity has nicknamed them "The Three." It is Peter, James, and John alone who witness the transfiguration (Mark 9:2–3), the raising of a little girl from a coma (Luke 8:51–55), and the agonizing final night of prayer in the garden of Gethsemane (Matthew 26:37).

All three men are bold, assertive, entrepreneurial, and aggressive, natural leaders with sharp edges that Yehoshua will polish like waves on sea rock.

5. Philip

John 1:44 says Philip was also from Bethsaida, perhaps suggesting he is already friends with brothers Simon and Andrew. Philip is clearly the "Bethsaida Boy"—before Yehoshua feeds the five thousand in Bethsaida, it is Phillip he seeks out to inquire about local provisioning (John 6:5), assuming he knows where one can buy bread in such quantities. This undesigned historical coincidence is one of the hundreds of Easter eggs that analytic philosopher Lydia McGrew says speak to the gospel's reliability. Here's another in John 12:20–21: "Now among those who went up to worship at the feast were some Greeks. So these came to Philip, who was from Bethsaida in Galilee, and asked him, 'Sir, we wish to see Jesus.'" Why did they go to Philip and not one of the other eleven? As it turns out, Philip is a Greek name. John 12:22 says that Philip talks to his (Greek-named) friend Andrew about these Greek fans, and together they go tell Yehoshua.

Philip, meaning "lover of horses," has a missionary's heart and, after becoming a disciple, he immediately recruits his friend Nathanael to join the gang.

6. Nathanael Bartholomew

Nathanael, meaning "given by God," is from Cana in Galilee (John 21:2) and may have been a guest at the wedding Yehoshua attends with his mother in John 2:1.

John 1:45–46 paints Nathanael's recruitment by his friend Philip in hilarious detail: "Philip found Nathanael and said to him, 'We have found him of whom Moses in the Law and also the prophets wrote, Jesus of Nazareth, the son of Joseph.' Nathanael said to him, 'Can anything good come out of Nazareth?' Philip said to him, 'Come and see.'"

Lighthearted Yehoshua applauds Blunt Bartholomew's forthrightness in verse 47: "Behold, an Israelite indeed, in whom there is no deceit!"

Guileless Nathanael evidently agrees with the assessment, because his response is simply, "How do you know me?"

We know almost nothing about Nathanael, aside from the fact that he may be the son or descendent of someone named Talmai or Tolmai. Another speculation is that he has Egyptian connections, because his family name sounds like Alexander the Great's successor Ptolemy. Nathanael's claim to fame is that he is the first person to declare that Yehoshua is the Son of God (John 1:49). His name always follows Philip's in the New Testament, and tradition pairs them up to head out as missionaries to Armenia after Yehoshua's murder. Legend says Nathanael is skinned alive. Today, he is quite horrifically remembered as the patron saint of . . . wait for it . . . leather makers.

7. Matthew/Levi bar Alphaeus

Disciple number seven is given two names in the gospels, and there are numerous reasons this may be. Perhaps he belongs to the Jewish tribe of Levi. Perhaps Matthew is a Yehoshua-assigned nickname. Perhaps Matthew/Matthias is his Greek name (*Maththaios*) and Levi is his Hebrew name. He is a tax collector for the Romans (Matthew 9:9) and was probably known by both names. The Hebrew *Matityah* means "gift of YHWH."

Matthew's father's name is Alphaeus (Mark 2:14), which is of Syrian origin. Matthew is the presumed writer of the Gospel of Matthew; his record-keeping experience as a grifter for the enemy is redeemed in the testimony he pens. Matthew's description of his recruitment by Yehoshua is lightning fast. "As Jesus passed on from there, he saw a man called Matthew sitting at the tax booth, and he said to him, 'Follow me.' And he rose and followed him" (Matthew 9:9). Luke 5:27–28 cuts it even shorter: "And Jesus said to him, 'Follow me.' And leaving everything, he rose and followed him." In the next verse, they throw a farewell party in the wealthy man's house, inviting Matthew's former colleagues and other "deplorables" (Matthew 9:10). Mark 2:15 adds that there were many such people who followed Yehoshua. Two words—*follow me*—and Matthew leaves a well-paid job to follow a street preacher who immediately raids his larder like Bilbo Baggins's dwarves? There must be more to the story. Either Matthew is fed up with being a turncoat for a murderous regime, or the reputation and presence of Yehoshua are so overpowering that the cost-benefit analysis says go. It is reminiscent of the farmer Elisha who, when called to follow Elijah, immediately burns his plow and cooks his oxen in celebration (1 Kings 19:21).

8. Thomas

The uncommon Hebrew name *Ta'om* means "twin" and, despite the fact that Yehoshua doesn't have another brother or disciple named Thomas, Thomas is called by the nickname *Didymus*, the Greek equivalent of *Ta'om*. We don't know if Thomas actually had a twin (he's always paired with Matthew in the gospel lists), if he just looked like someone else in Yehoshua's entourage, or if the whole crew just loved wordplay.

Thomas's major contribution to Scripture arises from a question he asks at the Last Supper in John 14 5–6, and from which Christians will derive their original name, the Way: "Thomas said to him, 'Lord, we do not know where you are going. How can we know the way?' Jesus said to him, 'I am the way, and the truth, and the life. No one comes to the Father except through me.'"

Poor Thomas isn't with the other disciples when post-crucifixion Yehoshua reveals himself to the them (John 20:24), and Thomas gains the scornful nickname "Doubting Thomas" for questioning the resurrection. (In other words, he is the disciple with whom we ourselves should most identify.) We shouldn't be quick to judge brave Thomas. When all the other disciples try to talk Yehoshua out of returning to Jerusalem for fear of assassination, John 11:16 says Thomas stands up to all of them: "Let us also go, that we may die with him." And die he eventually will, traveling farther east than any of the disciples before being murdered in India.

9. James bar Alphaeus

James's father's name is Alphaeus/Clopas, though not the same Alphaeus as Matthew's father. The group nicknames James "The Less"—in our parlance, Little James—to differentiate him from thunder son James, brother of John. Whether this James is shorter, younger, or less thunderous is unclear. Like Yehoshua, Little James has a brother named Joses (Matthew 27:56), and to add more confusion, his mother's name is also Mary (Mark 15:40). According to several second-century Christian writers, Little James's father, Clopas, is Yehoshua's stepfather Joseph's brother, making Yehoshua's mother Mary Little James's aunt, and Yehoshua Little James's cousin.

The number of nicknames employed by Yehoshua for his disciples suggests a lighthearted filiality that exceeds the usual teacher-student relationship. Even in our highly informal modern education settings, not many college students in today's lecture halls receive a nickname from their economics professor. That said, Yehoshua is being practical—after all, he has brothers named Simon, James, and Judas, and six disciples named Simon, Simon, James, James, Judas, and Judas.

10. Judas Thaddaeus

Poor Thad. The man is interchangeably named Thaddaeus, Jude of James, Jude Thaddaeus, Judas Thaddaeus, and Lebbaeus. His name is actually Judas, but clearly Judas Iscariot commands the main claim to this name. And since Yehoshua also has a brother named Judas/Jude, the group gives Thad all sorts of heart- and chest-related nicknames, potentially signifying a special tenderness or earnest love.

Thaddaeus has just one line of dialogue in the gospels, and it is spoken during the Last Supper: "Lord, how is it that you will manifest yourself to us, and not to the world?" (John 14:22). That is quite literally all we know about him, other than the fact that he is the son of yet another James (Luke 6:16).

11. Simon

We know even less about this second Simon than we do about Judas Thaddaeus. He never speaks a recorded word or performs a recorded action, but that is not to say he wasn't as active as the rest. Luke 6:15 says he is "Simon who is called the Zealot." Mark 3:18 and Matthew 10:4 call him "Simon the Cananaean" in some translations, which is Aramaic for *zealot*. Even though that is all we know about Simon, we know plenty about the extremist political party from whence his identifier arises. Known for their burning zeal for Jewish political independence, the Zealots were a fanatical, ecclesiastical militia hellbent on theocratic rule, always spoiling for a fight. While conspiracy theorists have written bestselling books in which they claim Yehoshua was himself a Zealot, we will see in chapter 9, "The Political Josh," that this is not at all likely. Does Simon abandon politics in the same way the other Simon abandons fishing? Does Simon turn his zealot ways into real zeal for the kingdom of God? Or did Simon become a Zealot *after* Yehoshua died? We simply do not know.

12. Judas Iscariot

Quite tellingly, Judas is mentioned last on every single list of disciples in Scripture. Iscariot is not his last name, and there are several intriguing theories about the identifier. The leading thought is that it comes from the Hebrew *ish qri'yot* and means "man of Kerioth," which was a village in southern Judea (Joshua 15:25). If this is true, it makes him the only non-Galilean in the core crew, an outsider from day one.

There is another far more intriguing (and probably less likely) explanation. As if the Zealots weren't militant enough, a splinter group broke away in the mid-first century and called themselves the Sicarii. They carried concealed curved daggers called *sicae* and would covertly murder Romans and Roman sympathizers in public before blending back into the crowd. In other words, they were the world's first organized assassination squad. (This is where the Spanish term for a hitman, *sicario*, originates.) If Judas was a bloodthirsty "Judas the Iscarii"—and that's a big *if*—it wouldn't be a surprise to most readers.

That said, both terms—Zealots and Sicarii—are too anachronistic to be applied to Yehoshua's disciples. Neither group emerges until several decades after the murder of Yehoshua. But both were well established by the time the gospel writers sat down to pen their works. So whether Judas and Simon were precursors of the two violent factions, or just bore characteristics similar to their political descendants, we cannot say with certainty.

Judas's father's name is Simon Iscariot (John 6:71), so either father and son are from Kerioth, they are early adopter Sicarii, or they are Sicarii from Kerioth. Unlike Yehoshua's brother Judas and his other disciples named Judas, this Judas gets to keep the name. He is the group's treasurer, tasked with carrying petty cash in a moneybag (John 13:29). Though he feigns concern for the poor (John 12:5), Yehoshua's cousin-disciple John has always suspected Judas is a thief (John 12:6). Even

Yehoshua knows Judas is trouble, calling him "a devil" in John 6:70.

So there are the inner twelve disciples. In English: Simon, Simon, James, James, Judas, Judas, John, Andrew, Bartholomew, Matthew, Philip, Thomas.

If Rabbi Josh recruited these men today, perhaps he'd call them Rocky, Andy, Thunder Sons, Little James, Matt, Phil, Thad, Bart, the Twin, the Zealot, and the Devil.

For those who are keeping score, the group contains three business partners, two sets of brothers, two sets of friends, three of Yehoshua's cousins, and six fisherfolk. In other words, these men are already fairly well connected before Yehoshua brings them all into his fold.

How old are the inner twelve? We cannot say for sure, but there is reason to believe most of them were still teenagers when they answered the call to follow. Yehoshua is around thirty when he starts his public ministry; it is unlikely he would recruit older men and call them "little children" (John 13:33). Exodus 30:11–16 says the half-shekel temple tax was for people age twenty and older, and only Simon and Yehoshua have taxes owing despite other disciples being present (Matthew 17:27). Though 1 Corinthians 9:5 makes it clear that the rest of Yehoshua's disciples and brothers eventually get married, Simon is the only one who is listed as married when Yehoshua recruits him. (The Talmud suggests eighteen is when men get married.) Matthew owned a house and worked as a tax collector, but several other disciples still worked with their fathers (suggesting a younger age). John mentions he beat Peter in a footrace in John 20:4, which is typically something that only concerns younger men. He also lives extremely late into the first century, with the math suggesting he was around fifteen at the start.

Most rabbis recruited young teenagers as their disciples (thirteen to fifteen in the Talmud), and it would be out of the ordinary for Yehoshua not to do something similar. It might be helpful to shave the beards off our mental images of the Twelve and replace them with a bit of peach fuzz.

We cannot imagine how much internal conflict exists among these young men. One is a zealot, another a Roman colluder. Some are Galilean, some Judean. Some are hotheads, others are cool. One is a thief, and another knows it. If they are mostly late-adolescent males, there is much wrestling and jibes about acne, but few cerebral cortexes fully formed and planning for the future. Hormones run wild, yet very few of the disciples are married. If this picture is accurate, Yehoshua spends his days acting as part rabbi, part referee, part policeman, and part father.

The Seventy-Odd

Please do not for a second think there are only twelve disciples! The gospel writers are clear that Yehoshua attracts and retains seventy disciples in short order, but we shouldn't be too religious about the number seventy either. Some texts say he had seventy-two. Seventy may simply be symbolic, perhaps a shout-out to Moses's seventy elders in Exodus 24:1.

At least two of the seventy-odd were disciples since the days of John the Baptizer, having followed Yehoshua from his baptism in the Jordan. In other words, they'd been Yehoshua's disciples for *longer* than many of the inner twelve had been disciples. Their names are Joseph (called Barsabbas, also nicknamed Justus) and Matthias, both of whom remain faithful straight through the crucifixion and resurrection. Both are nominated in Acts 1:21–23 to replace Judas Iscariot, and both are of such high character that the apostles have to leave it to a game of chance to decide who they should choose. The dice (or more likely, tablets in an urn) fall to Matthias (Acts 1:26), meaning that six of the apostles are now Simon, Simon, James, James, Matthew, and Matthew. Not that it's much better for poor Judas Thaddaeus, who John 14:22 now calls "Judas (not Iscariot)."

Why does Yehoshua select twelve apostles and not, say, seven, fifteen, or forty? As it turns out, the decision is symbolic. There are twelve tribes of Israel, and this new gathering promises renewal for the sons of Jacob. Note that Yehoshua says "follow me" to only half of the inner twelve in the gospel texts—Simon and Andrew, James and John, Philip, and Matthew. The remaining six apostles are chosen from among the seventy-ish (Luke 6:13). His reason for appointing twelve and naming them apostles is elucidated in Mark 3:14–15: "He appointed twelve (whom he also named apostles) so that they might be with him and he might send them out to preach and have authority to cast out demons."

In other words, he is training apprentices so he can delegate the work of announcing the kingdom of God.

The Women

Several well-meaning men in Christian history have tried to compile lists of the original seventy disciples by combing through the New Testament and plucking out the names of anyone mentioned who could've been disciple-age at the time of Yehoshua. They should certainly be applauded for their efforts, but we may rest assured that they are wrong, because almost none of them contain the names of any women.

In chapter 8, we will more thoroughly meet the women who generously bankroll Yehoshua's public ministry, but suffice it to say, his female disciples play a central and sustaining role in his rabbidom (Luke 8:1–2). Here are the names we do know: Mary of Magdala, Joanna wife of Chuza, Susanna, Aunt Salome (mother of thunder cousins James and John), and Aunt Mary (mother of cousin Little James). Mark 15:41 states that these women had followed Yehoshua since way back in Galilee, and Matthew 27:55 confirms it.

There are *five* named female disciples. (If we add the two sisters of Lazarus, Mary and Martha, we have seven—four of whom are named Mary.) As we will see, we know more about some of the female disciples than we do about several of the inner twelve. This is an extraordinary fact considering the era and custom.

It is also a real mind-bender for most churchgoers. We traditionally think of Yehoshua tramping around with a dozen mature men, but in reality, the mostly teenaged troupe traveled with a not-inconsiderable number of women, including *several of their own aunts and moms.* When you add Mary Magdalene, Joanna, Susanna, Salome, Mary, and the "many other women" that both Mark and Matthew mention, you realize Yehoshua's male disciples may have actually been outnumbered amidst his seventy-strong company.

And speaking of women . . .

Was Jesus married?

While it is tantalizing to speculate that Yehoshua was married and sired a secret family that exists to this day, the hard evidence is nonexistent. There floats in the ether the notion that men like Yehoshua had to be married to be rabbis, but that isn't true. This belief is an anachronism, as the formalized rabbinical system didn't emerge until decades after Yehoshua's murder. Plus, we will permit theologians to argue that Yehoshua took no earthly wife because he already had a bride: his church.

The would-be earthly wife could be no other than Mary Magdalene, the "Apostle to the Apostles." The marriage-obsessed, third-century, non-canonical, Gnostic Gospel of Philip calls her Yehoshua's "companion," "partner," or "consort"—one of the word's connotations can even mean "business partner"—but never the regular Coptic word for wife. (To give you an idea of "Philip's" reliability, this is the same text that claims the Holy Spirit is a woman named Sophia, that the Garden of Eden contained animal-bearing plants, and that Jesus invented bread.)

There is also speculation that Mary is the unnamed "disciple whom Yehoshua loved," as mentioned many times in John's gospel, but this cannot be the case because Yehoshua and Simon Peter both refer to the loved disciple as a man (John 21:20–22). Mary's name, of course, was not actually Mary Magdalene. Luke 8:2 says that that she is *called* Magdalene, presumably after the Galilean seaside town of Magdala from which she likely hailed. Did Yehoshua give her this nickname? We don't know. But knowing his proclivity for giving playful names to his closest friends—and having three other Marys in his entourage—it is not outside the realm of possibility that he referred to her as, more or less, Maggie.

What is Maggie like, and what is her relationship with Yehoshua? For one thing: She is decidedly her own woman. The gospel writers mention her twelve times, and unlike most of the other women mentioned in the Bible and in all other ancient documents, not once is she attached to a husband, father, or child. She is Miryam, from Magdala, and she follows Yehoshua. We must never project our cultural values onto the past. For Yehoshua not to have pursued sexual fulfillment is unthinkable for many moderns, but this doesn't change the facts of history.

Despite their lack of wedded union, there should be no doubt Maggie is the most committed and courageous of all Yehoshua's disciples:

1. He heals her of the greatest brokenness (Luke 8:2).
2. She helps supply his needs for years (Mark 15:40–41).
3. While the rest of the disciples flee, she is there at the foot of the cross for the duration of Yehoshua's horrific murder (Matthew 27:56; John 19:25; Luke 23:49).
4. She is the one who bravely follows and spies out Yehoshua's burial location (Mark 15:47; Matthew 28:1; John 20:1).
5. She is the first to arrive at the tomb with spices to embalm the body. The Yehoshua-was-married faction insists this is "proof" that Mary was his wife because only family would dare make themselves unclean by touching

the naked body of a deceased rabbi. While this hardly constitutes proof of nuptials, these folks also seem to forget she isn't alone at the tomb but is accompanied by Yehoshua's aunt Salome (Mark 16:1).

6. Maggie is named by all four gospel writers as the first disciple to encounter the resurrected Yehoshua (Mark 16:9; Matthew 28:9, Luke 24:10; John 20:18). The fact that the gospel writers name a woman in an age when a woman's testimony wasn't valid in a court of law belies the impossibility of usurping her place in Yehoshua's innermost circles. But there should be no doubt of the sort of relationship they shared. In John 20:16, when she realizes it is Yehoshua, she does not exclaim "Husband!" or "My love!" or even "Yehoshua!" but rather "Rabbi!"

Who is this Maggie, this Miryam of Magdala? She is healed. She is independent. She is generous. But above all, she is a disciple of Yehoshua ben Yehoseph. It's no wonder she is one of the most celebrated women in history, with countless churches and colleges named in her honor.

While there is absolutely no proof of any bloodline descendants from Yehoshua himself, it is likely that he had many nieces and nephews. Eusebius writes in his *Historia Ecclesiae* that Yehoshua's brother Jude's two grandsons are nearly killed by Caesar Domitianus for their relation to the long-gone Messiah, but that he lets them go when the grandsons assure the emperor that Yehoshua's kingdom is "not of this world." While most of us would be over the moon to discover we were the great-great-etc.-grand-nephew or niece of Yehoshua, leaving a physical bloodline is simply not his priority. He offers all of his followers a far more intimate relationship: sonship.

All told, Yehoshua's motley crew of seventy-odd includes at least half a dozen teenage fisherfolk, a tax collector, a political extremist or two, a whole bunch of wealthy women, several moms and aunts, and one undeniable disciple who will risk her life to ensure her Lord's legacy lives on. By the time their three to five years of life and ministry together come to an end, Yehoshua no longer considers them disciples, mere apprentices. In John 15:15, he gives them a new title: friends.

But friends are not the only relationships in Yehoshua's life. He also has mortal enemies.

Enemies

> *"Blessed are you when people hate you and when they exclude you and revile you and spurn your name as evil, on account of the Son of Man!"*
>
> Luke 6:22

> *"If the world hates you, keep in mind that it hated me first."*
>
> John 15:18

Yehoshua's list of enemies runs so long that he could easily be confused for a drug-running mob boss turned informant. While he loves everyone and counts none his enemy, the number of distinct groups who hate him runs to at least nine: the Romans, the Herodians, the Samaritans, the Pharisees, the Sanhedrin, the Sadducees, the elders, the scribes, the high priestly family—plus every sinner on earth.

Romans

To start, there are the political rulers of Judea and Galilee: Rome. When you are a hammer, everything is a nail. When you are a Roman, everyone not Roman is either a current or future enemy. Yehoshua, of course, does not see Romans as his enemy (even though they will eventually torture him to death). In fact, he betrays zero anti-Roman sentiment, having no qualms about eating with their tax collectors (Matthew 9:10), paying taxes to them (Mark 12:17), or healing their paralyzed servants (Matthew 8:5, 13).

The key Roman in Yehoshua's life will be his judge and executioner, Pontius Pilatus. Even the undeserving Pilate gets nothing but respect and honesty from Yehoshua, despite sentencing him to death after declaring the rabbi innocent of all crimes (Luke 23:14). Pilate is likely from a military family and may have been a personal bodyguard of the Emperor. We know nothing about his life before he is selected by Tiberius or his Praetorian Prefect, Sejanus, to govern Judea, a low-prestige position he will hold for more than a decade before being deposed for slaughtering a group of Samaritans. He is a bit of an oaf, not particularly sensitive to his touchy subjects and their religious customs. On more than one occasion he will slaughter innocents to enforce the *Pax Romana*. He is the man who appoints the High Priest, and he keeps the High Priest vestments in his Antonia Fortress, letting the Jewish top man borrow them for special occasions.

It is unlikely that Pilate loves his job. The deeply unstable Judea is probably the worst province in the empire to govern. Over seventy years, it will change hands from a singular king (Herod the Great), to a gaggle of client kings (Herod's sons), to a Roman prefect (Pilate) surrounded by client kings, to client kings again, then Roman procurators, then a Jewish revolt, then a Roman recapture.

Herodians

Under the Romans are the boot-licking Herodians, an insufferable party of power-hungry Jews who swear allegiance to the House of Herod. Herod Antipas is Galilee's Tetrarch (meaning "ruler of one-fourth" of his father's empire). Antipas is the one who murders John the Baptizer; Yehoshua refers to Antipas as "that fox" in Luke 13:32. The Herodians are deeply corrupt and far more political than religious, but they lurk around the temple because it's a major power center in ancient Israel. They have no complaints when Herod Antipas murders Yehoshua's kinsman John the Baptizer. All they want is comfort, and they believe the people should submit to the Herodian dynasty so Rome will leave everyone alone. Like many politicians, they have no problem buttering up their enemy before trying to frame him for tax evasion (Matthew 22:16–17).

Samaritans

The Samaritans are the multi-century enemies of their Jewish cousins. Yehoshua, of course, does not see Samaritans as his enemy, even though a Samaritan woman is rude to him in John 4:9 and an entire village refuses his presence in Luke 9:53. As we have seen in chapter 4, he possesses a countercultural love for the Samaritans that his disciples cannot yet fathom.

Up next on the list of people who hate Yehoshua are the Jewish religionists—temple elites who care more for the law than for the people it was created to protect and serve.

It cannot be said that the religionists are a unified bloc, but rather a hodgepodge of overparticular moralists who've crossed the Rubicon into religious sin. They bicker among themselves constantly, fighting over resurrection versus reincarnation, which books should and shouldn't be in the library of Scripture, and whether they should read said books in Greek, Aramaic, or Hebrew. The religionists also have strong opinions on their relationship with Rome, with some wanting open revolt at one extreme to total capitulation on the other.

The temple hierarchy roughly breaks down into six main categories: the Sanhedrin, the Pharisees, the Sadducees, the elders, the scribes, and the High Priests.

The Sanhedrin

The Sanhedrin is Judaism's ruling council, but the entire organization is a shambolic bastardization of Moses's council of elders

(Numbers 11:16). As the self-appointed supreme court of Israel, the body is composed of seventy mostly rotten religionists, though Yehoshua does have at least two secret supporters amidst their ranks. The Sanhedrin meet every day except Sabbaths and holy days, but they will make an exception to pass judgment on Yehoshua under cover of night. Their mandate is wide-ranging, and they have the final say on all Jewish matters both religious and political, with no separation of church and state. About the only thing they can't do is execute people, because the Romans alone retain that right. The Sanhedrin court is split along party lines; it is essentially a two-party system that is majority Shammai and Hillel Pharisees, yet is deftly controlled by the minority Sadducee party.

At least, that's what most churchgoers believe. All of this is true, but it is a tad anachronistic. Our Sanhedrin here is not the Great Sanhedrin of Jerusalem, comprised of seventy-one Jewish leaders who will be described in the Talmud several centuries after the time of Yehoshua. At this point in our story, the *synedrion* is still in a nascent phase of development. The Greek word means "sitting with," and in the time of Yehoshua, it is more of an ad hoc advisory group for the high priest. Synedrions weren't limited to Jewish high priests either—even Herod and Augustus convened synedrions of varying sizes at various times and places. Philo mentions a synedrion of friends in *Every Good Man Is Free*. The gospel writers are also aware that there are multiple synedrions throughout Israel (Matthew 10:17; Mark 13:9), and they never mention the number seventy. So which synedrion are they referring to in relation to Yehoshua? It is the high priest's synedrion, comprised mostly of politically aligned religionist friends, lawyers, fellow aristocrats, and nepotistic family connections. Luke calls it *their* synedrion in Luke 22:66. To differentiate between the later Sanhedrin of Seventy and our current high priestly synedrion, we will stick with the latter term for the rest of this book.

The Elders

It is best not to think of the temple elders as godly, wizened old men. The *presbuteros* are simply aristocratic Jews from prominent families. In our parlance, elders are "old money." When they are mentioned by the gospel writers in connection with the high priest, we may substitute the word *elders* for "elites," and in the gospel story, all the so-called elders simply play yes-men to their temple bosses. As such, the elders are likely a small group comprised of older men who are loyal to the high priestly family, be they members of the high priest's own family or those of politically and economically aligned families.

The Scribes

If the synedrion technically runs the nation of Judaism, the scribes execute its will at the ground level. The scribes are the bookish fellows who spend their days studying the Law, transcribing it, and writing commentaries about it. They know how to keep the letter of the law, but they know nothing of its spirit. With at least one scribe in every village, they can draw up divorce contracts for a price, along with marriage certificates, mortgage documents, land deeds, loans, and more. Imagine if your worst seminary professor was also a corporate lawyer—this should give you a bit of an idea of how much the commoners must have loathed the scribes. Some were likely also members of one of the two religiopolitical parties. The scribes started out protecting the Law of God and ended up nullifying it with so many man-made legal traditions. When the gospel writers mention scribes, they are talking about the corrupt lawyers who do the legal bidding of the high priestly family.

The Pharisees

As one of the two main parties, Pharisees are the religionist's biggest bloc. Pharisee comes from *Pharisaíos*, meaning quite literally, "the separatists." They start off as a movement to make the Jewish nation sacred again, but their literalist adherence to the written law and unwritten tradition quickly turns them into religionists. Most are conservative Shammai followers, but there are some kindlier Hillel folk scattered in. This, of course, puts Yehoshua in a tricky place within the house of Phariseeism. If he sides with Hillel on an issue, the majority of the Pharisees can beat up on him. If he sides with Shammai on an issue or believes the House of Hillel is not liberal enough—especially when it comes to giving women equal rights at the table—Hillel's people get their turn to take shots. If he steps one foot outside the Pharisaical world, the Sadducees can snap at his heels.

In *Antiquities*, Josephus estimates there are six thousand Pharisees and that they are the most popular party among the people, perhaps because they are appalled by Herodian compromise. Jewish independence could never involve the Romans. According to Mark 3:6, the Pharisees and Herodians seem to agree on only one thing: "The Pharisees went out and immediately held counsel with the Herodians against him, how to destroy him." Yehoshua tracks this unholy alliance and tells his disciples to watch out for the rancid yeast that both parties are trying to work into the dough of the nation (Mark 8:15).

The Pharisees are perhaps not all quite as bad as most churchgoers tend to believe. To be sure, the majority of the Pharisees were probably happy to be rid of a nuisance reformer like Yehoshua, but there were genuinely good men in their number, including some who warn the rabbi about a Herodian death threat (Luke 13:31), one who argues against his arrest (John 7:50–51), and two who will personally pay the costs of Yehoshua's burial (John 19:38–42).

It is important to remember that, while others make an enemy of Yehoshua, he counts no man his foe. In fact, he expressly welcomes his main opposition into the fold in Matthew 13:52 (NIV): "Every teacher of the law who becomes a disciple in the kingdom of heaven is like the owner of a house who brings out of his storeroom new treasures as well as old." In other words, members of the temple elite were well positioned to be powerful missionaries in the Yehoshua movement if only they would embrace its founder. This truth is borne out nowhere so powerfully as later in the life of the apostle Paul, a former Pharisee who reminds his audience of their Jewish heritage and their heavenly future.

The Pharisees are definitely conspiratorial plotters (John 11:47), but when push comes to shove, they may have a significantly bigger bark than bite. Their murder plan with the Herodians evidently comes to naught, as the Pharisees play almost no role in Yehoshua's actual murder, with not a single mention in Mark or Luke, and only one in Matthew (Matthew 27:62, but this happens *after* the murder). Even John, who has a serious beef with the Pharisees, says their only involvement is supplying some guards and officials for Yehoshua's arrest (John 18:3).

So if the leading party of the temple elite aren't the ones to actually pull off the assassination, who is?

The Sadducees

While the Pharisees focus on obeying the letter of the Law, the Sadducees are far more interested in wielding said law for personal gain. Contrary to popular belief, the bulk of the religionist bickering wasn't between the Pharisees and Sadducees, but between the houses of Hillel and Shammai *within* Phariseeism.

In *Antiquities*, Josephus depicts the Sadducees as worldly, elite, and upper-class, and they tended to be extremely wealthy, hypernationalistic, and deeply secular: "The Pharisees have delivered to the people a great many observances . . . which are not written into the laws of Moses . . . that the Sadducees reject. . . . The Sadducees are able to persuade none but the rich. The Pharisees have the multitude on their side."

Indeed, the Sadducees ignore every Jewish teaching except the first five books of the Bible, roundly rejecting Joshua, Judges,

Samuel, Kings, Isaiah, Jeremiah, Ezekiel, and more than a dozen other books of the Old Testament. They are decidedly more political than the Pharisees. They are keen on "heathen" Greek philosophy and don't believe in angels or spirits, or in the afterlife. In other words, they are thoroughly secular grifters masquerading as faithful Jews.

On the religious side, their job is to take care of the temple and preside over the three pilgrim festivals, which they use as an opportunity to siphon untold wealth from followers of YHWH. On the political side, they do everything from collecting taxes to mediating for Israel with the Romans—presenting evermore chances to skim and extract from the working poor. While the Pharisees produce bossy rabbis, the Sadducees produce brutal politicians.

Josephus, in *Antiquities,* says the Sadducees are "more heartless than any of the other Jews," but there is no Sadducee more heartless than their murderous leader.

The High Priest(s)

There is a chess master behind the scenes, a man of political cunning and unfathomable violence who wears the disguise of a faithful Jew. He is a wolf in sheep's clothing, who preys on the poor and devours the houses of widows yet is seen by the public as a holy and righteous man, the greatest in the land. We will dwell on this future murderer for a lengthy moment here, because this man is the chief antagonist in Yehoshua's story, and yet almost no Christian has ever heard of him.

His name is Annas ben Sethi, High Priest Emeritus of Israel, and he is the most powerful Jew in the world. Ironically, his Hebrew name, Hanan/Hananiah means, "the grace of YHWH," but he is a legalistic, anti-God tyrant who quietly rules Judaism with an iron will.

Annas (sometimes Ananus, Ananias, Hanan, Chanin) is born into a wealthy family and in his mid-twenties comes to power as high priest in 6 AD, having gotten himself appointed by the Roman governor Publius Sulpicius Quirinius. Such a thing is not possible without vast amounts of capital with which to purchase said post. In 175 BC, a fellow named Jason of the Oniad family out-bid his own brother for the Jerusalem high priesthood by promising the Greek king Antiochus Epiphanes 440 talents of silver. Weighing in at nearly 33,000 pounds, the high priest seat cost him $13.3 million in today's dollars. High Priest Jason likely more than recouped his investment in less than three years.

As high priest, Annas's job is to collect tithes and taxes, oversee the temple, liaise with the Romans, and serve as president of the Jewish ruling council. Annas is a harsh judge who has no problem meting out capital punishment for religious infractions. He is a deft political mover, easily able to manipulate the court and the mob to achieve his aims, as he will do after Pilate declares Yehoshua innocent. The aristocratic Annas rules his synedrion for nearly a decade before he is deposed in 15 AD by Valerius Gratus, who flips high priests with the frequency of a blackjack dealer.

Now no longer titled, Annas sets his sights on building a political dynasty. In his late thirties, the nepotistic *éminence grise* gets the Romans to appoint his son Eleazar the high priest in 16 AD. Valerius Gratus deposes Eleazar the next year, and Annas wins the seat for his son-in-law Joseph Caiaphas. Joseph has a particularly long tenure—a whopping eighteen years, from 18–36 AD, covering the entire span of Yehoshua's public ministry and then some. That said, John 18:19 makes it clear that Annas is anything but retired from active control. Luke agrees. After finishing his prologue in chapters 1 and 2, he launches into *the story* with this sentence: "In the fifteenth year of the reign of Tiberius Caesar, Pontius Pilate being governor of Judea, and Herod being tetrarch of Galilee, and his brother Philip tetrarch of the region of Ituraea and Trachonitis, and Lysanias tetrarch of Abilene, during the high priesthood of Annas and Caiaphas, the word of God came to John the son of Zechariah in the wilderness" (Luke 3:1–2).

All the leaders in this sentence check out historically, except Annas and Caiaphas. The temple can have only one high priest. But Luke writes, "During the high priesthood of Annas and Caiaphas . . ." Why the discrepancy? Because Jews believe a high priest serves for life, whereas the Romans select and depose high priests at will. Annas *leverages the people's faith in God* to maintain his high priestly position, abusing their trust to maintain his influence and affluence. Caiaphas holds the office; Annas holds the power. In the same way that Italian bankers will buy themselves the papacy around the Renaissance, the Jewish High Priesthood goes up for sale on an annual basis. Annas the so-called High Priest is a despotic master of the arts of dark power and will use political machination to get five of his sons appointed to the lofty position. Despite being a Sadducee in a Pharisee-majority court, Annas's family dominates the high priest seat for *six decades*. Considering many high priests are deposed in less than a year, it is clear that Annas is well-versed in nation-state diplomacy and industry-scale bribery.

Such a sacred-secular position comes with a prodigious package of pecuniary perks, including myriad ways to economically exploit the Jewish faithful. He can get his tax collectors to overcharge and skim. He can get his moneychangers to jack up their exchange rates and charge commissions. He can get his people to steal copious amounts of meat from the sacrificial roasting altar like Eli's wicked sons in 1 Samuel 2:12–17. He gets the first pick of all the hides of the sacrificed animals, ensuring top-quality leather for furniture and resale. He can get his festival salespeople to charge obscene prices for sacrificial supplies. He decides who receives the nation's tithes. He controls the temple treasury, essentially acting as the central banker for the Jewish nation. Josephus describes the temple treasury's contents: "An immense quantity of money, and an immense number of garments, and other precious goods, there deposited; and to speak all in a few words, there it was that the entire riches of the Jews were heaped up together" (*Wars*, 6.5.2). Annas controls it all, charging protection fees and interest on loans. Yehoshua makes a point of sharing several teachings right beside the treasury (Mark 12:41) despite knowing the danger in it (John 8:20). Ever willing to protect their master's profits, Annas's temple treasury guards (John 7:32) are the ones sent to arrest Yehoshua in the garden of Gethsemane (John 18:3).

To say that Annas is the Jewish equivalent of Crassus is not a stretch—he is by far the greediest Jew in first-century Palestine. His family's thirst for money is unquenchable; they even go so far as to collect all the sacrificial blood, dry it out, and sell it to gardeners as fertilizer. Annas is also supposed to maintain Jerusalem's infrastructure, but he lets so much work remain undone that at one point, Pontius Pilate robs the temple to pay for an aqueduct to bring water to the citizens under Annas's supposed care. (Josephus, *Wars* 2.9) In 1973, the remains of a first-century priestly mansion were discovered in Jerusalem and are thought to belong to Annas. The building's two-story floor plan boasts over 13,000 square feet of living space, making it the largest private residence ever excavated *in the entire nation of Israel*. What first-century Jew in an agrarian economy under Roman occupation could possibly possess such a spectacular place? Only someone who truly hates God and actively hates people. But because Annas doesn't believe in the afterlife (Acts 23:6–8), he doesn't care at all about who suffers or dies while he amasses evermore wealth and power. *Now* is all that matters.

Everyone in first-century Israel knows their high priests are illegitimate mafiosos. When John 11:49 mentions Caiaphas, "who was high priest that year," John assumes what his audience already knows—that the Romans lease the high priesthood to the highest bidder on an annual basis, and the House of Annas has won the seat for yet another year. The House of Annas isn't the only wretched crime family in the era, of course. Of the twenty-five high priests in Herodian-Roman times, twenty-two were from four families, with none holding more offices than Annas and Sons.

The House of Annas is the obvious target of Yehoshua's barely veiled parable of the rich man and Lazarus in Luke 16:19–31. Caiaphas represents the fabulously wealthy man dressed in high priestly garb, the father's house is the House of Annas, and the five sons in the story are Annas's sons who only believe in the first five books of the Bible but don't believe in the prophets or the resurrection. If you read the parable, it's quite clear that Yehoshua thinks Annas and his greedy cartel are going to burn in hell for their crimes against God and humanity.

Yehoshua isn't the only person who sees Annas for who he really is. One of the main reasons the Dead Sea Scrolls-creating Qumran community splintered from mainline Judaism was because they despised high priestly corruption and their obsession with looted wealth (1QpHab 8–12, translated by Géza Vermes in *The Complete Dead Sea Scrolls*, in English):

> *The Wicked Priest, who at the beginning of his office was called by the name of truth. But when he ruled in Israel, his heart became puffed up and he deserted Elohim and betrayed the Laws for the sake of riches. And he stole and collected the riches of the men of violence, who rebelled against Elohim. And he took the riches of the peoples, heaping upon himself guilty sinfulness.*

Or consider this popular ditty in the Talmud (Pesahim 57a):

> *Woe to the house of Annas!*
> *Woe to their serpent's hiss!*
> *They are high priests;*
> *their sons are keepers of the treasury,*
> *their sons-in-law are guardians of the temple,*
> *and their servants beat people with staves.*

Annas's goal is to personally rule an independent Israel, and he will stop at nothing—not theft, not systemic injustice, not corruption, not murder, not the wholesale slaughter of his enemies, and not temporary political alliance with the Romans—to get it. In the meantime, he will use his family's position of power to loot the land by monopolizing all temple trade.

Annas receives only four named mentions in the gospels, because the gospel writers assume everyone knows the overlord of Jerusalem is the lead antagonist in this story. Whenever the gospels mention the high priests—and as we will see, they mention them a lot—they are talking about Annas, Caiaphas, and their family cartel of future high priests, some of whom are named in Scripture (Acts 4:6), and all of whom dominate the temple within the lifetime of the gospel writers.

Annas will come to see Yehoshua as yet another fly to squash and, as we will see, all four gospel writers know it. When the upstart rabbi threatens Annas's expanding economic empire, Annas will use his synedrion, his lawyers, his thousands-strong administration, and his high priest son-in-law to set in motion a plot to have Yehoshua tortured and publicly murdered while bolstering his own reputation as a holy defender of the one true God.

The Everyday Josh

"May you live all the days of your life."
—Jonathan Swift

The Caucasian Christ

We know exactly what Yehoshua ben Yehoseph looked like. Hasn't everyone seen commercial advertiser Warner Sallman's 1941 *Head of Christ* Sunday school painting? Yehoshua is a handsome, light-skinned thirtysomething with soft eyes, a forked beard, long brown hair parted in the middle, and wearing a robe with a classy sash.

Because that indelible image sold more than a half billion prints and spawned a whole series of sequels, it may therefore come as a shock to many that Yehoshua likely had short black hair, brown eyes, darker skin, and that he actually mocked religionists who wore long robes.

Not one of the biblical authors spends a word on Yehoshua's physical description. Biblical authors tend to mention when people are exceptionally tall (Goliath, Saul), voluptuously fat (Eli, Eglon), climb-a-tree short (Zacchaeus), above-average hairy (Esau), ridiculously strong (Samson), incredibly handsome (Moses, David), exceedingly beautiful (Rebekah, Tamar, Esther), or have particularly luscious locks (Samson, Absalom). When someone in the Bible has an extraordinary physical trait, it is usually mentioned.

Yet nothing is said of Yehoshua. If he was exceptionally good-looking, the authors could have strengthened their spiritual case by saying he appeared kingly and regal in appearance. If he was profoundly ugly, they could have redeemed this hideousness. Plato, for instance, mentions Socrates's looks on many occasions, describing his bulging eyes, piggish nose, potbelly, and balding head. Yet these are not seen as losses in the world of philosophy but advantages—with no prettiness to attract a crowd, Socrates's ugliness proves the attractiveness of his wisdom.

Preachers have made much of Isaiah 53:2, which suggests a physical description of the future Messiah: "He had no form or majesty that we should look at him, and no beauty that we should desire him." Notice the prophecy does not say, "The Messiah will be repulsively grotesque," simply that he is no Brad Pitt in *Fight Club*. So if Yehoshua is described neither as the Hunchback of Notre Dame nor a Middle Eastern male model, is this, perhaps, because Yehoshua was so undistinguished that there was nothing physically special to point out?

If this is a case—and one should certainly not build a theology on it—we can conjure up a pretty fair picture of what the Nazarene may have looked like.

We simply need to ask: What did Jewish men look like? More specifically, what did an average adult male Jew from the tribe of Judah look like in first-century Judea?

For this, we turn to the excellent work of Professor Joan E. Taylor. Based on skeletons recovered from the time and place, she reports the average male was a mere five feet five inches tall. This aligns well with the Roman historian Suetonius, who considers five seven to be respectably tall. So if Yehoshua is neither tall nor short, he's somewhere between five four and five six.

Biologically, the people group that best approximates Yehoshua's skin tone are today's Iraqi Jews—the descendants of the Jews forced into Babylonian exile in 586 BC. Iraqi Jews have beautiful honey-colored or olive-brown skin, brown eyes, and black hair.

If he kept his hair in the style of the surviving portraits of other men from his era, then his hair was clipped short and wasn't the flowing mane we see in the paintings. Long hair was considered culturally unmanly (1 Corinthians 11:14); Roman coins from the era reflect this. Coins depicting Jewish men of the era also display short to shaggy hair and moderate-length beards, sort of a Middle Eastern peasant take on the Greek philosopher look.

It is likely that Yehoshua had a beard, as the Levitical law commands it. A prophecy in Isaiah suggests the Messiah's torturers will rip out his beard and spit on his face, and while Matthew notes the Romans did slap and spit on his face, there is no mention of hair-pulling. That said, Jewish historical records suggest men condemned to death were always subject to the shame of shaving or having their beards torn from their faces. If Yehoshua's presumed beard was particularly long, it likely would have been mentioned (as Pliny does of Euphrates). On the subject of hair, Professor Taylor points out that of the ten combs found in Judean desert caves, eight had lice.

What of Yehoshua's physique? He is a craftsman for a decade or more, connoting some semblance of rugged strength, and he walks long distances as a rabbi, connoting stamina and endurance. The gospel writers do not say he is either fat or emaciated, but we have hints that he may have been undernourished at times: the Lord's Prayer is one of subsistence—asking for daily bread like the manna of old (Luke 11:3); he pronounces woe on those who are well-fed (Luke 6:25); he tells his disciples not to worry about what they will eat (Luke 12:22); and Mark 11:12 and Matthew 21:18 explicitly say he gets hungry. Sometimes he is so busy that his disciples have to urge him to eat (John 4:31). Yet when he does manage to find the time, he is willing to eat with anyone, saint or sinner alike (Mark 2:15), and even gains a reputation as a glutton (Matthew 11:19).

If he is the highly active peasant preacher depicted in the gospels, and he has no business, home, or wife to supply sufficient and consistent calories, might he have been one of those who occasionally hungered and thirsted for something in addition to righteousness?

The Rabbi's Clothes

"For the apparrell oft proclaimes the man."

—Shakespeare's Polonius in *Hamlet*

While the gospel writers are silent on Yehoshua's physical appearance, they have much to say about his sense of fashion, or perhaps more accurately, his lack thereof.

It is ironic that artists have dressed Yehoshua in voluminous robes for the past sixteen centuries, considering we know he wore the opposite. In Mark 12:38–39, Yehoshua derides people who dress to impress. "Watch out for the teachers of the law. They like to walk around in flowing robes and be greeted with respect in the marketplaces, and have the most important seats in the synagogues and the places of honor at banquets" (NIV). The Greek word for *robe* here is *stolai*. Not once in Scripture is Yehoshua caught wearing an attention-seeking *stolai*. Instead of swishing around in a sartorial status symbol, he wears the commoner's covering: a *chiton*.

A chiton, or tunic as it's called in many Bibles, was a basic knee-length covering made from two pieces of wool with stripes down the side, leaving the arms and legs uncovered for the hard-scrabble work of peasant subsistence under an extractive overlord. Unless, of course, you are Simon "Rocky" Peter and chose to fish in the nude (John 21:7).

We know from John 19:23 that Yehoshua's tunic is seamless, that is, made from a single piece of cloth instead of two—a cost-cutting measure usually reserved for children. Archaeologists have recovered one-piece bag tunics from the time and area; they're incredibly cheap, almost underwear-like, and certainly appropriate for the poor.

On top of their tunics, Jews wore a rectangle of wool for warmth, called a *himation*. We may guess that Yehoshua's cloak isn't very valuable because the Roman soldiers who steal it simply cut it into four pieces (John 19:23). As an obedient Jew, Yehoshua would have tassels on the corners of his cloak. Why? Because Moses wants the Israelites to remember and perform YHWH's commands (Numbers 15:38–39). But even beautiful reminders of God's loving law can become tainted. In Matthew 23:5, Yehoshua again judges the religionists for their showy fashion: "They do all their deeds to be seen by others. For they make their phylacteries broad and their fringes long." In other words, they were showing off a luxury, because lengthening a tassel showed you had the money to buy expensive blue thread. Yehoshua doesn't say not to wear tassels, just not to bling them out. We know Yehoshua wears tassels on his cloak because Mark 6:56 says the crowds try to touch them in hopes of a healing, no doubt because word had spread of a woman being healed of internal bleeding for doing just that (Mark 5:27).

We can guess that Yehoshua's clothes weren't high-count linen, nor fancily embroidered or dyed in eye-catching colors. Mark 9:3 suggests his cloak was undyed and unbleached, and when speaking of his kinsman John the Baptizer in Luke 7, Yehoshua scorns such luxuries. "What did you go out to see? A man dressed in fine clothes? No, those who wear expensive clothes and indulge in luxury are in palaces" (v. 25 NIV). Yehoshua's brother will echo this indictment of fancy dress in James 2:2–4 (NIV): "Suppose a man comes into your meeting wearing a gold ring and fine clothes, and a poor man in filthy old clothes also comes in. If you show special attention to the man wearing fine clothes and say, 'Here's a good seat for you,' but say to the poor man, 'You stand there' or 'Sit on the floor by my feet,' have you not discriminated among yourselves and become judges with evil thoughts?"

If his fashion instructions to his disciples in Mark 6:8 are any indication, Yehoshua also wore a leather belt and carried a walking stick. On the footwear front, Matthew, Mark, and John all suggest Yehoshua wore sandals. John the Baptizer says in Mark 1:7 that he is unworthy to untie the Messiah's sandal straps. The leather versions discovered in Dead Sea caves are thonged between the big toe and index, with a heel strap around the ankle.

Knowing what Yehoshua wore, can we make a guess at the condition of his clothing? Mark 2:21 betrays Yehoshua's knowledge of how to patch worn cloaks, a task usually reserved for women. The mid-second-century anti-Christian philosopher Celsus interviewed people who knew people who may have had recollections of what Yehoshua looked like, and came to the conclusion that he "wandered about most shamefully in the sight of all."

There are lessons in Yehoshua's appearance for us today. The first and most important is to not judge and discriminate based on outward appearances. In reality, very few of the most impactful people in history have been particularly pretty or well-dressed. William Shakespeare wasn't confused for Aphrodite. Winston Churchill was no Cary Grant. Mother Teresa wasn't a Victoria's Secret model. Proverbs 31:30 says that "charm is deceitful, and beauty is vain." Isaiah 57:15 says YHWH is with those who have "a contrite and lowly spirit," not a three-piece button-down or a maxi and stilettos.

The second fashion lesson is to lift our gaze from earthly things to heavenly ones. Yehoshua does not tell his followers to dress to impress. Instead of storing up a wardrobe full of clothing for moths to eat and thieves to steal (Matthew 6:19), we should store up treasures in heaven.

The third lesson is that we should wear nothing that distracts from the message we are trying to embody or distances us from the people we are called to reach. Yehoshua does not care what is de rigueur in the world of fashion. Pastors are not celebrities. A church platform is not a fashion runway. Clothing choices carry a message: Throwaway fast fashion and high-priced haute couture are both declarations of disregard for the poor. Anything attention-seeking takes attention away from God.

The fourth lesson is that Christians should wear clothing that reflects the values of their leader. If Yehoshua eschewed the long robes of the religionists of his day, what would he say about the dog collars, embroidered robes, sky-high mitres, bejeweled vestments, and gold chains of today's clergy?

Clothing is a powerful signaler of values. This is why the gospel writers use their precious space to make note of Yehoshua's clothing. Why did Mohandas Gandhi, a London-trained lawyer, dress in hand-spun Indian peasant garb? Why did Martin Luther King Jr., a Baptist pastor from Atlanta, dress like a Wall Street banker? Because they were trying to convey a message—that the Indian poor are worthy of self-sovereignty and that American blacks are equal to American whites.

From everything we read in the text, Yehoshua did not favor the rich, powerful, and well-dressed. If we continue to give Yehoshua the makeover of a powerful, regal, well-off European philosopher-prince, we broadcast the wrong signal on the wrong channel.

What does Yehoshua look like in our average-Jew scenario? He is around five and a half feet tall, thin but strong, with olive-brown skin, brown eyes, shortish brown-black hair potentially plagued with lice, and a scruffy beard. He carries a walking stick and wears an undyed, tasseled cloak over a cheap, knee-length tunic, with well-worn leather strap sandals. His clothing is rough, his deportment perhaps shabby, his overall look a tad vagabond. In other words, he looks like the revolutionary Middle Eastern rabbi he is.

So how in the world did Yehoshua end up looking like the baggy-sleeved male equivalent of Mona Lisa?

Unbelievably, it all comes down to a piece of fan fiction from the late-fourteenth century called "The Letter of Lentulus." Supposedly written by a Roman governor of Judea (who never actually existed), it contains anachronisms several hundred years out of touch with the period from which it claims to originate. Are you ready for this governor's description of Yehoshua? He is tall and handsome. His hair, parted in the middle, is the color of "unripe hazelnut," falling in curls to his shoulders. He has a forked beard. His skin is wrinkle-free. His eyes are bright and serene.

This is exactly the Yehoshua that Leonardo da Vinci captures in *Salvatore Mundi*—perhaps, as novelist Alexandre Dumas speculated, sketching with the aid of a handsome Italian model in the person of Pope Alexander VI's son Cesare Borgia. While the cultural appropriation of Yehoshua begins almost immediately after his death, da Vinci is truly off to the races to erase the lowly rabbi's religion, race, and raison d'être.

The reality is that we do not know exactly what Yehoshua looked like, despite our best guesses. The gospel authors remain unanimously silent, aside from his clothing. But perhaps this is on purpose. Second Corinthians 5:7 says we walk by faith, not by sight, and as YHWH told Samuel, "People look at the outward appearance, but YHWH looks at the heart."

The Language(s)

Turning from the heart to the mouth, let's discuss the language (or languages) by which Yehoshua communicated his message.

Yehoshua didn't speak English. He didn't speak Yiddish either. He probably didn't even speak Rome's native tongue, Latin. Despite the empire's massive power, the lingua franca that greased the wheels of international trade was still Alexander's Koine Greek, which Yehoshua may have picked up during his decade or so as a commercial craftsman.

The other candidate language in first-century Judea was Hebrew, the ancient mother tongue of King David. This was the posh language of Yehoshua's day, the classical one used by the Jewish ruling class in Jerusalem. In other words, it was temple-speak. If Yehoshua preached in synagogues, read scrolls, and dined with religious leaders, he probably knew Hebrew.

Classical Hebrew ran the linguistic show from the Jordan to the Med for centuries, but its days were numbered. The Babylonians gutted Judah in 586 BC; the Babylonian captivity is an astounding event worth mentioning. Not only did Nebuchadnezzar II crush the Judean army, raze Jerusalem, obliterate Solomon's temple, and murder Zedekiah's sons before blinding and enslaving the king, but he oversaw a mass deportation of at least 14,600 Jewish elites to service his empire. (Thus, the despair-filled book of Lamentations.) While the peasants remained on the now-redistributed land in Judah, the formerly wealthy priests and professionals (including Ezekiel and Daniel) worked for the profit of their captors. The brahmins remained stuck in captivity for fifty-odd years until Darius I and Cyrus the Great of Persia ransacked Babylon and allowed 42,360 Jews to return home.

By this point, the Aramaic language was flourishing in the north (Yehoshua's Galilee and Samaria), and when the Babylonian exiles returned, the majority Hebrew tongue found itself swamped by Aramaic speakers, which allowed the freedmen to communicate with folks throughout the Persian world.

Alexander the Great subjugated Judah in 332 BC and introduced Greek, and then, of course, the Romans came to power, leaving Israel with four competing languages: Latin, Greek, Hebrew, and Aramaic. Which language people spoke fell along locational and class lines: Northern Jews in Galilee and Samaria, plus the Babylonian Jews, spoke Aramaic; the Hellenized intellectuals spoke Greek; and the religious classes like the Sadducees and Pharisees spoke and read Hebrew. In other words, Yehoshua may have been trilingual or more.

But there is little doubt as to Yehoshua's everyday vernacular: He spoke Aramaic. Originally the language of the Arameans, Aramaic was eventually used throughout the Persian Empire and was the go-to language of the Near East for nearly thirteen hundred years. Of the Bible's more than 23,000 verses, Aramaic accounts for just over 1 percent—a mere 268 verses, two hundred of which are in Daniel. Still, a tantalizing whisper of Yehoshua's Aramaic breaks into most English Bibles as the gospel writers keep some of Yehoshua's Aramaic words intact, and in doing so give us a fascinating glimpse into how he spoke: "*Talitha cumi*" (Mark 5:41), "*Raca*" (Matthew 5:22), "*Ephphatha*" (Mark 7:34), "*Abba*" (Mark 14:36), "*Eli, Eli, lema sabachthani*?" (Mark 15:34). When Maggie encounters the risen Yehoshua in John 20:16, the text specifically says she exclaims in Aramaic, "*Rabboni*!"

Aramaic words and phrases like these help us realize Yehoshua was a foreigner from our point of view, and that he spoke a language far removed from our own. Upwards of 500,000 people still speak variants of Aramaic, so if you'd like to get a stronger sense of Yehoshua's language, head either to southern Syria or YouTube.

Not only did Yehoshua speak Aramaic, but he likely did so with the same Galilean accent as Peter (Matthew 26:73). Galilee was a hotbed of insurrection, and Yehoshua is rejected by the Jerusalem cognoscenti in large part because of his Galilean ethnicity. His message is the equivalent of a Deep South redneck marching into Manhattan to tell Wall Street bankers and Broadway actors how to live, and he is by and large rejected by everyone but the poorest of peasants.

Food Fit for a King

What did Yehoshua eat? Did food ever get stuck in his teeth? What foods caused him gas? What were his tastes and preferences? Was food a big part of his life?

By my count, the gospels record at least fifteen meals Yehoshua ate, not including the myriad mentions of Passover Seders and other Jewish feasts that any good rabbi would have hosted. Yehoshua consistently uses mealtimes to generate spiritual meaning.

When the disciples are eating grain on a Saturday in Mark 2, he confronts Pharisees on the meaning of the Sabbath.

When a sinful woman anoints his feet during a meal at Simon the Pharisee's house in Luke 7, he uses the encounter to tell a parable about debt and forgiveness.

When Mary sits at his feet while her sister Martha busybodies in the kitchen in Luke 10, he lovingly helps Martha reprioritize what's truly important.

When he heals a man with dropsy over a Sabbath supper at the house of one of the chief Pharisees in Luke 14, he turns it into a conversation about pride and humility.

When he hosts the last Passover supper in Mark 14, he uses the opportunity to announce his forthcoming betrayal, predict Simon Peter's betrayal, inspire the Eucharist ritual, and teach his disciples about servanthood by scrubbing their feet.

But what did—and didn't—he eat at these meals? Mark 7 is conventionally interpreted as Yehoshua striking down the Jewish food laws (and plowing into a plate of pulled pork?), but if you read the text, this is clearly not a closed case. Scripture never says that Yehoshua tells his disciples to stop eating kosher, and not once in Scripture does Yehoshua tuck into a spread of forbidden food.

Religionists had convinced the Jewish public that the unkosher foods themselves were sinful—that the words *muttar* and *tahor* meant spiritually "pure" and "impure" instead of simply "permitted" and "forbidden"—and Yehoshua is just making the point that it isn't the foods we put into our mouths that make us soul-polluted before YHWH. Yehoshua isn't changing the food rules of Judaism; he's saying that's what the Pharisees have been doing. In the words of New Testament professor Robert A. Guelich, "No foods, even those forbidden by the Levitical law, could defile a person before God."

So bearing in mind that Yehoshua likely did not eat sautéed slugs, bat confit, or buffalo-basted vulture wings, what did he eat?

The Bible mentions all sorts of delicious things like salt, cilantro, cinnamon, rue, apples, grapes, beans, gourds, leeks, corn, millet, spelt, partridge, pigeon, quail, dove, goat, venison, oxen, butter, milk, grape juice, vinegar, raisins, dates, honey, and cheese (hallelujah). Almonds get seven mentions in the Bible, and pomegranates make an appearance in Song of Songs 6:11. Pistachios are mentioned in Genesis 43 and were so popular in the first century that they made their way all the way to Emperor Vitellius's Rome. It's possible Yehoshua even chewed gum-like bits of frankincense or myrrh resin, though the text doesn't say.

In Egypt, the Israelites ate cucumbers, melons, leeks, onions, and garlic, which Yehoshua may have at least tried as a child refugee. (Cucumbers are an excellent source of portable water and were popular in Judea.) The former Egyptian slaves in Genesis also complain that they no longer have figs, grapevines, or pomegranates, and early one morning in Matthew 21:18–19, Yehoshua hurls a curse at a fig tree for failing to produce figs.

Yehoshua evidently had a penchant for seasonings, as he sprinkles them into his teachings quite a bit. In Matthew 5:13

he talks about salt losing its saltiness. In Matthew 13:31 he mentions mustard seed. In Matthew 23:23 he mentions mint, cumin, and either anise or dill, depending on the taste of the translator.

Olives and olive oil are mentioned over 150 times in the Bible—for eating, cooking, lamp-lighting, and ceremonial anointing. Poor people would have consumed olive oil sparingly, as it was extremely valuable. During the Last Supper, we assume Yehoshua dipped the bread in olive oil, but the text doesn't say; it just as easily could have been the more affordable lentil puree or chickpea hummus.

I'd like us to pause at the Last Supper for a moment, with the full disclosure that I plan to push a piece of lost theology on you. While today's church communions consist of a sip of wine or juice and an anemic cracker, this is hardly the lavish dinner enjoyed by upwards of seventy of Yehoshua's disciples. Their feast likely included roast lamb, flatbread, fruit sauce, bitter herbs, and at least four cups of wine, and the communion happened near the end of the Final Dinner (Luke 22:20). This theme of "abundance before remembrance" is grasped nearly immediately by the early church (Jude 1:12; Acts 2:46; and some 2 Peter 2:13 manuscripts), and for the next 150 years or so, Christians ate a full celebratory meal, called the Agape Feast, before taking communion. In every society in human history, eating is the primary way we start and maintain relationships, with the dinner table as a society in microcosm. The Christian lovefeast or *agapæ* took things to the next level, celebrating Yehoshua's unconditional love while offering an opportunity to practice radical fellowship across socioeconomic lines.

Sadly, it didn't always work out that way, and Paul has to play referee for a church potluck in 1 Corinthians 11:20–21: "When you come together, it is not the Lord's supper that you eat. For in eating, each one goes ahead with his own meal. One goes hungry, another gets drunk."

Agape abuses aside, eighty years after Yehoshua's death, this lovefeast is still mentioned both by early church fathers like Ignatius of Antioch and secular Romans like Pliny the Younger. Hippolytus of Rome and Tertullian both mention the lovefeast, but by this point, the Western church had begun to separate it into a morning communion and an evening supper.

These communal evening meals get quite outrageous by the time of Clement of Alexandria, with so much gluttony and drunkenness and so little focus on Yehoshua that Augustine of Hippo believes they should be stopped. The Councils of Laodicea, Carthage, and Orléans all ban lovefeasts in church buildings, with the Trullan Council of 692 AD excommunicating anyone who continues to share a meal together.

It would take more than a thousand years and a Protestant Reformation to see the *agapæ* make its reemergence, first with the German Brethren, who believed the Agape Feast required a good foot scrubbing, a hearty communal meal, and a proper Eucharist celebration. Ludwig von Zinzendorf brought the practice to his legendary Moravian community, which is how John Wesley picked up the torch and brought it to the Methodists. Unfortunately, the global church never revived this important New Testament tradition and instead settled for a mere coffee hour. I say we bring Yehoshua's *agapæ* back.

With that plug for holy feasting accomplished, let us return to what Yehoshua likely ate. We know that bread was likely his main sustenance. Whole grain bread—wheat for the upper crust and barley for the working class—was made with water and yeast and perhaps a little olive oil on special occasions. On Saturdays it was made without yeast. Mark 8:14 suggests the disciples usually packed multiple loaves for their journeys.

Unless Yehoshua did a gap year abroad in the not-yet (re) discovered Americas, he never had the pleasure of tasting coffee, chocolate, tomatoes, potatoes, corn, peppers, pumpkins, or cane sugar. Even tea hadn't been introduced to Israel yet, and rice wouldn't arrive in the region until the Persians bring it over five hundred years after Yehoshua's death.

While the Genesis authors may have initially envisioned an all-vegetarian world (Genesis 1:29), a strong case cannot be made that Yehoshua was a vegetarian like Daniel. If a youngish Yehoshua dabbled with the Essenes, he may have been vegetarian for a time, but after his crucifixion, he eats a piece of fish (potentially with honey, depending on your translation) to prove he's not a ghost (Luke 24).

We also know that he eats roasted lamb shank at least once per year at Passover, and if Yehoshua spent time with kinsman John's community, he probably tried desert locusts at least once.

That said, Judea was roughly plant-based at the time because meat was expensive. Then again, Yehoshua attended an untold number of feasts and weddings at the homes of rich people, so who knows what he might have been served there. In Luke 11:12 he mentions eggs, and we know the hard-boiled variety were used in Passover Seder meals. While it is almost certain that he did not eat pork, he, unlike his peers, says in Mark 7 that doing so doesn't make you a sinner bound for hell. (Other animals forbidden by Jewish custom included shellfish, rabbit, snails, camel, sturgeon, catfish, eels, shark, marlin, reptiles, eagles, vultures, kites, falcons, ravens, owls, gulls, hawks, rats, and bats, which I can safely say makes me an obedient and kosher disciple.)

Fishing on the Sea of Galilee today is heavily restricted due to pollution and overfishing, but excavated fish bones suggest it once contained carp and catfish—and the lake was best known for its tilapia, now nicknamed St. Peter's Fish. (It seems Yehoshua would have gotten his omega-3s.) The most common way to cook fish would have been to roast it on coals, but there's evidence for salting, smoking, and air-drying fish along its shores as well. (Indeed, it seems unlikely that the boy at the feeding of the five thousand handed Yehoshua a pair of putrid uncooked fish in the midday heat.)

Then there is the question of alcohol. Was Yehoshua a drinker? Some argue that the ultra-strict Nazarite vow precluded adherents from imbibing booze, but nowhere in Scripture does it say Yehoshua took the Nazarite vow. He was from Nazareth and thus a *Nazarene*, not a *Nazarite*. We have evidence of distillation from twelve hundred years before Yehoshua's time, but spirits didn't start to become popular until more than twelve hundred years after his death. Though bread was plentiful in Israel and beer can be made from the same ingredients, there is no archaeological evidence that brewing was widespread in his time. Wine is mentioned 231 times in the King James Bible, whereas beer is mentioned only seven, and only then in the New International Version.

Culturally, men at the time may have drunk as much as a quarter-gallon of wine per day, which would explain why the New Testament warns against drunkenness on several occasions. Nowhere in the text does it say Yehoshua drank alcohol of any kind, but considering he plays bartender at a wedding in Cana (John 2), contrasts himself to his non-drinking kinsman John (Luke 7), and serves Passover wine while telling his disciples he won't drink *again* until after his resurrection (Mark 14), it is certain he enjoyed a wee tipple every now and then.

So we know what Yehoshua eats, but can he cook? It was typical at the time for Jews to eat only breakfast and supper, and the one instance in Scripture of Yehoshua cooking is, in fact, a post-crucifixion breakfast fry-up: Clothes-free Peter and some other disciples have evidently returned to fishing after their rabbi's passing, and they spot Yehoshua grilling fish on a beach, which he serves with bread on the side (John 21:19).

Yehoshua uses food as a symbol to great effect. Perhaps the most poignant of his culinary metaphors is John 6:35, "I am the bread of life; whoever comes to me shall not hunger, and whoever believes in me shall never thirst." By identifying himself with the two staples of first-century cuisine, he sends the message that even more than food and water itself, he is the essential ingredient in the life of his disciples.

Means of Transport

There is no mention in the gospels of Yehoshua owning or even riding a horse, let alone commanding a chariot. The fact that he borrows a donkey in Mark 11:4 for a brief jaunt into Jerusalem suggests he did not own any means or mode of transportation except his own two feet.

And what a prodigious ambler he is. According to Arthur Blessitt, the Guinness world record holder for the world's longest walk—some 43,340 miles—Yehoshua sauntered an estimated 21,525 miles in his lifetime, nearly equal to the distance around the earth at the equator. He walks to the temple in Jerusalem (Mark 11:27). He walks by the sea to recruit disciples. He walks on water to show them he's God. He walks around Galilee to avoid Judea (John 7:1). He walks with ramblers on a country road after his crucifixion (Mark 16:12). Aside from walking and his one-time donkey ride, there is only one other recorded mode of transportation for Yehoshua ben Yehoseph: boats on the Sea of Galilee.

The Sea of Galilee is a misnomer in the extreme—even a cursory glance at a map reveals it is not a sea at all. At 1/113th the size of Lake Ontario, and a little larger than Loch Ness, Canadians and Russians may be excused for seeing it as little more than a large pond. While first appearing in the Bible in Numbers 34:11 as the Sea of Kinnereth, it is called the Sea of Ginosar in Flavius Josephus's histories, but the well-traveled gospel writer Luke cannot bring himself to honestly call it a sea, and instead calls it the Lake of Gennesaret. By the time John writes his gospel in the mid-to-late first century, he goes with the Sea of Tiberias, named after the resort city Herod built on its western banks.

At just eight miles wide, the storm-prone lake is a pleasure to sail on a nice day, but it quickly becomes a nightmare as cool upland air whips down on the water and churns it into a frothing gale. The lake is the largest body of freshwater in Israel (and the lowest freshwater lake in the world), and the majority of Yehoshua's ministry takes place on and around it. It's where he recruited many of his disciples, preached to crowds, calmed the storm, walked on water, and helped Peter haul in a massive number of fish. It was a bustling place in Yehoshua's time, with Josephus calculating at least 230 fishing boats working the lake.

In the year of my birth, 1986, a first-century, mud-preserved boat containing a lamp and a cooking pot was discovered on the northwest shore. It was immediately named "The Jesus Boat." At nearly eight feet wide and twenty-seven feet long, the flat-bottomed cedar craft theoretically could have held thirteen men. Even though there is no proven connection to the rabbi or any of his disciples, it gives us a good idea of what sort of craft Yehoshua could have used as his commuter vehicle.

Boats are mentioned more than fifty times in the New Testament, and by my count, Yehoshua takes at least five boat trips in the gospel of Mark alone (4:36; 5:21; 6:32; 6:51; 8:10). We know that long walks tired him out (John 4:6), and it is my hunch that he liked to be on the water because it was significantly less tiresome than walking everywhere. It also gave him a much-needed reprieve from the constant crowds (Mark 6:31). That said, it didn't stop an armada of fans from chasing after him in small boats in Mark 4:36, until a wicked storm drove them back to shore. On another occasion, a whole fleet of boats follows him from Tiberias all the way to Capernaum (John 6:23–24).

We don't know who owned the boat or boats on which Yehoshua and his disciples zipped up and down the so-called "Sea" of Galilee, but it could have been Simon Peter, James and John's father, or perhaps one of the wealthy women who bankrolled Yehoshua's rabbinical operation. (More on them in chapter 8.) Being on the water also gave him a chance to catch up on sleep (Mark 4:38), and on at least one occasion he was so exhausted that he slept soundly even though a squall nearly swamped the boat (Luke 8:23).

No doubt after this brush with death, the non-fishermen disciples, like their Noahic ancestors, were all too happy to be back on dry ground.

The Sustaining Work

If the Romans hadn't crucified him, Yehoshua could have just as easily worked himself to death. The physical and spiritual needs of the Judean populace under dictatorship were immense, so it's no surprise that "great multitudes" and "large crowds" swarmed Yehoshua wherever he went. We know he taught and fed at minimum tens of thousands of people. We know he was mobbed wherever he went, chased across a lake on at least two occasions, and was nearly crushed to death at least once.

As an extremely popular rabbi, the workload was immense: teaching, healing, exorcising, feeding, mentoring, hanging out with sinners, walking, sailing, eating, and sleeping, plus the expectations of a Jewish rhythm of life including the many pilgrimages to feasts. And all this while moving from house to house, never knowing where the next meal and next bed will come from. Add the psychological pressure of being seen as a rebel against the Judaism of your ancestors, experiencing constant scorn and shame in an honor-and-shame culture, having your own family think you've gone mad, and anticipating when the Romans will arrest, torture, and murder you for speaking blessing over the poor and oppressed. For most of us, this level of pressure would end in a mental breakdown, a heart attack, an aneurysm, or suicide.

How did Yehoshua do it? How did he manage to keep a sustainable pace amidst an outrageously busy public life? How did he avoid the soul-crushing workaholism that pervades our day? As it turns out, we can know quite a bit about the rituals and routines that kept Yehoshua serving at a sustainable pace. I've taken the liberty to tabulate a few of these with classic preacher alliteration.

1. Sabbath

Yehoshua honors the Shabbat to the letter of its *original* biblical meaning. He doesn't work, and he doesn't force others to work for him. Instead, "as was his custom," he visits local synagogues (Luke 4:16), heals individuals (Mark 1:29), eats with friends (Mark 2:23), and attends parties (Luke 14:1). By rejecting the slavery of ceaseless toil, he takes one full day each week to remember the Creator and enjoy the created. The Sabbath is a day to look forward to, a day to look back on, and a day to dwell in. The Sabbath becomes a weekly rhythm, a steady beat of rest and recuperation amidst weeks of hard labor.

2. Sleep

"Have courage for the great sorrows of life and patience for the small ones; and when you have laboriously accomplished your daily task, go to sleep in peace. God is awake."

—Victor Hugo

YHWH designed the human body for sleep. Though our money-hungry age is one of ceaseless sleep-shaming, the Bible is very much in favor of sufficient rest for weary bones.

The Qoheleth of Ecclesiastes 5:12 (NIV) says, "The sleep of a laborer is sweet . . . but as for the rich, their abundance permits them no sleep."

King David's song in Psalm 4:8 says the reason he can sleep so restfully is that YHWH alone makes him dwell in safety.

King Solomon says, "In vain you rise early and stay up late, toiling for food to eat—for [God] grants sleep to those he loves" (Psalm 127:2 NIV).

The prophet Jeremiah glories in a good night's rest (Jeremiah 31:26).

Yehoshua believes there is a time for everything under the sun (Ecclesiastes 3:1), and simply assumes that sleep is part of humanity's God-given routine (Mark 4:27). Prior to Edison's lightbulb, Americans averaged ten hours of sleep per night, and we should not assume that Jews in the pre-electricity first century got any less. Jerusalem gets a little over fourteen hours of daylight in June and just ten through the winter season, and like all Jews, Yehoshua believes there are twelve hours in a day (John 11:9) and therefore twelve hours of night. Knowing all this, we cannot assume a homeless rabbi and his flock of peasants can afford to burn several hours of oil, candles, or firewood each night.

Occasionally, Yehoshua gets up before sunrise to go off and pray (Mark 1:35) or arrives at the temple by dawn (John 8:2), but one gets the impression he is a bit of a night owl, considering he goes for post-3 a.m. walks (Mark 6:48), prays in moonlit gardens (Luke 22:39), prays all night under the stars (Luke 6:12), and makes himself available after nightfall for mighty people who need to keep a low profile (John 3:2). That might help explain why he takes noonday breaks when he's weary (John 4:6) and naps when the opportunity avails (Mark 4:38).

3. Solitude

Perhaps the greatest anti-weariness weapon in Yehoshua's arsenal is his practice of retreating to remote wilderness locations. Do a word study on the phrase "desolate place" and you will be shocked by how much it crops up in the four gospel testimonies. The word here is *erémos*, from which the Desert Fathers will become *hermits*, and it connotes a strong sense of solitude and desertion. (Isn't it interesting that the Bible is filled with stories of deserts being the place of much spiritual fruit? Abraham and Moses immediately spring to mind, as do Elijah and David hiding in caves. What seems to be a place of scant redeeming value becomes a place of ultimate redemption.)

It is John the Baptizer who preaches in the *erémos* (Matthew 3:1). Yehoshua spends forty days in the *erémos* before the start of his public ministry (Mark 1:13). He feeds the five thousand in the *erémos* (Matthew 14:15). After his disciples return from their first missionary outing and are so pressed by crowds that they can't even find a moment to eat, he tells them to come with him to get some rest in the *erémos* (Mark 6:31). When he receives word of John's beheading, he immediately withdraws to the *erémos* (Matthew 14:13). Luke 5:16 says he would *often* "withdraw to desolate places." But what is Yehoshua doing on all these escapades?

Without fail, he is praying.

In hiddenness, he seeks revelation.
In strategic retreat, he makes his advance.
In aloneness, he communes with his Father.

Read the gospels—really read them—and you will see this steady ebb and flow of advance, retreat, advance, retreat. Once you see it, it is forever unmissable. He dives into the fray in Jerusalem or Decapolis or Jericho, then he withdraws to the outskirts of Nowheresvilles and Nazareths to be alone in prayer with God.

In the cities, it's mayhem and miracles. Outside the centers of power, he enjoys a slower pace of life. He's like a middleweight boxer, dipping in and out of the melee, punching strategically. Eventually, this method proves so effective that he doesn't need to venture into soldier-heavy cities anymore. Mark 1:45 says that after healing a man of leprosy, Yehoshua "could no longer openly enter a town, but was out in desolate places [the *erémos*], and people were coming to him from every quarter." A nowhere became a somewhere because someone showed up.

4. Supper

After a long day, nothing restores the soul more than a hearty meal with good friends. A whole day of drudgery or disaster can be wiped away by a plate of pasta and a bottle of Bordeaux. There is a curious phrase in the English Standard Version that turned me on to the regularity with which Yehoshua rejuvenates himself with food and fellowship. The term is "at table," and it occurs roughly a dozen times in the gospels. Why not at *the* table? The two words are *sunanakeimai* and *katakeimai*, both meaning "to recline with." Time and again throughout Scripture, Yehoshua "at tables" himself with others. What better way to end a long day of teaching and healing than to feast with friends?

5. Shalom

One gets the sense from reading the gospels that Yehoshua was probably known as a person of peace. He was, in the breathtaking phrase (and book title) of pastor Mark Sayers, a "non-anxious presence."

What does he tell his disciples-turned-missionaries to say the second they step into a host's home? "Peace be to this house!" (Luke 10:5).

Sabbath, sleep, solitude, supper, shalom. These are a few of the human means by which Yehoshua manages to stay sane and work effectively without burnout. He is sustainable because he possesses sustaining rhythms, but more so because he is connected to his ultimate sustainer: God the Father and his Holy Spirit. Rather than pursuing ruthless efficiency—knifing the gift of time and getting covered in its entrails—Yehoshua spiritually redeems time and makes his life truly effective by constantly dwelling in the presence of God. He trusts his Father's provision and does God's will in God's way.

After my mother was diagnosed with a brain tumor and the doctors were unsure if it was cancerous and/or removable, my father said something quite profound about how they planned to live their potentially limited days together: "From now on, we are going to live lightly." It reminded me of Yehoshua's word to the crowds in Matthew 11:28–30: "Come to me, all who labor and are heavy laden, and I will give you rest. Take my yoke upon you, and learn from me, for I am gentle and lowly in heart, and you will find rest for your souls. For my yoke is easy, and my burden is light." Yehoshua lived lightly, and he invites us to do the same.

The Philosophical Josh

"A little philosophy inclineth Man's mind to atheism, but depth in philosophy bringeth men's minds about to religion."

—Francis Bacon, "On Atheism," *The Essays Or Counsels, Civil and Moral*

Yehoshua the Philosopher

It is tantalizing to picture Yehoshua as a Judean-born, Greco-Roman philosopher. Indeed, entire books have been written to convince us this is all he ever was. For the sake of pure philosophical pleasure, let us for a moment strip Yehoshua of his short *chiton* and *himation* and drape him in several bedsheets of *toga*.

He and his disciples are now Kappa Sigma frat brats during Greek Week, and we can picture them philosophizing in an American university garden over goblets of Merlot and pots of bubbling brie.

Nathanael scratches his head. "If prayers are just words, why are people so hell-bent on keeping them out of schools?" Little James nods with resonance. "You raise a good point, Bar-tholomew. If morals and ethics are all negotiable, why do secularists press so hard for Christians to approve of their behavior?" Simon the zealot slams his fist on the table. "Because it's actually about power and control instead of trust and surrender." Thomas muses in a gentler tone, "If it is reasonable to not believe in God, then it is not unreasonable to believe in God." Andrew agrees, troubled. "To deny the mere possibility of God is to deny all that is spiritual." Simon Peter throws up his hands in disgust. "There goes personhood and the self, democratic values, faith, hope, and—" Maggie interrupts. "Don't forget women's rights and love!" Matthew is confused. "How can people rationalize their belief in hundreds of other spiritual concepts yet hold to the opinion that a belief in God is somehow irrational?" The Thunder Sons answer in unison: "Because it's all faith!"

Though our eyes may quickly glaze over at the very thought of philosophy, few subjects could be more interesting, helpful, or happiness-inducing. The goal of philosophy is, after all, to learn how to live "the good life." But before we get into it, let's freshen up on three key terms:

Philosophy: From *philo-sophia*, meaning the love of wisdom. Wisdom is the ability to know and do what is right and true. In its ultimate sense, philosophy is a search for God's perfect standard of right-way-of-livingness (Matthew 6:33).

Morals: From *moralitas*, meaning character or proper behavior. Personal principles or goodness guidelines for individuals.

Ethics: Culture-based rules, actions, and behaviors of what is right and wrong in groups, communities, and societies.

With these in mind, what is Yehoshua's philosophy of the good life? What are his morals and ethics? And what sort of philosopher is he? We will start with the last.

Yehoshua the Cynic

> *"The most useful piece of learning for the uses of life is to unlearn what is untrue."*
>
> —Antisthenes

Unlike Epicurus, Aristotle, or Zeno, Yehoshua ben Yehoseph did not work to establish a school of thought or a philosophical system for living the good life. Still, there is a sect of scholars who believe Yehoshua was little more than a Hellenistic sage. In particular, they believe he was a Cynic philosopher.

Laying aside the fact that it would be quite the feat for one man to be both a Jewish rabbi and a leading Middle Eastern Greek philosopher, the notion is tempting to consider.

Nominally founded by a pupil of Socrates named Antisthenes, Cynicism's greatest moment belongs to Diogenes of Sinope, a homeless iconoclast who lives in a ceramic barrel and hurls not-unwarranted insults at well-to-do passersby. So famous is his poverty that Alexander the Great pays him a visit, towering over the reclining philosopher in the afternoon sun. Alexander asks Diogenes if he wants anything, and Diogenes replies, "Stand out of my light."

Cynics embrace voluntary poverty and simplicity, oppose the corruptions of power and wealth, and reject complicated theology and rote ritual for personal virtue. Cynics do not travel with a wallet, staff, or cloak. They commit themselves to poverty, self-sufficiency, and freedom of speech. Four hundred years later, Yehoshua embraces all these values.

Yehoshua lives at the end of the Hellenistic period, which ceases just two years before his death, and even though Cynicism has been in decline for three hundred years, Greek philosophy witnesses a revival among Athens-obsessed first-century Romans. Just a day's walk from Nazareth, a Cynic school springs up and produces leading Cynics like Menippus, Meleager, and Oenomaus. Does this school of thought directly or indirectly influence Yehoshua more than the Galilean political messiah complex or the Jewish prophet identity? Is it a mix of all three, or none of the above?

The Cynic goal is a life of virtue, which can only be achieved through a rejection of, well, pretty much everything. Cynics see themselves as teachers on a mission to convince the public that they should reject money, power, fame and even basic cultural norms. Instead, people should live a possession-free life of virtue at one with nature. Is this where Yehoshua gets the idea of selling everything you have and giving it to the poor? (Matthew 19:21) Cynics inveigh against honors and political power, and rail against preening and posturing. Is this why Yehoshua tells his followers to pray in secret in their closets instead of on street corners? (Matthew 6:5) In the Cynic model, wealth is seen as a serious impediment to virtue because it is so corrupting. In Yehoshua's house of philosophy, wealth is seen as a serious impediment to loving God (Matthew 6:24).

Indeed, Yehoshua can be seen as an expression of Jewish peasant Cynicism, but it cannot be said Yehoshua was a full-on Cynic philosopher. Cynics are obsessed with *oligarkia* (self-sufficiency), but Yehoshua makes no attempt to wean himself off the loving support of others. He is never indecent, never urinating in the streets like Diogenes just to make a point. He never publicly humiliates the rich, never causes shame. He believes people can change and holds out generous amounts of hope for all. The Cynics are known for their pithy sayings, but Yehoshua's complex character cannot be reduced to a handful of quips and quotes, as biting and universal as his words may be. To reduce him to something we can understand is to make him far less than he is.

So if he is not a proper Cynic philosopher, what is he?

Yehoshua the Stoic

> *"If a man can reduce his needs to zero, he is truly free: there is nothing that can be taken from him and nothing anyone can do to hurt him."*
>
> —John Boyd

If Yehoshua bears some resemblance to a Greek Cynic, the same can be said of the Stoic school.

Diogenes hands off his Cynic school to Crates, who teaches it to Zeno of Citium. Zeno starts teaching under the colonnade of the Athens marketplace, the Agora, around 301 BC. Shaded from the beating Athenian sun by the Painted Porch (*Stoa Poikile*), they adopt the name *Stoics.* If they started today, we'd call them the Porch Poets.

Over four successful centuries, Stoicism gains a wide audience by proving itself nearly universal in application. Consider the two most famous of all Stoics—Epictetus and Marcus Aurelius. One is a slave, the other the emperor of Rome. Stoicism is the most popular form of philosophy among elites in the Roman Empire and is focused on logic and rationalism, which tends to create rather even-keel and even emotionless adherents. Paul of Tarsus is well-versed in Stoicism, having been born in the land of Chrysippus and Athenodorus. He debates a gaggle of Stoic philosophers in Acts 17:18 and quotes a Stoic poet in Acts 17:28. Yehoshua's cousin John nabs the Stoic focus on the *logos* (the natural law of the universe) and starts his gospel with, *In the beginning was the logos, and the logos was with God, and the logos was God.*

The goal of Stoicism is the achievement of an ideal state of being called *eudaimonia.* The word means "good spirit," connoting tranquility of mind, immunity to circumstance, and a steadfast outlook in the presence of pain or pleasure. When Yehoshua calmly faces Pontius Pilate and refuses to defend himself, he is acting like a Stoic and then some.

Stoics believe an ideal state can be attained through practicing virtue and the twin disciplines of imperturbability and freedom from passion. The good life is achieved through detachment from this world and pure alignment with the *logos*.

This imperturbability can go to astounding lengths, as in the case of Stilbo, who after witnessing the sacking of his city and the murder of his wife and children, can still say to his barbarian enemy with zero emotion, "Nihil perditi." *I have lost nothing.* How is this possible? Because he still has his Stoic virtue. This hard-core freedom from attachment is similarly expressed by Yehoshua when he says in Matthew 10:39, "Whoever finds his life will lose it, and whoever loses his life for my sake will find it." That said, Yehoshua does not tell his disciples to pursue detachment. As we will see shortly, he has far higher aims for his followers.

Yehoshua is not always the unflappable Stoic. He gets angry when the religionists try to stop him from healing on the Sabbath (Mark 3:5). He is indignant when people try to stop children from coming to see him (Mark 10:14). He is deeply troubled and weeps at the tomb of Lazarus (John 11:33, 35). Unlike Socrates and Seneca, who meet their forced suicides with gentle aplomb, Yehoshua is in anguish in the garden of Gethsemane (Luke 22:44).

So it cannot be said Yehoshua was a full-on Stoic philosopher.

Yehoshua the Epicurean

"Pleasure, we declare, is the beginning and end of the happy life."

—Epicurus

If Yehoshua is both a square peg in Stoicism's round hole and a round peg in Cynicism's square hole, is he perhaps an Epicurean?

Founded by Epicurus roughly a half-decade before Stoicism in 307 BC, Epicureanism is the lightest of the philosophies in the sense that one of its major goals is human happiness. Epicurus is far ahead of his time, believing the world is comprised of "atoms and the void." Unlike the other academies, Epicurus builds his contrarian school in his house outside the Athens city walls. He calls it "The Garden," and it is essentially a precursor to today's monasteries. He lives with his friends, working and learning and enjoying life, and he scandalously welcomes women and slaves into his ranks. The philosophy becomes stupendously popular, with upwards of 400,000 people living in hundreds of communes across the ancient world. Epicureanism lasts over eight hundred years, until Emperor Justinian finally shuts down the garden in 529 AD.

Despite Epicureans being depicted as depraved hedonists addicted to bodily pleasure, Epicureanism is not the wine-glugging, orgiastic cult we may now envision. Many Epics were vegetarians, and Epicurus usually chose water over wine. His one occasional extravagant luxury was a mere "pot of cheese." As Epicurus wrote in his letter to Menoeceus, "For it is not drinking bouts and continuous partying and enjoying boys and women, or consuming fish and other dainties of an extravagant table, which produce a pleasant life, but sober calculation which searches out the reasons for every choice and avoidance and drives out the opinions which are the source of the greatest turmoil for men's souls."

The goal of Epicureanism is neither to maximize pleasure or virtue but to minimize pain. *Aponia* (absence of pain) is the ideal state of mind and body. For Epics, the pursuit of happiness requires the purging of pain. So relax, enjoy life, and stop worrying so much.

Yehoshua's philosophy overlaps with Epicurean thought in many ways. Both agree that anxiety is useless (Matthew 6:25), that wealth is a distraction from what really matters (Matthew 13:22), and that seeking political power is a waste of time (Matthew 4:8). Yehoshua lives in close relationship with his disciples. He enjoys life, spends time with women and other second-class citizens, and feasts and drinks when the opportunity avails.

But unlike the Epics, Yehoshua believes in the afterlife (John 11:25–26), that there is one ultimate right way to live (John 14:6), that ultimate peace doesn't arise from the absence of trouble

(John 16:33), and that God cares about people (Matthew 6:26, 30). Unlike the Epics, Yehoshua believes in appropriate fear and reverence for God (Matthew 10:28), and he doesn't try to avoid the ultimate pain—crucifixion (Hebrews 12:2).

Josh and the Three Schools

Is Yehoshua a devotee of Cynicism, Epicureanism, or Stoicism? It appears that when it comes to philosophy, Yehoshua raises no flag, commits to no team. He is cynical, but not a Cynic. He is epicurean, but not an Epicurean. He is stoic, but not a Stoic. He is all three—a *Harmonian*, as I like to call him.

Philosophies are simply different approaches to life, and Yehoshua offers a nod of approval to bits and pieces of other frameworks while offering a fully coherent way of living the good life.

Why would a Hebrew Galilean messiah want to lower himself to the position of a toga-wearing Greek philosopher? The answer is that he wouldn't. Yehoshua is certainly philosophical, but he doesn't set out to invent a philosophy. He starts no academy, writes nothing down, makes fun of Greek garb, and appoints no individual successor to run a namesake school.

Still, one can assemble a rather wonderful way of life from his philosophical teachings. Shall we assemble his academy and build him a school? If he blends Epic, Cynic, and Stoic thought into a unified system of philosophy called the House of Harmonianism, can we give him a philosophical motto? "Enjoy what you will, scorn what you can, bear what you must." This seems to more or less sum up his philosophical outlook. Having constructed him a somewhat disjointed motto and academy, let us now populate it with his morals and values.

Yehoshua's Morals

Is Yehoshua moral? Certainly not by eighteenth-century Puritan standards, and certainly not by first-century Jewish standards either. He eats, drinks, and makes merry, even with corrupt government officials and prostituted women. He seemingly breaks the sabbath, and even hangs out with those filthy, backstabbing Samaritans.

That said, if Yehoshua showed up today, we would write him off as a prude. He is against wealth accumulation. He is a rigorous keeper of the Jewish law. He believes charitable giving is nonnegotiable. He is strongly against divorce.

Humans have a tendency toward moralism, and that is not usually a bad thing. It is an extremely healthy thing to want to know right from wrong and to seek the good and not evil. Indeed, I would rather my son marry a moral woman than an immoral or amoral woman. But there are at least three major problems with trying to live a simply "moral" life.

The first trouble with morals is that they are never enough. It is far easier to focus on rule-keeping than on maintaining healthy relationships. Morals are the fruit. Relationship is the root. If the heart never changes, morals are a temporary shellac atop rotting wood.

The second trouble with morals is how we define them. We live in a Samson-like age where everyone does what is right in their own eyes. There have been seasons of humanity when certain cultures raped virgins and immolated children and thought this was the moral thing to do. In my own nation, I watched agog as my nominally represented officials rose in a standing ovation for the so-called morality of murdering unborn infants. Without YHWH as the sole arbiter of what is right and what is wrong, everything is open to negotiation, and it is this lack of common morality that inevitably bring nations to their knees.

The third trouble with morals is that if you choose the wrong ones, it leads to disaster. The law of gravity doesn't care one bit about my opinions and feelings about gravity. If someone throws me off a building, all claims that gravity isn't real won't stop me from decorating the pavement like a work of modern art. The spiritual world is no less objective than the physical one.

We moderns have lost the plot. Our universities produce good scholars but not good people. Our histories convey facts and dates, but not moral meaning. Morality is seen as a *negative*—that is, when it is not being actively redefined to mean the opposite of historical morality.

Let us then build Yehoshua a university, or at least, a philosophical school. What can we glean from his teachings that can be slotted into the category of philosophy? Without attempting to prioritize, order, or systematize his teachings, what are a few of his moral principles?

More than Eudaimonia

What is the aim of Jesus's philosophy? While the Cynics seek virtue, the Stoics seek tranquility of mind, and the Epicureans seek an absence of pain, Yehoshua's house seeks something far higher than the rest: *shalom*.

The Hebrew word *shalom* occurs 237 times in the Bible and is woefully translated as "peace." But it is so much more than a temporary cessation of war. It is safety, justice, reconciliation, delight, rightness, calmness, soundness, wellness, goodness, wholeness. It is ease and favor and order and welfare and security and prosperity and good health and rest. In other words, it is oneness with God and others. So while the Hellenists aim to strip away negative qualities, YHWH injects his peace-making presence *into* the worst situations.

That everything will be made right is *the* great Jewish hope, the national dream for which they have been striving since the days of Abraham, Isaac, and Jacob. It is a transcendent vision of human flourishing, the high and universal aim to which every civilization should strive with all its might.

This uniquely special Hebrew word appears not once in our New Testament, of course, because we only have Greek copies.

But if we accept that the word *eirene* is the Greek equivalent, it pops up ninety-two times in the New—a 30 percent greater density than the Old. In approximately 10 percent of cases, it is used as a greeting or a farewell. A quarter of the time it is used in the context of relationships. The remaining two-thirds are devoted to the concept itself.

Looking forward to Yehoshua, the prophets Isaiah, Jeremiah, and Micah all predict that the coming Messiah will be the "prince of shalom." Looking back at Yehoshua, Paul of Tarsus in his letter to the Ephesians says Yehoshua's purpose was to "create in himself one new man in place of the two, so making *shalom*. . . . he came and preached *shalom* to you who were far off and peace to those who were near" (2:15, 17). Luke writes in Acts 10:36 (NLT): "This is the message of Good News for the people of Israel—that there is *shalom* with God through Jesus Christ, who is Lord of all."

Jeremiah's letter to the exiles in Babylon exhorts them to "seek the shalom of the city where I have sent you into exile, and to pray to YHWH on its behalf, for in its shalom you will find your shalom." Isaiah 45:7 says it is God himself who brings shalom. If Yehoshua is the Messiah his disciples think he is, he is the prince of shalom prophesied in Isaiah 9:6. If he is the living embodiment of shalom, he has a self-generating source of inner peace, no doubt hard-won from his eremitic times in deep communion atop remote wilderness mountains.

What do the holy messengers tell the shepherds in Luke 2:14? "Glory to God in the highest, and on earth *shalom* among those with whom he is pleased!"

In the Sermon on the Mount, who will be called the children of God? The shalom-makers.

What does he say in Luke 19:42 as he weeps over the Jerusalem that will soon crucify him? "Would that you . . . had known on this day the things that make for *shalom*!"

After his Last Sermon in John 16:33, what is Yehoshua's reason for having taught his disciples all these years? "I have said these things to you, that in me you may have *shalom*."

What does Yehoshua say to his disciples in John 14:27, right before concluding the Last Supper? "*Shalom* I leave with you; my *shalom* I give to you." That's it. That's the gift. *Shalom*.

What is the first post-resurrection thing he says to the gathered disciples in Luke 24:36? "*Shalom* to you!"

Yehoshua's goal is not rule-keeping, a tranquil mind, the absence of pain, or a withdrawal from humanity. He seeks the shalom of God.

Love

I love my infant son, Concord. My firstborn is nearly six months old as I write these words, and every day is a radiant miracle, pleasure, and joy. I love his smiles and giggles and coos and squeals. I love his squished ear, his lopsided smile, and the dent in his forehead from the brutal forceps delivery that ended his mother's punishing thirty-eight hours of labor. I even love his whimpering cries, wolfish howls, and pterodactyl screams.

In addition to loving my son, I also love burritos.

Specifically, chipotle chorizo burritos from *Zarape* in Marlborough, Massachusetts.

I love my swaddled baby boy . . . and I love tortilla-wrapped meat.

How is this possible?

I love my father . . . but I also love *The Godfather*.

I love my wife . . . but I also love *Walden* by Henry David Thoreau.

Doesn't this strike you as odd? Doesn't it make you wonder what in the world Western postmodernists did to the word *love*?

The ancient Greeks, Romans, and Jews didn't see love the way we do. We see it mostly as a word and a feeling. This is very sad. In the ancient mind, love wasn't so much an emotional sentiment as an energetic action. It was a verb, not a noun. We understand this notion, at least in some shallow sense. You can't tell your spouse you love them but then never lift a finger to help around the house. You aren't really loving your friends if you don't commit regular time to them. For the ancient Greeks, love was far more than just a word, feeling, and active pursuit. Love was so nuanced and multifaceted that one word wasn't enough: It was so meaningful that they gave it *seven* words. Let us camp on them for a minute so we can appreciate their meaning when we encounter them in Yehoshua's teaching.

The first love is *philautia*—the love of self. Do you love yourself? Do you realize how special and unique you are? You are fearfully and wonderfully made (Psalm 139:14). While *philautia* can easily stray into sociopathic narcissism (think: politicians and social media influencers), a healthy amount of love for yourself is vital to maintaining self-esteem, confidence, positivity, hope for the future, and a commitment to self-care. This love of self must not be based on performance or what others think of you (Galatians 1:10), otherwise it is destined to fail. It has to come from the innate worth ascribed to all human beings—that you are stamped with the image of God (Genesis 1:27).

Don't let *philautia* turn into selfishness (Philippians 2:3). "Me time" can only go so far. Let your love of self be motived by a love of others —loving yourself well (getting enough sleep, sun, nutrients, movement, meaning, etc.) makes you a far better servant of others.

The second love is *ludus*. Do you have a fun friend who's good for sports or camping trips and pretty much nothing else? Or how about a high school flirtation that lasted for years without a serious thought about dating? Or that time you gave yourself over to the whims and danced your heart out with a total stranger? That's *ludus*, from the same root as the word *ludicrous*. *Ludus* isn't long-lasting, and that's the point. The shared goal is fun—we *ludus* stand-up comedians for this very reason. *Ludus* is all about levity. We desperately need a greater sense of playfulness in our oh-so-serious world. As Proverbs 17:22 says, "A joyful heart is good medicine."

The third love is *pragma*. *Pragma* is the opposite of *ludus*. It's where we get the word *pragmatic*. *Pragma* is wonderful and important because it fosters commitment and companionship and drives us to do the right thing even when we'd rather yield to an easier path. While *ludus* can never last, *pragma* often finds a way. In our noncommittal times, people are giving up on each other far too easily. They block and ban each other online, cancel each other in universities and the entertainment industry, break up, divorce, and unfriend. *Pragma* sees the bigger picture—that there are benefits to commitment rather than the instant gratification of always walking away.

The fourth love is *eros*. *Eros* is how babies get made. This is the romantic, passionate, sexual word for love, from whence we get the word *erotic*. This type of love can often spark a fling, but *eros* doesn't have the fuel to maintain a committed relationship through work, commuting, deadlines, travel, weariness, pregnancy, postpartum, sickness, erectile dysfunction, menopause, injuries, disability, and old age.

Eros can also start a fire that burns your life to ash in a matter of minutes. *Eros* is the Roman equivalent of Cupid in the Greek pantheon, and is often depicted blindfolded for a reason—he fires arrows to and fro without discernment, maiming just as often as he strikes for good. We must shield ourselves from this oft-illogical form of love. Sadly, media corporations are obsessed with *eros*. From Netflix to porn and the narrow gap in between, addiction culture tries to twist all forms of love into mere sex because it's incredibly profitable to do so. (I wish we still used all seven Greek loves if only to watch hormonal high school boys try to pressure girls into sex while saying, "Baby, I agape you!" only to get slapped upside the head by intelligent females who retort, "All you want is eros, you noncommittal tool!") For Yehoshua, *eros* is such a holy flame that the only place it is permitted to burn is within the sanctuary of marriage (Matthew 19:5; Matthew 5:27–28).

The fifth love is *storge*. Parents and guardians experience *storge* in its fullest sense, though some grandparents, aunts, uncles, or rabbis like Yehoshua may get a glimpse. This is the overwhelming love that a parent feels for their newborn; that immediate and unconditional sense that they would sacrifice anything and everything for this child without thinking twice. It is not a mutual exchange sort of love —it is entirely one way, from the parent to the child, with all the responsibility on the former. *Storge* generates a seemingly unlimited amount of patience, compassion, and forgiveness, and is probably the top reason why nearly everyone should have or adopt a kid.

The sixth love is *philia*. This is one of the most important and long-lasting loves. Have you ever had an intimate, authentic, affection-filled friendship that was built on active mutual pursuit? That's *philia*. If we are brutally honest, most people have never had a classically true friend in their entire lives. It is the sort of David-and-Jonathan brotherhood that philosophers like Cicero craved and raved about in books on the subject. It's the sort of love that siblings can also come to enjoy, particularly after they lose their parents and start to grow old themselves. It is sweet, platonic, secure, enduring—a friend who sticks closer than a brother (Proverbs 18:24). While many marriages fade, many *philia* friendships hold fast. In fact, many of the best marriages are filled to the brim with *philia*. Paul tells the church in Rome to "love one another with *philadelphia*. Outdo one another in showing honor" (Romans 12:10).

The seventh and final love is *agape*. This is the motherlode, the pièce de résistance, the magnum opus, the gold standard, the apotheosis of love. For Greeks and Romans, it is the highest love. Yehoshua will take this secular word and completely redefine it. Now, it is the love of YHWH himself. Unconditional, godlike *agape* drives us to acts of selflessness great and small. It compels us to love unconditionally and to love in the fullest possible sense. Incredibly, it doesn't respond to perceived worth or value but *creates* value and drives us to self-sacrifice. In other words, it is the antithesis of our hyper-individualist consumerist age (Romans 12:2). Without *agape*, we are just clanging symbols (1 Corinthians 13:1). *Agape* awakens within us a definite universality—a strong feeling of connection to every living thing in existence (Acts 17:28)—and makes us able to transcend any circumstance (Romans 8:38–39). Most people will never experience *agape*. It is *agape* that drives Yehoshua to the cross.

Now that we understand the nuance and depth of love as Yehoshua conceives of it, and knowing his culture sees all seven loves more as verbs than nouns, let us return to our philosopher-rabbi and see what he has to say about love.

The Chief Commandment

When asked by a fair-minded scribe to pick out the most important commandment in Judaism (Mark 12:30–31), Yehoshua quotes Deuteronomy 6:5 and Leviticus 19:18: "You shall *agape* the LORD your God with all your heart and with all your soul and with all your mind and with all your might," and "You shall *agape* your neighbor as yourself."

If shalom is the goal, agape is how we attain it. Love is the way to peace.

How do we attain shalom? By loving God and loving people.

How do we embody our love for YHWH? By loving him with all our heart (in prayer and affection), soul (passion and ambition), mind (study and thought), and strength (words and deeds).

How do we actively love our neighbors? Well, first we must determine who is our neighbor. The parable of the good Samaritan says it's everyone, enemies included (Luke 10:37). With the target of our love now understood, we go to the Golden Rule, Yehoshua's improvement on Hillel's "don't treat other people the way you don't want to be treated." "So whatever you wish that others would do to you, do also to them" (Matthew 7:12). It's not enough to follow Google's former motto of "Don't be evil." This philosophy requires active love.

Yehoshua is deadly serious on this point. Consider this passage in Matthew 25:31–45, one of the longest teachings in the gospels, subtitled in many Bibles as "The Last Judgment."

> When the Son of Man comes in his glory, and all the angels with him, he will sit on his glorious throne. Before him will be gathered all the nations, and he will separate people one from another as a shepherd separates the sheep from the goats. And he will place the sheep on his right, but the goats on the left. Then the King will say to those on his right, "Come, you who are blessed by my Father, inherit the kingdom prepared for you from the foundation of the world. For I was hungry and you gave me food, I was thirsty and you gave me drink, I was a stranger and you welcomed me, I was naked and you clothed me, I was sick and you visited me, I was in prison and you came to me." Then the righteous will answer him, saying, "Lord, when did we see you hungry and feed you, or thirsty and give you drink? And when did we see you a stranger and welcome you, or naked and clothe you? And when did we see you sick or in prison and visit you?" And the King will answer them, "Truly, I say to you, as you did it to one of the least of these my brothers, you did it t o me."
>
> Then he will say to those on his left, "Depart from me, you cursed, into the eternal fire prepared for the devil and his angels. For I was hungry and you gave me no food, I was thirsty and you gave me no drink, I was a stranger and you did not welcome me, naked and you did not clothe me, sick and in prison and you did not visit me." Then they also will answer, saying, "Lord, when did we see you hungry or thirsty or a stranger or naked or sick or in prison, and did not minister to you?" Then he will answer them, saying, "Truly, I say to you, as you did not do it to one of the least of these, you did not do it to me."

You say you love YHWH? Yehoshua says *prove it with active agape*. His brother James (real name: Yakob ben Yehoseph) will later build on this theme in James 2:16–18. "And one of you says to them, 'Go in peace, be warmed and filled,' without giving them the things needed for the body, what good is that? So also faith by itself, if it does not have works, is dead. But someone will say, 'You have faith and I have works.' Show me your faith apart from your works, and I will show you my faith by my works." Agape, for the ben Yehoseph boys, is active.

Even enemy love must be active: "*Agape* your enemies, do good to those who hate you" (Luke 6:27). For some Israelis, this means blessing Palestinians. For some Mexicans, it means blessing Americans. For some blacks and whites, it means blessing whites and blacks. For some rich and poor, it means blessing the poor and rich. While the courts can try to coerce these sorts of unifying behaviors, agape can do what the law can never do.

To what lofty height can this new definition of love attain? What is Yehoshua's conception of the greatest possible act of love? He shares his answer under the cover of night with a non-religionist Galilean synedrion leader named Nicodemus in John 3:16: "For God so loved the world, that he gave his only Son, that whoever believes in him should not perish but have eternal life."

The highest form of love is not to enjoy a burrito or sleep around or rewatch *The Godfather*, but to sacrifice your own son as God the Father . . . *and* to sacrifice yourself as God the Son . . . *for your enemies*.

Fellow philosophers, lovers of wisdom and right-way-of-livingness: Love *is* the ultimate moral and ethic.

This truth will lead Yehoshua's cousin-disciple John to pen some of the most breathtaking verses in all of Scripture.

> Beloved, let us love one another, for love is from God, and whoever loves has been born of God and knows God. Anyone who does not love does not know God, because God is love. In this

> the love of God was made manifest among us, that God sent his only Son into the world, so that we might live through him. In this is love, not that we have loved God but that he loved us and sent his Son to be the propitiation for our sins. Beloved, if God so loved us, we also ought to love one another. No one has ever seen God; if we love one another, God abides in us and his love is perfected in us. By this we know that we abide in him and he in us.
>
> 1 John 4:7–13

The word for love here is *agape*, every single time. Fifteen *agapes* in seven verses.

YHWH is *agape*. We *agape* because Yehoshua *agaped*. If we *agape* like Yehoshua, YHWH lives in us and perfects his *agape* in us. I'm sure you can see the ripple effect. As more and more people begin to *agape*, the world fills with shalom. This is the life vision of our philosopher-rabbi.

We have camped on love for quite a few pages because it is the most important value in Yehoshua's philosophy. Yehoshua's entire school of philosophy is summed up in actively *agape*-ing God and others. Knowing this is the case, we may rest assured that all other philosophical concepts, morals, virtues, and ethics flow from this fountainhead. Let us look now at just three—three that, two thousand years later, society continues to violently resist.

Radical egalitarianism

Yehoshua is troublingly egalitarian, not only by first-century Jewish standards but also by our own. He has no problem associating with women, be they posh aristocrats (Joanna), the wives of businessmen (Salome), prostitutes (Luke 7:37), demoniacs (Luke 8:10), cripples (Luke 13:11), divorcées (John 4:18), adulteresses (John 8:3), or little girls (Mark 5:41). Of the thirty-seven miracles detailed in the gospels, a third of them expressly involve women. He heals Simon's mother-in-law (Mark 1:29), a widow's son (Luke 7:11), a daughter of a Syrian woman (Mark 7:26), and his most committed disciple, who suffered from internal demons (Mark 16:9).

Yehoshua's first public miracle is performed at the request of a woman (John 2:1–11). His greatest miracle ever (raising Lazarus from the dead) is at the request of two women (John 11:1–44). The first person he tells he is the Messiah is a woman (John 4:25–26). The first person to see him alive after his crucifixion is a woman (John 20:1–16). The first commissioned evangelist is a woman (John 20:17). As we have seen, he has plenty of female disciples from start to finish.

Yehoshua sees men and women not as the same, but as entirely equal in value. This leaves not only Hillel and Shammai in his dust, but also the vast majority of Greek and Roman philosophers.

Yehoshua also has a heart for children, the cultural nobodies of first-century Palestine. No matter how busy he is, he invites the children in for an embrace and a blessing (Mark 10:14–16). He heals the children of foreigners (Matthew 15:28). He casts demons out of children (Matthew 17:18). He raises children from the dead (Mark 5:41–42). He involves children in his miracles (John 6:9–10). He tells his disciples to become like children (Matthew 18:3–4). He lets them make noise in church despite the scolding of religionists (Matthew 21:15). He tells the Twelve that welcoming children in his name is *the same as welcoming God himself* (Mark 9:37).

Paul of Tarsus picks up on this radical egalitarianism in Galatians 3:28: "There is neither Jew nor Greek, there is neither slave nor free, there is no male and female, for you are all one in Christ Jesus." That is not to say that passports and egregious inequalities and chromosomes magically disappear, but that *anyone and everyone's value is equalized* in Yehoshua.

Let us not pretend for a moment that our commodified society views everyone with such radical equality. People are only as valuable as the profits they produce. Where are all the Hollywood paralytics? Where are all the Congresspeople with dwarfism? Where are all the impoverished black female Christian authors with speech impediments and facial deformities? Why do we still see refugees and people with disabilities as "other"? The gospel writers suggest it is because we are human, fallen, and in need of a philosopher-equalizer named Yehoshua.*

In the kingdom of God, Yehoshua's radical egalitarianism equalizes men and women without the need for suffragette marches and equal pay for equal work. It equalizes blacks and whites without the need for affirmative action or desegregation. It equalizes freedmen and slaves at the stroke of Paul's pen. Though society cannot yet fathom a world where coercive action simply isn't necessary, that same world will never be more outwardly equal as when everyone's inner value is equalized in Yehoshua. This fact is borne out by Yehoshua's global faith family, which is far and away the most diverse group of uncoerced humans in history.

Radical sharing

If all people have equal value in Yehoshua's philosophy, then their wealth and possessions will sooner or later reflect this reality. I have yet to meet a father who allows one son to own multiple

* Perhaps the starkest example of this reality in Scripture is the scandal that Paul summarizes in his letter to Philemon. Philemon is a godly follower of the Way, who hosts a church plant in his Colassae home with his wife, Apphia. But Philemon is also still deeply enculturated and has yet to become a fully loving Christian—i.e., he still owns a slave. (If you own a pair of Nikes or an iPhone, don't be too quick to judge the slowness of his sanctification.) This slave, named Onesimus (meaning helpful or profitable), robs Philemon and escapes to the bustling metropolis of Rome. There he meets the imprisoned apostle Paul, along with his partners, Timothy, Epaphras, Mark, Aristarchus, Demas, and Luke. They all become fast friends, and Onesimus is so transformed by faith that he *willingly* goes back to Philemon, risking a brutal beating if not crucifixion as punishment for his "crimes." Mercifully, he is armed with a letter from Paul that doesn't try to guilt or shame or cancel Philemon but begs him to now see Onesimus as a man and a brother (Philemon 1:16). Unbelievably, Paul also asks Philemon to take Onesimus back not as a slave but *as a son*. Paul is so confident of the *agape* that is growing in Philemon that he voices his expectation that Philemon will do *even more* than he asks (Philemon 1:21).

hyper-yachts in Monaco while his daughter starves to death in a Nigerian slum.

As we will see in the next chapter, Yehoshua files a total claim over the assets of his disciples and demands as much on the socioeconomic front as he does of sex and legal status (Matthew 16:24). I will not belabor the point here but simply say this: There is no place for wealth accumulation in the life of Yehoshua's disciples (Luke 12:15–21). In Yehoshua's philosophical garden, everything is shared with those in need—housing, clothing, food, wealth, time, all of it. Whoever earns it doesn't necessarily keep it. Whoever needs it most, gets it. Paul picks up on this theme of spirit-led wealth equality in 2 Corinthians 8:13–14: "I do not mean that others should be eased and you burdened, but that as a matter of fairness your abundance at the present time should supply their need, so that their abundance may supply your need, that there may be fairness."

This Christ-centered communalism dredges up that dreaded word: *redistribution*. Rest assured, Yehoshua does not hold out any hope that state-run poverty prevention programs will fix the root issue of sinful, selfish, self-seeking hearts. While taxation feels punitive and confiscatory, radical sharing becomes second nature to those who truly understand that they are the beneficiaries of the most radical act of redistribution in history—the shifting of the penalty of sin from themselves to their savior.

Radical pluralism

It is extremely important to note that Yehoshua's teachings do not apply to those outside his "school." He never scolds a Gentile, a Phoenician, a Samaritan, or a Roman for their bad behavior. His ethical teachings are almost exclusively directed at his disciples, and his harshest denunciations are for those within his religious context, namely, the Jewish religionists. Yehoshua has no moral expectations of those who haven't yet joined the family. As my mother likes to put it, "You can't clean a fish until you catch it."

So how is a moral student of Yehoshua to live in a world of immorality, amorality, and redefined morality? Yehoshua answers the question with a pair of parables.

> "The kingdom of heaven is like a man who sowed good seed in his field. . . . When the wheat sprouted and formed heads, then the weeds also appeared. The owner's servants came to him and said, 'Sir, didn't you sow good seed in your field? Where then did the weeds come from?' 'An enemy did this,' he replied. The servants asked him, 'Do you want us to go and pull them up?' 'No,' he answered, 'because while you are pulling the weeds, you may uproot the wheat with them. Let both grow together until the harvest. At that time I will tell the harvesters: First collect the weeds and tie them in bundles to be burned; then gather the wheat and bring it into my barn."
>
> Matthew 13:24, 26–30 NIV

In case his disciples are unclear about this parable's meaning, he explains it in Matthew 13:36–43, then uses another metaphor to emphasize the separation.

> Once again, the kingdom of heaven is like a net that was let down into the lake and caught all kinds of fish. When it was full, the fishermen pulled it up on the shore. Then they sat down and collected the good fish in baskets, but threw the bad away. This is how it will be at the end of the age. The angels will come and separate the wicked from the righteous and throw them into the blazing furnace, where there will be weeping and gnashing of teeth.
>
> Matthew 13:47–50 NIV

In other words: Plant seeds and urge people to repent and believe, but let people believe what they want to believe; live and let live. Let God decide when it is all over.

Yehoshua never forces behavior change. Yehoshua never punishes dissidents. Yehoshua never issues a gag order or censors his critics. He doesn't even defend himself when religionists at his trial hurl false accusations that lead to his murder. He simply urges his followers to make sure they are wholesome wheat and not noxious weeds, spotless lambs and not mangy goats.

No one is forced to follow Yehoshua or believe he is God. All we know for certain is that whenever and wherever people stop practicing his philosophy, things tend to fall apart. Still, he doesn't demand love and fidelity. To be clear, Yehoshua never condones sin or avoids inviting people to live sanctified lives, but he adores sinners. He believes so strongly in their right to reject him that he would rather be murdered than force his views upon them.

This is the sort of radical pluralism that even the most liberal-minded college professor cannot fathom putting into practice. Everyone is battling for ideological supremacy, and almost none of it is driven by self-sacrificial love and everlasting patience. If ever there were a champion and defender of radical free speech and free thought—even the dangerous delusions of morality like those held by Jewish religionists and murderous Romans—it is Yehoshua ben Yehoseph.

Yehoshua the Not-Philosopher

Yehoshua is humanity's greatest philosopher because he teaches the human race how to live the ideal life. How does one live as a follower of Yehoshua? They seek first their philosopher-king's kingdom and right-way-of-livingness and actively agape everyone, enemies included. As their lives fill with the active agape of YHWH himself, this naturally fills the world with joy, patience, kindness, goodness, faithfulness, gentleness, self-control, radical egalitarianism, radical sharing, radical pluralism, and ultimately total global shalom.

Isn't this clearly what the ideal philosophy—dare I say the philosophy of heaven—might look like?

The Economic Josh

"There are three conversions necessary: the conversion of the heart, the conversion of the mind, and the conversion of the purse."

—Attributed to Martin Luther

Josh the Builder

How did Yehoshua ben Yehoseph make money and pay his bills? What did he do for a living? What were his thoughts on robo-investing and day-trading cryptocurrency?

The Sunday school answer to the first question is that if you stitch together Mark 6:3 and Matthew 13:55, Yehoshua takes after his stepfather Yehoseph and becomes a carpenter. But the Bible never says Yehoshua worked specifically with lumber. In a *Christianity Today* article entitled "The Stonemason the Builders Rejected," pastor-professor Jordan K. Monson makes a compelling case that Yehoshua was not so much a wood guy as a stone man. As Monson points out, Yehoshua refers to wood only twice in the gospels: once in his famous log-in-the-eye illustration, the other a passing mention of dried-out wood in Luke 23:31. Not a single one of his forty-eight parables is about carpentry. On the other hand, he references rocks constantly, speaking of cornerstones (Mark 12:10), towers (Luke 13:4), walls (Matthew 21:33), building on rocks (Matthew 7:24–27), stones (Luke 19:40), winepresses (Matthew 21:33), millstones (Luke 17:2), and foundations (Matthew 7:24). As we saw in chapter 5, he even nicknamed his lead disciple Rocky.

Monson notes that Galilee was so lacking in trees that it had to import wood from elsewhere, that most houses in Yehoshua's day were built of stone, and that King Solomon had to hire Sidonian carpenters to teach his Israelite workforce how to work with timber because they simply didn't know how. So why are Sunday school teachers around the world still telling children that Yehoshua was a carpenter?

Once again, we may blame the translators of King James's Bible. When the English scribblers arrived at the Greek word *tektón*, from which we get the beautiful English word architect (chief builder), they translated it as *carpenter*. And it makes sense. Greece was a nation covered in trees, and at least in 1611 when the KJV was published, England was a nation well forested. Plus, isn't there something evocative and poetic about a humble man hammering nails into wood, only later to be nailed to a wooden cross?

But Yehoshua wasn't Greek. His daily tongue was Aramaic, which means he would have called himself a *haras/kharash*—a builder-craftsman. There is a Greek term specifically for wood craftsmen, but Yehoshua is always given the more general term.

While it is deliciously romantic to picture the lone figure of Yehoshua sanding tables in silent solitude with God, it is much more likely that he worked alongside others. If he was of middling skill, he would have worked under an arch-*tektón*.

A little higher up the ladder and he may have managed a few underling day laborers and apprentice craftsmen. I am of the view that with a father as a guide and fifteen years of hard practice, it is not unreasonable to think Yehoshua could have made foreman on a project or two. At this point we might as well go straight to Monson's article: "Jesus's knowledge of building did not seem to stop at the materials themselves. He spoke constantly of financial practice, of management of both projects and people; payment, debt, wages, investment, hiring and firing, relationships between managers and staff and masters and bondservants."

That is not to say Yehoshua possessed an occupation of high standing. In fact, the word for builder/craftsman used to describe Jesus's occupation may have been derogative at the time, connoting a relatively lowly tranche in the Roman social order. In Mark 6:3, after Yehoshua gains fame as a rabbi and returns to Nazareth to preach in his hometown synagogue, the people scoff. "Isn't this the builder, the son of Mary?" Note the double disparagement: that he is a mere laborer who has to supplement his preaching income, and that he is not worthy of his father's name. This thread of elitist superiority toward the working class is carried into the second century by the anti-Christian philosopher Celsus, who in Origen's *Contra Celsum* is quoted as labeling Yehoshua as "only a *tektón*"—a mere day laborer, a gypsy-like handyman, even if in truth he was a well-respected foreman who earned his keep by contributing to his community.

We may assume that this is how Yehoshua spent much of his adolescent and early adult life, laboring with stone and wood and mud from sunup to sundown, six days per week, from Sunday through Friday, until at least his late twenties, forever erasing from our minds the medieval iconography of a fragile and emaciated weakling academic.

Josh the Teacher

By the age of around thirty, Yehoshua is ready to drop the hammer and/or chisel and embark on a new and more eternal vocation. Did he continue to work on houses and temples as a Paul-style, self-funding "tentmaker" (Acts 18:3–4) after becoming an itinerant spiritual teacher? Perhaps, but the text doesn't say. What it does admit is that Yehoshua's public ministry was scandalously bankrolled by a troupe of rather wealthy women, no doubt making Yehoshua appear to some as the righteous Rasputin of first-century Palestine.

Yehoshua's supporters receive scant mention in the New Testament, but if they were anything like the gospel patrons in every generation who have silently partnered in the good work of disciple-making since, they probably wanted it that way. The fact that Scripture records the unseemly detail that Yehoshua's ministry was funded by women only adds to its credibility. If you wanted to confer social proof on a rabbi, you would assign him patrons of the highest order, such as the high priest, King Herod, or even Caesar himself.

Instead, Yehoshua is supported by Maggie, Jo, and Sue.

We may accept that Luke interviewed the most eyewitnesses for his gospel, and it is obvious that he pays careful attention to the testimony of women in the Yehoshua community. In Luke 8:1–3 (NIV), he reports that as a traveling rabbi, Yehoshua "traveled about from one town and village to another, proclaiming the good news of the kingdom of God. The Twelve were with him, and also some women who had been cured of evil spirits and diseases: Mary (called Magdalene) from whom seven demons had come out; Joanna the wife of Chuza, the manager of Herod's household; Susanna; and many others. These women were helping to support them out of their own means."

This is an extraordinary passage that deserves our keen attention.

First, let us banish from our minds the idea that Yehoshua simply wandered around with twelve young men when in fact it was a mixed brigade of dozens.

Second, note that three women are named, while the inner circle disciples get lumped into "the Twelve."

Third, note the named women.

We have Maggie, the most committed and courageous disciple.

We have the English Susanna, whose name in Hebrew was likely Shoshana, and we know nothing about her. She is attached to no man yet is wealthy enough to travel with a revolutionary rabbi and feed and shelter seventy-odd hungry lads and lasses. The specific mention of her name—the only time she is mentioned in Scripture—suggests she was well known to the fledgling faith community, either for her special devotion, her social rank, or both.

And we have Joanna. Who is she? Likely a resident of the Galilean capital of Tiberius, she is or was the wealthy wife of Chuza, household manager for the wretched King Herod Antipas. This is an extraordinary bit of information. Yehoshua's ministry is partially bankrolled by enemy money? It is the equivalent of the Dalai Lama receiving funds from Xi Jinping's business manager, or a backwoods preacher in Ukraine being funded by Vladimir Putin's Moscow accountant. If the reader feels uncomfortable with the idea of Yehoshua accepting blood money, this is a sign of a working conscience. It is hard to know why Yehoshua decides to accept these funds, but perhaps he has Proverbs 13:22 in mind: "The sinner's wealth is laid up for the righteous."

Yehoshua is on a holy mission to redeem everything in the universe, blood money included. A case can also be made that each person is accountable before God for how they earn their money, and in this case, the earner in question is Chuza, not Yehoshua, and that Yehoshua didn't court the funds in the first place. Further, there is no sign that Yehoshua keeps any of the money for himself but instead uses it to meet the needs of the very people Chuza and his bosses regularly exploit.

Joanna won't be the only person in the royal court to come to faith—by cross-referencing Acts 13:1 with Roman history, we learn that Herod's foster-brother joins the church at Antioch. But Joanna's specific mention in Luke 8:1–3 brings up all sorts of questions: What evil spirit or disease did she have? How did she first make contact with Yehoshua? As a member of Herod's court, did she remember the murder of John the Baptizer? Was it John himself who turned her on to the candidate for Messiah? (After all, even King Herod was happy to listen to the locust-eating prophet at first.) How did Joanna get away with following Yehoshua on his Galilean roadshow, essentially funding the enemy as he stirred up an army, without getting caught? Did Chuza divorce her, or was he secretly a follower of Yehoshua as well? Why is she named in the text, anyway? Is the Greek-named Joanna the Latinized Junia, who Paul greets in his letter to the Romans and calls "outstanding among the apostles"?

Every one of these questions is maddeningly unaddressed by Luke. But perhaps that is the point. We cannot help but adore these women who quietly fund the work of the kingdom, yet the lens remains rightfully focused on their rabbi. What we do know about these gospel patrons is that they were not only faithful to Yehoshua with their money, but also with their lives. It is the same Maggie and Jo who Luke places at the tomb on the morning after Yehoshua's execution, ready with expensive spices and ointments to embalm their murdered master.

There is another woman who shows up for the macabre memorial. Mark calls her Salome—the wife of Zebedee, the mother of the disciples James and John, and likely Yehoshua's aunt. Mark mentions in 15:40 that Salome, along with Aunt Mary, the mother of Little James, had been with Yehoshua since Galilee, and had "followed him and ministered to him." Matthew confirms in

27:56 that Salome and Little James's Mary followed Yehoshua from Galilee to care for his needs.

In other words: Yehoshua and his disciples are supported by their aunts and mothers.

Going forward, we should not skim over these special names in our Sunday sermon readings. For are these women not history's first gospel patrons and the inspiration for all those to follow?*

All this heavenly largesse can be traced back to the generosity of Maggie, Jo, Sue, and many other far-seeing women who gladly traded temporary riches for eternal glory. In doing so, they remind us that we are God's method for funding the work of the gospel. As John Rineheart reminds us, Yehoshua could have been born into a rich or even royal family. He could have started a zero-cost restaurant by multiplying fish and bread. He could have started a winery whose only input was well water. Instead, he humbles himself and accepts donations from "mere" women and invites us into partnering and co-laboring to advance the mission of one first-century rabbi. In doing so, Yehoshua sets an uncomfortable example for the rest of us: He lives a life of voluntary poverty so that others can find blessing.

So that is how Yehoshua funded his adventures. He worked first as a journeyman construction worker, and later as a donation-based traveling teacher. The mid-second-century anti-Christian philosopher Celsus is quoted in *Contra Celsum* as believing Yehoshua "obtained his means of livelihood in a disgraceful and

* Author John Rineheart has made a colossal effort to reintroduce the Christian world to stories of gospel patrons, including the quiet supporters behind the apostle Paul (a woman named Phoebe), the church at Thessalonica (a fellow named Jason), the apostle Peter (a tanner named Simon who owned a house by the sea), the gospel writer Luke (a friend of God named Theophilus, who funded the writing of Luke and Acts), the first English Bible as translated by William Tyndale (an English merchant named Humphrey Monmouth who owned a huge fleet of ships), and the funders of work accomplished by George Whitefield, John Newton, Bill Bright, R. C. Sproul, and dozens more.

importunate way," which Professor Taylor reads as begging or receiving donations. Yehoshua sees the gifts as an investment in the kingdom of God and an invitation to join in the exciting work of kingdom-building. They are rarely flat broke, but they are never rich either. When Yehoshua instructs his followers to feed the five thousand, they estimate it will cost two hundred denari (roughly six months' wages) to feed the crowd. The disciples don't say, "We don't have cash," they just worry that it's a lot to spend for one speaking gig. We know they buy food on the road (John 4:8), and John 12:6 suggests they carry some sort of float in petty cash, likely in the money bag carried by Judas.

We may guess that Yehoshua's needs on the road were few. He is depicted as walking everywhere and has to borrow a colt for his triumphal entry into Jerusalem, so we can be assured he didn't own wheels (that is to say, a chariot). It is also doubtful that he owned a sailboat, though he seems content enough to nap "on a cushion" in the stern of a borrowed vessel in Mark 4:38. When they are extremely low on money, the disciples nab a bit of wheat while they walk.

The story is recorded in Matthew 12:1–8. "At that time Yehoshua went through the grainfields on the Sabbath. His disciples were hungry, and they began to pluck heads of grain to eat." When the Pharisees saw this, they didn't say, "You dirty, rotten thieves! How dare you steal from a farmer?" No, what they say is, "Look, your disciples are doing what is not lawful to do on the Sabbath."

The religionists had worked themselves into such a traditionalist frenzy that picking a few grains of wheat was, in their addled heads, the same thing as harvesting a whole crop, which was forbidden work on a Saturday. Yehoshua, of course, disagrees. Work is work. Lunch is lunch.

Poverty and hunger were so rampant in first-century Judea that it was neither illegal nor immoral to nip a bit of food when you truly needed it. Despite the existence of private property, the Jewish faith family collectively agreed that the real sin was allowing a fellow Jew to starve to death. Can I get an amen?

There were, of course, reasonable limits to protect farmers from total ruin. Deuteronomy 23:24 says you can enter a vineyard and eat your fill of grapes, but you can't put any in your basket. Deuteronomy 23:25 says you can pluck a few heads from a grainfield, but you can't bring a sickle. Leviticus 23:22 commands farmers to leave the edges of all fields unharvested so the poor and the foreigner won't starve to death. If you extrapolate the data, it appears that Yehoshua and his seventy-odd don't starve but sometimes live right near the edge.

Where do they sleep? Yehoshua intimates in Luke 9:58 that he doesn't own a house. But does the troupe occasionally rent or couch surf? Almost certainly. Matthew 4:13 says Yehoshua moved to Capernaum and lived there after leaving Nazareth. There are at least three houses available among the Twelve. It appears Simon Peter's Capernaum house becomes a bit of a northern base camp for the ever-growing flock. Simon is evidently married and has a hospitable mother-in-law, so it makes logistical sense. Simon's is the first place Yehoshua sleeps over (Mark 1:29) and when he returns to Capernaum after his first tour of Galilee, Peter's Mark says that "he was at home" (Mark 2:1). Matthew/Levi, the wealthy former tax collector, also has a house, which Yehoshua commandeers for a dinner party in Matthew 9:10. Yehoshua's thunder cousin John also has a house, which will become the home of Yehoshua's mother, Mary, after her son is crucified (John 19:27).

In addition to at least three disciple homes, Salome and Zebedee are likely rich enough to host, and the same might apply to Joanna, Susanna, Maggie, and Aunt Mary.

John 4:40 says Yehoshua stays two days in a Samaritan village, and it is likely that plenty of other hearers (such as Zacchaeus) would have opened their homes to the rabbi and disciples. In an age before hotels, true hospitality was significantly more developed, and who wouldn't want to entertain a famous celebrity known for turning water into wine?

There is nothing in the gospels that says they didn't camp, rent, or even chip in and buy a house, though that last one seems most unlikely. That said, John 19:27 suggests Yehoshua has been supporting his presumably widowed mother, Mary, so maybe he occasionally stays at the place she resides. We simply don't know, but there is enough evidence to suggest he was not *entirely* homeless.

Shall we now take a sidestroke and dive for deeper waters?

What did Yehoshua believe about money? What was its purpose? How should his disciples manage it? And most important—to us, at least—how much of it do we get to keep for ourselves? It is to the vitally important spiritual topic of financial stewardship that we now turn.

Contrary to what prosperity gospel televangelists and radio money gurus would have us believe—there's even a book called *The Millionaire from Nazareth*—Jesus Christ did not come into the world to make us rich in earthly possessions.

Yehoshua ben Yehoseph makes no attempt to institute a new set of systematized earthly economic policies, but he has a lot to say about money. In fact, it is an act of economic sabotage that will lead the high priests to set in motion his assassination. There is no doubt that Yehoshua was a financial radical in his day, but in our modern, hyper-commodified society, his teachings on money are considerably more radical than they were twenty centuries ago.

Yehoshua told somewhere between thirty-eight and forty-six parables in the Synoptic Gospels (depending on how you define a parable), over a quarter or more of which can be applied to financial stewardship.

In total, there are 288 verses about money in the gospels, which, quite deliciously for those who practice tithing, works out to about one in every ten verses. It is at this juncture in the conversation that the give-me-the-minimum-standard church-goer immediately raises his hand to ask the tired old question, "Does Jesus command us to tithe?"

The answer is yes and no. Some scholars have suggested that when Yehoshua speaks of money, his hyper-religious audience would have immediately known he was hinting at the tithes and offerings passages found in Leviticus 27:30 and Deuteronomy 16:16–17. But the strongest case can be made from Matthew 23:23 (emphasis added): "Woe to you, scribes and Pharisees, hypocrites! For you tithe mint and dill and cumin, and have neglected the weightier matters of the law: justice and mercy and faithfulness. These you ought to have done, *without neglecting the others.*" In other words: Do not neglect tithing, but more important, work on the matters of character that keep you from giving *all* of yourself away.

With tithing out of the way (or back on the menu), can we try for a moment to put Yehoshua's thoughts on money in some sort of order? What are the financial principles we may glean from his teaching?

Here are twelve of his economic principles, in no particular order, and bearing in mind this is by no means an exhaustive list.

1. God's kingdom is more valuable than our empire.

Yehoshua drops a powerful pair of back-to-back parables in Matthew 13:44–46. The first: "The kingdom of heaven is like treasure hidden in a field, which a man found and covered up. Then in his joy he goes and sells all that he has and buys that field."

To drive home the point to his disciples, he immediately paints a similar picture: "Again, the kingdom of heaven is like a merchant in search of fine pearls, who, on finding one pearl of great value, went and sold all that he had and bought it."

The shared meaning of the parables of the pearl and hidden treasure could not be clearer: The kingdom of heaven is worth liquidating all of our earthly assets to attain. That is not to say that we can buy our way into heaven, of course. If anything, it is Yehoshua who is surrendering everything, even his body to the Roman cross, in order to secure the kingdom for his disciples.

2. There is a far higher authority than Caesar.

Mark 12 tells us the chief priests and their entourage send some Pharisees and pro-Roman Herodian partisans to frame Yehoshua for tax evasion. Yehoshua's answer is the stuff of legends. He grabs a denarius coin—Rome's standard silver coin from 211 BC to around 240 AD (weighing 0.125 troy ounces, worth around three dollars at today's prices, and from which we derive words such as the North African dinar and the Spanish dinero)—and asks the crowd whose face is on it. We don't know which particular minting Yehoshua held up, but whether the image was of Augustus or Tiberius, everyone recognizes the face of a tyrant. "Give to Caesar what is Caesar's," he says, "and to God what is God's."

Many a preacher will close his Bible right there and tell you this means Christians should pay taxes—even to a government as corrupt as Rome's—but there is always more to the story when Yehoshua drops the microphone. For what, after all, belongs to God? The Jewish elite would have known David's answer in Psalm 24:1 (NIV): "The earth is the LORD's, and everything in it, the world, and all who live in it." What bears the image of Caesar? A mere lump of metal. What bears the image of God? All of humanity. Yehoshua is challenging his inquirers not so much to pay taxes to authorities like Caesar as to submit themselves to his ultimate authority.

By answering as brilliantly as he does, Yehoshua not only sends the religionists scrambling in retreat, but advances the idea that there is an authority far higher than Caesar: the one true King of kings and Lord of lords.

3. Make a budget, or rather, count the cost.

In Luke 14:25–35, huge crowds have been stalking Yehoshua from village to village, and he now wheels on them to winnow the flock. The former *tektón* tells his fans that no contractor worth his salt will start building a tower without first counting the cost. What is the cost of discipleship to this particular rabbi?

First, you must love your master so much that you appear to hate your own life and family in comparison.

Second, you must carry your own cross. (And where do all crosses lead but crucifixion?)

Third, you must renounce all your possessions.

If you will not do these three things, you cannot be his disciple.

Yehoshua is well within his rights to demand such terms. After all, no one is forced to follow him. His warning is, if anything, kind. If he is God, he knows that this new relationship will end in torture and murder for ten of the inner twelve disciples.

Luke does not say if the crowds immediately abandoned Yehoshua after this budgetary bludgeoning, but they disappear from the text by the start of chapter 15.

4. Use your money to show mercy.

Yehoshua holds court and challenges all comers. A religious law expert steps up to test the rabbi, though not necessarily in a hostile way, in Luke 10: "Teacher, what must I do to inherit eternal life?"

Yehoshua, like the Jewish rabbis around him and the Socratic philosophers before him, replies to the question with two more questions. "What is written in the Law? How do you read it?" The lawyer answers correctly: "'Love the Lord your God with all your heart and with all your soul and with all your strength and with all your mind,' and 'Love your neighbor as yourself.'"

Spot on, Yehoshua replies, "Do this and you will live."

The legal eagle raises his hand for a quick point of clarification. "And who is my neighbor?"

As the *Cambridge Greek Testament Commentary* puts it, "He wants his moral duties to be labelled and defined with the Talmudic precision to which ceremonial duties had been reduced."

Staying true to his method, Yehoshua tells a story to answer the question: A man, presumably Jewish, heads down the sixteen-mile road from Jerusalem to Jericho. (If the lawyer is truly the legal expert he claims to be, he catches the allusion of descending from the heavenly city of David's Psalms to the cursed city of Joshua 6.) The traveler gets brutally mugged on the way, stripped naked, beaten senseless, left for dead. By pure and total coincidence—note Yehoshua's playful cheek—a Jewish priest *happened* "to be going down the same road." Unfortunately for his semi-conscious Jewish brother, the priest changes lanes and passes right on by. Up next comes a bona fide Levite, a heavy hitter from the priestly line of Aaron. This fellow does the opposite of the priest. He steers close enough to stop and inspect the man lying there. But then he too crosses over and continues on. Now it's time for the climax. The lawyer isn't stupid. He can hear the music heading toward its crescendo. Who will come and rescue the dying Jew?

"But a Samaritan, as he journeyed, came to where he was, and when he saw him, he had compassion" (Luke 10:33).

The lawyer goes wide-eyed. A Samaritan? *Those half-Jew, half-Gentile mutts? Those keepers of the fake Torah who opposed the rebuilding of Jerusalem and later aided Alexander in his conquest? The people we Jews have hated for more than six hundred years? You must be joking.*

The Samaritan "went to him and bound up his wounds, pouring on oil and wine. Then he set him on his own animal and brought him to an inn and took care of him. And the next day he took out two denarii and gave them to the innkeeper, saying,

'Take care of him, and whatever more you spend, I will repay you when I come back'" (vv. 34–35).

Yehoshua then reverts to questioning, asking the lawyer, "Which of these three, do you think, proved to be a neighbor to the man who fell among the robbers?"

The Jewish legal expert can't even say the word *Samaritan*. "The one who showed him mercy."

The rabbi nods. "Now go and do the same."

In other words, the answer to the question, "What must I do to inherit eternal life?" is: Love God with everything you have, and love others so much that you can extend generous mercy even to your mortal enemies.

5. Financial faithfulness requires radical sacrifice.

If you doubt that Yehoshua took an interest in how the wealthy managed their money, just look at where Mark says Yehoshua took a seat when visiting the temple: "Jesus sat down opposite the place where the offerings were put and watched the crowd putting their money into the temple treasury. Many rich people threw in large amounts. But a poor widow came and put in two very small copper coins, worth only a few cents. Calling his disciples to him, Yehoshua says, 'Truly I tell you, this poor widow has put more into the treasury than all the others. They all gave out of their wealth; but she, out of her poverty, put in everything—all she had to live on'" (12:41–44 NIV).

Note the nonchalance with which the rich people "threw in" large amounts. One can almost imagine city elites tossing in an elastic-wrapped wad with a thump. But can the widow do anything less than tremble as she drops the last of her wealth into the pot? Her mites were worth one-fortieth of a denarius apiece. As we have seen, a denarius is worth about three dollars, which means she dropped in approximately fifteen cents. And it was all she had.

One can only imagine what would happen if Yehoshua appeared in our church and positioned himself with a direct eyeline to the offering plate. Who would be the greatest giver? I once attended a fundraiser for one of the most well-known megachurches in the world and ate dinner beside a wealthy divorcée. I asked her how much she planned to give, and without batting an eye, she said of the pastor, "If his speech is any good, he'll get six figures."

While any amount of generosity should certainly be celebrated, it is not the dollar figure that defines the sacrifice. The financial faithfulness Yehoshua wishes his disciples to aspire to is not that of my dining partner, but of the woman with so little that dinner was no longer an option. Should I make it to heaven's banquet, I hope I am seated beside the precious widow so she can have my portion.

What ever became of the poor widow who gave all she had? We could hope that the House of Annas took care of her needs through the temple's benevolent fund, but considering they stole tithes from their own priests, it is highly doubtful. It is just as likely that the opposite occurred, and she became one of the women Yehoshua refers to in Mark 12:40 when he says that the temple lawyers "devour the houses of widows."

6. Give and lend to the poor without question.

> *"If you have things your neighbor doesn't have, share them, because he or she has the right to the part of the world over which God has made you a temporary steward."*
>
> —Tim and Kathy Keller, *God's Wisdom for Navigating Life*

Yehoshua could not make clearer what he expects from his disciples when it comes to how they treat the poor: "Give to the one who begs from you, and do not refuse the one who would borrow from you" (Matthew 5:42).

This seemingly unreasonable command contains unmissable echoes of Deuteronomy 15:7–8, a passage Yehoshua would likely have read hundreds of times: "If among you, one of your brothers should become poor, in any of your towns within your land that the Lord your God is giving you, you shall not harden your heart or shut your hand against your poor brother, but you shall open your hand to him and lend him sufficient for his need, whatever it may be."

This is the brutal and blessed ideal to which disciples of Yehoshua are to strive.

Theologian Albert Barnes's winsome notes on this incredibly challenging text, written in *Barnes' Notes on the Whole Bible* in the 1800s, should erase from our minds the age-old conundrum of whether to give a few dollars to our homeless brothers and sisters when we pass them on the street: "It is better to give sometimes to an undeserving person than to turn away one who is really in need. It is good to be in the habit of giving."

There is, of course, more to the command than first meets the eye. It is the last in a series of four examples of how to deny the unrighteous desire to retaliate against our enemies, and it is from this hard-to-swallow passage that Tolstoy constructed his dreadfully biblical doctrine of non-resistance to evil by force. If someone slaps you, turn the other cheek. If anyone sues you for your jacket, give him your shirt as well. If a Roman forces you to carry his heavy pack for a mile, go two. If you are pressured into alms-giving or forced into making a loan, give and don't refuse. Money is part and parcel of loving your enemy, Yehoshua says. While you're at it, pray for those who persecute you. Otherwise, how are you any different from everyone else? Even tax collectors love those who love them. If you want to be perfect as God is perfect, you will learn to love even your enemies with your money.

Yehoshua is by no means done hammering home the point that giving to the poor is an essential mark of his disciples. In the following words of Matthew 6:2–3 (emphasis added), he simply assumes that his followers will do so. "*When you* give to the needy, sound no trumpet . . . . *When you* give to the needy, do not let your left hand know what your right hand is doing."

Scripture makes clear there is a time and place for public giving (Matthew 5:14–16)—just as there is a time for public and private prayer—but it is not while helping those in destitution. Do it secretly, Yehoshua says; this protects their honor and dignity in a world that has always shamed the poor.

7. There is only one Almighty.

In Yehoshua's vocabulary, all earthly money and wealth are mere *mammon*, which several scholars define as "the treasure in which people put their trust."

What is our most trusted treasure? *That* is the heart of Yehoshua's economic concern.

God or money. We must pick one and only one. We cannot put our trust in both.

In the mind of Yehoshua, *mammon* is a rival god that competes for our allegiance. People who follow Yehoshua must choose between the almighty dollar and the almighty God.

Matthew 6:24 says, "No one can serve two masters, for either he will hate the one and love the other, or he will be devoted to the one and despise the other. You cannot serve God and money."

These are incredibly hard words to swallow. The love of money will make you hate God. The love of God will make you hate money. Yehoshua seeks undivided devotion, yet most of us spend our lives never fully committing to one side or the other. It is no wonder that it can be easier for the sick and poor and lowly to love the Lord with undivided hearts compared with those of us with greater means. They have nothing to lose. And we wrongly think we have too much to lose.

If we are honest, most of us prefer the Sermon on the Mount in Matthew 5 (with an exalted rabbi raining down eight blessings on his disciples), but it is the Sermon on the Plain in Luke 6 (where that same lowly, servant-hearted rabbi is now looking *uphill* at his audience) that deserves just as much of our attention and sermon space. To start, the number of blessings is cut in half, and they are de-boned of the spiritual elements we read in Matthew:

> Blessed are you who are poor, for yours is the kingdom of God.
> Blessed are you who are hungry now, for you shall be satisfied.
> Blessed are you who weep now, for you shall laugh.
> Blessed are you when people hate you and when they exclude you and revile you and spurn your name as evil, on account of the Son of Man!
>
> Luke 6:20–22

Don't you see? Desperately poor people are blessed because it is easier for them to embrace the kingdom and its king. Yehoshua then follows up his four blessings with four warnings:

> Woe to you who are rich, for you have received your consolation.
> Woe to you who are full now, for you shall be hungry.
> Woe to you who laugh now, for you shall mourn and weep.
> Woe to you, when all people speak well of you, for so their fathers did to the false prophets.
>
> Luke 6:24–26

This is a dire warning to those of us who flush cleaner toilet water than half the world drinks. We have received our comfort. We are now well fed. Are we willing to risk it all? The statistics suggest we aren't. When it comes to money, we are the living definition of Matthew 15:8 (NIV): "These people honor me with their lips, but their hearts are far from me."

Luckily, Yehoshua's stewardship Sermon on the Mount gives us the antidote for a treasonous heart: "For where your treasure is, there your heart will be also" (Matthew 6:21). In other words, we can reallocate our treasure in order to lead our hearts. My wife calls this "the holy purpose of investment bias." If we want our hearts to treasure something new, we must give away that which we currently treasure most.

8. Do not hoard wealth.

The Christ-follower's bank is in heaven. Yehoshua values eternal riches more than temporary wealth on a scale that cannot be quantified. We are commanded in Matthew 6:19, "Do not lay up for yourselves treasures on earth, where moth and rust destroy and where thieves break in and steal." I do not know a single Christian who obeys this clear command, myself included. For centuries, theologians have qualified this in various ways, but even if you accept the notion that "treasure" means "anything above the basic necessities," we continue to disobey the command. Theological contortions to explain away this command continue to gnaw at our spirits, don't they? Yehoshua speaks the truth about our hearts in verse 21: "For where your treasure is, there your heart will be also."

Ours are undeniably hearts divided, and the prescription is terrifying: full economic reliance on God.

According to Yehoshua's parable of the sower in Matthew 13:22—one of the few that he explicitly explains to his disciples—money is one of the three main things that stops the *logos* from growing deep roots and ripe fruits in a person's life. "The seed falling among the thorns refers to someone who hears the word, but the worries of this life and the deceitfulness of wealth choke the word, making it unfruitful" (NIV).

That Yehoshua is firmly against the prosperity gospel is crystal clear to Paul of Tarsus, who lays it out for one of his apprentices in brutal terms:

> These are the things you are to teach and insist on. If anyone teaches otherwise and does not agree to the sound instruction of our Lord Jesus Christ and to godly teaching, they are conceited and understand nothing. . . . They have . . . been robbed of the

> truth and think that that godliness is a means to financial gain. But godliness with contentment is great gain. For we brought nothing into the world, and we can take nothing out of it. But if we have food and clothing, we will be content with that.
>
> 1 Timothy 6:2–4, 5–8 NIV

One cannot be a follower of Yehoshua and hoard wealth.

When faced with feuding brothers in an inheritance dispute in Luke 12:15–21 (NIV), Yehoshua issues a dire warning and a harrowing parable:

> "Watch out! Be on your guard against all kinds of greed; life does not consist in an abundance of possessions." And he told them this parable: "The ground of a certain rich man yielded an abundant harvest. He thought to himself, 'What shall I do? I have no place to store my crops.' Then he said, 'This is what I'll do. I will tear down my barns and build bigger ones, and there I will store my surplus grain. And I'll say to myself, "You have plenty of grain laid up for many years. Take life easy; eat, drink and be merry."' But God said to him, 'You fool! This very night your life will be demanded from you. Then who will get what you have prepared for yourself?' This is how it will be with whoever stores up things for themselves but is not rich toward God."

Yehoshua's brother James presses hard on this theme in James 4:13–14 and 5:1–3.

> "Come now, you who say, 'Today or tomorrow we will go into such and such a town and spend a year there and trade and make a profit'—yet you do not know what tomorrow will bring. What is your life? For you are a mist that appears for a little time and then vanishes. . . . Come now, you rich, weep and howl for the miseries that are coming upon you. Your riches have rotted and your garments are moth-eaten. Your gold and silver have

> corroded, and their corrosion will be evidence against you and will eat your flesh like fire."

What, then, are we to do with all the treasures we have heretofore laid up on earth? How does one store up treasures in heaven? The answer comes to us in Luke 12:33: "Sell your possessions, and give to the needy. Provide yourselves with moneybags that do not grow old, with a treasure in the heavens that does not fail, where no thief approaches and no moth destroys."

For readers who have managed to make it this far into an admittedly tough chapter in this book, there is no doubt a huge amount of anxiety and terror at the prospect of putting these words into action. Thus, it makes sense that Yehoshua would follow up this treasure teaching with a sermonette on worry:

> Therefore I tell you, do not worry about your life, what you will eat or drink; or about your body, what you will wear. [In other words: Do not seek financial security if it will change your allegiance or misplace your trust.] For life is more than food, and the body more than clothes. Consider the ravens: They do not sow or reap, they have no storeroom or barn; yet God feeds them. And how much more valuable you are than birds! Who of you by worrying can add a single hour to your life? . . .
>
> But seek his kingdom, and these things will be given to you as well.
>
> Do not be afraid, little flock, for your Father has been pleased to give you the kingdom. Sell your possessions and give to the poor. Provide purses for yourselves that will not wear out, a treasure in heaven that will never fail, where no thief comes near and no moth destroys. For where your treasure is, there your heart will be also.
>
> Luke 12:22–25, 31–34 NIV

This will strike many readers as cold comfort, knowing that sparrows do not have mortgages and that flowers lose their "clothes" each winter in cold climates. And has a Christian never starved to death, naked and freezing, despite seeking the kingdom of God and his right-way-of-living-ness? I cannot reconcile it in the rational realm, nor can any theologian, and that is why finance will always be faith's final frontier. Clearly, our relationship with money is extremely complicated and intensely personal, which is why it is vital for Christians to stay close to Yehoshua so he can show us what to do. But still the point remains: It takes a huge amount of faith to withdraw our wealth from temporary earthly accounts and deposit it in heaven's eternal trust.

But can anything be more sensible to a spirit-filled heart? We know that not a single person alive today, whether rich or poor, can carry a single U.S. dollar or Swiss franc into the afterlife.

9. Refuse to participate in exploitation.

When most Christians hear the word *stewardship*, their minds immediately head to Luke 19 and Matthew 25—a pair of vexing parables about a wicked nobleman who entrusts his slaves with talents and rewards them for multiplying his Smaug-like money hoard.

A talent, it must be said, was not a skill—one cannot simply hand over a skill to an employee and go on vacation—but was rather a weight of gold or silver. In the late Second Temple period, a *talanton* weighed 63.49 pounds and worked out to roughly seventy-five years of wages for a common laborer. (At today's gold price, the parable's five talents work out to around $9 million—and 375 years of labor for a commoner.)

When a modern, Western, capitalist-minded reader skims the two parables, they are left with the vague notion that the kingdom of heaven requires Christians to steward their possessions and multiply their assets for the sake of their king.

But that is not even remotely the point of the parable.

Luke makes it clear in 19:11 that this is not a parable about the kingdom of heaven. Yehoshua and company are nearing Jerusalem. His disciples are convinced that "the kingdom of God was to appear immediately." Picture a posse of passionate young people, having just spent several years in the politically charged Galilean backcountry, fomenting with rebellion toward the Jewish aristocrats and their Roman overlords, now descending on the capital city of Jerusalem, utterly convinced that their rabbi-Messiah is going to call down heaven's legions and set up a new Jewish empire to reign for all time.

So Yehoshua tells them a parable about how wicked people act. He describes an Annas-like ruler who is hated by his subjects, who is self-admittedly so hard and severe that the people lobby against his reign. He gives his slaves vast sums of money to invest on his behalf while he is away. Some of the slaves double and even multiply his money tenfold, while a conscientious objector squirrels away the principal for safekeeping. When the evil ruler returns, he predictably praises and promotes those who produced a profit.

But what of the one who refused to participate? A first-century hearer of Yehoshua's story would surely have known the near-impossibility of doubling multiple lifetimes of income in an agrarian context without aggressive exploitation of the weak and vulnerable. Who ever heard of a slave producing 375 years of income while his boss was on vacation?

The righteous servant rightly defends his decision: "You reap where you have not planted, and gathered where you have not scattered seed." In other words, Master, you are a lecherous extractor. The evil ruler rages at the servant, but notice that he doesn't say the indictment is untrue. "You knew that I take out what I did not put in, and reap what I did not sow? Then why did you not put my money on deposit with the bank exchangers, so that when I came back, I could have collected it with interest?"

At this juncture we may be assured there would have been a chuckle from at least the moneymen Judas and Matthew. After all, Levitical law rightfully forbade the poverty-promoting practice of interest-taking from fellow Jews. (The Hebrew word for *interest* literally means "bite.") "You shall not charge interest on loans to your brother, interest on money, interest on food, interest on anything that is lent for interest" (Deuteronomy 23:19). Only corrupt Jews like Annas run banks and collect interest from their own kin.*

Depending on which version of the parable of the talents you read, the story concludes with the wicked ruler either hurling the humble protestor into homelessness and deprivation or having him slaughtered while he watches. In both cases, the ruler proudly declares, "To everyone who has, more will be given, but from the one who has not, even what he has will be taken away" (Luke 19:26).

So what is the point of this strange story whose stated intention is to remind Yehoshua's disciples that the kingdom of God will not immediately appear when they step foot in Jerusalem? It is that when people play an active role in a system of exploitation, the rich get richer and the poor get poorer. Yehoshua's mind is not focused on overthrowing the Romans—he is thinking about the

* While we are on the subject, we simply must put to bed the tired debate: Yes, Yehoshua upholds the Old Testament injunction against charging interest to fellow Israelites—and just as he does with adultery and divorce and dozens of other laws, he raises the expectation, telling his disciples to loan without interest to Jews *and Gentiles* alike: "If you lend to those from whom you expect to receive, what credit is that to you? Even sinners lend to sinners, to get back the same amount. But love your enemies, and do good, and lend, expecting nothing in return" (Luke 6:34–35). Many churchgoers jump to a defense of interest, but clearly it is an activity in which faithful Christians simply cannot partake.

Obeying Yehoshua's affirmation of Deuteronomy 23:19's command against interest also has the effect of ruling out for-profit land-lording for followers of the Way. Yehoshua upholds and expands the dictates of Deuteronomy 23:19, which include the admonishment to not lend "anything that is lent for interest"—and this includes lending houses and expecting them back with rental profit. Rent and interest are one and the same. The German word for interest (*zins*) derives from *rent*. The French word for a public loan (*rentes*) originates with land-lording. The Babylonian word for *interest* and *rent* were one and the same. Adam Smith, the father of capitalism, who wanted markets to be free from feudal exploitation, called rent a form of "interest derived from monopolization." In *The Wealth of Nations*, he notes that "Landlords, like all other men, love to reap where they never sowed." Leviticus 25:35–37 takes it a radical step and prohibits turning *any* form of profit off the poor, which has got to be about the most grace-filled thing in the Old Testament. This, then, unearths an even scarier question: Who does Yehoshua consider to be poor?

House of Annas and its intolerable corruption of the House of God. As if to emphasize his point, not twenty verses later, Luke records Yehoshua overturning moneychanger tables in the temple.

Though long-enculturated churchgoers such as myself are apt to chafe at this interpretation of these passages, we will all do well to set aside our modern economic biases and study the texts at length. In this case, the reader will reach the unsettling conclusion that this is clearly *not* a parable about a heavenly king or how his perfect economy will operate, but about how evil men like Annas treat the powerless. Yehoshua sides with the exploited, not the exploiter.

10. Money is an opportunity to practice honesty.

Another of Yehoshua's vexing money parables is that of the dishonest manager. Found in Luke 16, it should first be noted that nowhere in the text does Yehoshua say this is what the kingdom of God is like. Indeed, it is the story of an accountant whose boss demands to see a balance sheet that he knows is unbalanced. The prideful, white-collar conman sweats at the terrifying prospect of first-century unemployment. "I am not strong enough to dig, and I am ashamed to beg." Thinking quickly, he rings up everyone on the accounts-receivable list and slashes their bills by 20 to 50 percent. The boss, no doubt with pursed lips, begrudgingly compliments the dishonest rascal for his shrewdness. He will still be fired, but he bought himself some friends in the process.

Several scholars have gone to great lengths to justify this bad behavior (for instance, by saying perhaps the manager just cut his commissions), but such justifications aren't necessary. Is Yehoshua condoning economic chicanery? No. He straight-up labels the accountant dishonest and ends the parable by noting that this is how worldly people tend to treat each other. His point is that we can learn spiritual lessons even from crooks who cook the books. If a fraudulent accountant can plan for the immediate future, how much more so can light-filled disciples plan for eternity? His call to action: Secure an eternal welcome for yourself by making faithful use of earthly money before it evaporates.

In saying this, Yehoshua reveals his personal investment strategy. Yehoshua's asset allocation techniques are decidedly non-exploitative and work out to an eternally long-only portfolio. Rather than pile up sixty years of serialized paper and bits of digital code, he says we should invest in human souls so we can enjoy the dividends for trillions of years (Luke 12:33). As John Piper wrote on DesiringGod.org, "Don't worry about being a shrewd investor in this age, where you can provide a future that will only fail. Instead, be a really shrewd investor by investing in people's lives. Use your resources to do as much good as you can for the glory of God and the eternal good of others."

Having ignored the first nine verses of Luke 16, prosperity preachers will now jump in and have us believe what follows is a promise of magical reciprocity, namely, that if we steward our money well, God will miraculously give us more: "Whoever can be trusted with very little can also be trusted with much, and whoever is dishonest with very little will also be dishonest with much" (Luke 16:10 NIV).

I have endured megachurch services in which pastors have told desperate congregants that a gift given by the end of the service will see a tenfold return within the year, and that parishioners must prove their trustworthiness by cutting a check. But Luke 16:10 is clearly not a universal promise for all people at all times. It is nothing more than a clear-eyed observation, a simple statement of fact. Whether with big or small amounts, trustworthy people are trustworthy and dishonest people are dishonest. In Yehoshua's mind, every person's character has eternal ramifications: "If you have not been trustworthy in handling worldly wealth, who will trust you with true riches?" (Luke 16:11 NIV).

In other words, if we can't be trusted to handle mere money in an eternal way, why should we think ourselves fit for any higher station?

11. It is impossible to buy our way into heaven or even get God to give us more money.

What we will not find anywhere in the financial teachings of Yehoshua ben Yehoseph is a promise of earthly benefit for giving back to God what is already his. The prosperity gospel's go-to verse on this front is Luke 6:38, "Give, and it will be given to you. Good measure, pressed down, shaken together, running over, will be put into your lap. For with the measure you use it will be measured back to you."

Contrary to the teachings of many televangelists, this is not a promise of fiscal reciprocity and a heavenly guarantee that your generosity will be rewarded with earthly riches. God is not a cosmic slot machine. If you read the two verses preceding this verse, you will see clearly that this is a promise about receiving grace: "Be merciful, even as your Father is merciful. Judge not, and you will not be judged; condemn not, and you will not be condemned; forgive, and you will be forgiven." Yehoshua is not saying that if you donate a hundred dollars, God will give you two hundred in return. You cannot game God, though plenty have tried. What Yehoshua is saying is to practice mercy, to forgive, to withhold judgment and condemnation, to give grace to all, and that when you give these good gifts to others, you will experience an overabundance of mercy and forgiveness and grace from the Father—surely a gift far more valuable than money.

What ultimately matters to him is our hearts.

Take, for instance, his encounter with the rich young ruler in Mark 10, Luke 18, and Matthew 19. The man in question is almost certainly not a Roman, having addressed Yehoshua as "teacher" while claiming to have a perfect track record at obeying all Jewish laws since childhood. The fact that he is young and rich and a ruler and not a Roman suggests he either inherited the wealth and power from a father or uncle or is involved in some sort of shady political affair.

The man asks Yehoshua what good deed he needs to do to

get eternal life, as though heaven were a trifle to be purchased with a few acts of piety.

Yehoshua tells him curtly to keep the commandments.

The young man's reply is telling of his heart: "Which ones?"

Yehoshua rattles off five of the Ten Commandments, plus he slyly throws in Leviticus 19:13 (do not defraud) before he is presumably interrupted. "I've obeyed all these commandments," the young man blurts. "What else must I do?"

It is extremely unlikely that this young cockerel is telling the truth. Have we not all dishonored our parents?

Listen to what Yehoshua says here, this time from Matthew 19:21: "If you would be perfect, go, sell what you possess and give to the poor." Yehoshua's definition of economic perfection is to sell your possessions and give to the poor. Therefore, economic depravity is to keep your possessions and actively exploit the poor. Everything in between falls short of God's economic perfection. The terrifying question that then confronts all Christ-followers is, Where am I on the spectrum? Am I taking active strides toward economic blamelessness, or am I defiantly marching away like the rich young ruler? While the rabbi is not commanding all Christians at all times in all places to sell all their possessions, it should make us pause to consider how far short of perfection we are, and see the immense opportunities we have to close the gap. This economic challenge is an invitation into life in the kingdom of heaven.

The rich young ruler, for his part, wanders into the mists of history, with all three synoptic gospel writers noting the reason for his departing sadness was because he had great wealth.

With so few words, Yehoshua impresses upon his listeners that it is extremely difficult for wealthy people to be wholehearted disciples of God. For what does he immediately say to Simon and the others as the rich kid slinks back to a life of temporary leisure and eternal loss? "Truly, I say to you, only with difficulty will a rich person enter the kingdom of heaven" (v. 23).

Perhaps money-minded Matthew and Judas weren't listening.

"Again I tell you, it is easier for a camel to go through the eye of a needle than for a rich person to enter the kingdom of God. When the disciples heard this, they were greatly astonished" (Matthew 19:24–25). And who wouldn't be?

Theologians have worked themselves into paroxysms of ecstasy trying to explain away this verse in order to cram rich people into heaven. *A camel through the eye of a needle*? Surely he meant cable, not *camel*, and by cable, we may substitute a string. (That was a real argument put forward by some wonderfully creative scholars, though not a single manuscript reads it as such.) Others raise the notion that some Syrian cities may have had human-sized doors in their gates called "needle's eyes," therefore allowing the rich to play contortionist as a means of squeezing in. Whether Yehoshua meant a rope through a needle or a camel through a doorway, or genuinely a camel through a needle's eye, his hyperbolic point has found its mark.

The flabbergasted disciples sputter, "Who then can be saved?"

The answer, of course, is no one. Heaven isn't for sale. No one of their own volition can buy or force their way into Yehoshua's kingdom. The text says he looks at them—perhaps with a gotcha smile—and replies simply: "With man this is impossible, but with God all things are possible" (v. 26).

Simon decides he's a better man than the rich young ruler and hits back with both a guilt trip and a shaky attempt to extract some prosperity promises from his master in Mark 10:28: "See, we have left everything to follow you."

And do you know what? He actually wrings a reciprocity pact from his teacher in Mark 10:29–30, though not without a proviso: "Truly, I say to you, there is no one who has left house or brothers or sisters or mother or father or children or lands, for my sake and for the gospel, who will not receive a hundredfold now in this time, houses and brothers and sisters and mothers and children and lands, with persecutions, and in the age to come eternal life."

In other words: *Give up everything you have, and I will give you my now and forever faith family, the Church.*

12. Reparations are a sign of salvation.

On one of Yehoshua's ambles from Galilee to Jerusalem, no doubt sauntering along the River Jordan path, he passes through the bustling metropolis of Jericho, located in what is currently the West Bank. Thanks to its many springs, it may very well be the oldest permanent city in the world, and it definitely has the oldest known wall. It was once the home of Yehoshua's most scandalous ancestor, Rahab, the prostituted woman turned human smuggler who bravely helped Israel overthrow the city. Evidently the good folks of Jericho have heard of Yehoshua, for Luke tells us in chapter 19 that the rabbi is swarmed by a crowd as he heads west through town. Former tax collector Matthew also mentions the Jericho jaunt, and the huge crowd, and that Yehoshua heals two blind men as they exit the walled city, but Matthew makes no mention of the episode to which we now turn in Luke.

These heavy crowds are no good for a short little fellow named Zacchaeus. This, we will note, is a Romanized name like Caesar, Aeneas, and Aesop. In Hebrew, it is Zakkai, and means "an Israelite." But this is no mere Israelite. This man is a turncoat, a traitor who refuses to use his own Jewish name, a man who shakes down his fellow Israelites on behalf of their Roman overlords. But he is not a mere tax collector either; he is the *chief* tax collector, and he is infamously rich. Jericho was then the center of a lucrative balsam industry, and Zacchaeus is the monetary bottleneck.

Zacchaeus has no idea which celebrity has come to town because he cannot see over the crowd. Left with no choice, he runs ahead and scrambles up a sycamore-fig tree, an astoundingly big, beautiful, and easily climbable species compared with the mighty palms for which Jericho was famous (Deuteronomy 34:3).

Yehoshua looks up at this despised traitor, a little man living large on extortion and theft and the bankruptcy of desperately poor peasants. He tells him to come down so they can do lunch. Zacchaeus's response is, frankly, strange beyond measure. Not only does he host Yehoshua and an unknown number of hungry disciples, but he pledges to give half his possessions to the poor and pay fourfold restitution to anyone he has defrauded.

What prompted such an outburst of generosity? I don't know anyone who came to faith in Jesus and immediately liquidated half their stuff. Something must have happened that rocked Zacchaeus to the core.

Once again, we find our English translations have failed us. In verse 2, Luke calls him Zacchaeus. In verse 8, Luke calls him Zacchaeus. But in Luke 19:5, Yehoshua uses Zacchaeus's true name: "*Zakkai*, hurry down, I must stay at your house today." Luke does not say how Yehoshua knows his true name, nor does it matter, but Zacchaeus is stunned. He knows he is a traitor to Israel, worthy of scorn and shame and hatred. And yet this famous friend of the poor has called him by his original name, Zakkai. *You are an Israelite.*

Zacchaeus, a man so despised and now ennobled, scrambles down and gladly welcomes Yehoshua into his undoubtedly palatial home. The crowd's grumbles echo in the streets.

But Yehoshua does not care about labels, only hearts. What's interesting is that as soon as Yehoshua calls Zakkai a true Israelite, Zakkai starts acting like a true Israelite. This invitation stirs something deep within Zacchaeus's heart, for he now stands and declares, "Look, Lord! Here and now I give half of my possessions to the poor, and if I have cheated anyone out of anything, I will pay back four times the amount" (Luke 19:8 NIV). There are clear echoes here of the faithful Judaism expressed in Exodus 22:1—that if a man steals a sheep, he must repay with four sheep. Zakkai is acting like a faithful Israelite again.

This is a good enough sign for Yehoshua; he affirms the traitor Zakkai's reintegration into the faith family's fold. "Salvation has come to this house, since he also is *a son of Abraham*. For the Son of Man came to seek and to save the lost" (Luke 19:9–10).

And that is the moral of the story, isn't it? That Yehoshua came to seek and save the lost—even those of us who are so lost that we've changed our name and forgotten our deepest identity. If Yehoshua can do that for a traitorous tax collector—even one who enriches the same regime that murdered his kinsman John the Baptizer—he can do it for us.

Let us affirm that Zakkai was not saved *because* he made restitution. It is the other way around: Restitution, in this case, was a sign of salvation.

There can be no doubt that Zakkai had a radical change of heart. Do you know anyone who has inspected their assets for injustice, restituted the abused therein fourfold, and given half their stock portfolio to the poor just for safety?

This story raises troubling questions for the reader, namely, *Who am I in this story?* We are all Zacchaeus, invited to give up our injustices and re-take the family name. If our main sin is economic in nature, a true change of heart will likely manifest as reparations. And do we not play an active and passive part in an economic system built on unfathomable amounts of exploitation? Just as people claimed to be Christians and profited directly and indirectly from slavery in the antebellum South, so do we through our unconsidered purchases and investments.*

* I have no doubt that a day of reckoning is coming for the Christian church, as the portfolios of denominations, churches, pastors, and parishioners are exposed to public scrutiny. What will be found in our purses? The reality is that the overwhelming majority of Christians who own pension plans, retirement funds, mutual funds, 401(k)s, RRSPs, education trusts, giving foundations, and other diversified investments are profiting from a huge range of anti-Christ activities. The Fortune 500 alone—America's largest five hundred companies in which nearly every mutual fund, pension plan, and index fund is invested—contain some truly troubling companies, funding and profiting from pornography to abortion, weapons, slavery, offshore tax havens, democratic destruction, the pollution and

After reparation comes reallocation, from the kingdom of darkness to the kingdom of light, regardless of the personal pay cut. We do not know what became of Zakkai, the tax collector to tax collectors, but he seems to have given up making a living via tax exploitation and put his managerial skills to better use: A fourth-century Apostolic Constitution says he moved fifty-six miles northwest to Caesarea and became a pastor to pastors.

The Most Purposely Misinterpreted Verse in the Bible

What would happen to a community of Christians if they valued God's kingdom more than their personal empires, served a higher authority than Caesar, counted the true cost of discipleship, used their money to show mercy, practiced radical sacrifice, gave and lent to the poor without question, made God their only trust, stopped hoarding wealth and banked their riches in heaven, gave until it hurt, refused to participate in exploitation, saw money as an opportunity to practice honesty, stopped trying to game God for money, and paid reparations to those they'd economically exploited?

I would venture to guess there would be no poor people among them.

"Tut-tut," the theologian interrupts triumphantly. "Have you never read Matthew 26:11? The poor will always be among us!"

Well, good.

The poor will always be among us.

Case closed.

Is the follower of Yehoshua satisfied with this callous justification of systemic poverty?

---

poisoning of God's creation, and the entrapment of hundreds of millions of people in debt. How much longer will we continue to be loan sharks and war profiteers before joyously repaying the costly price of a God-honoring retirement fund?

Scripture is quite clear: After confession and repentance comes restitution. Reparation is not a requirement of salvation; it is the proof that follows.

Does the devoted disciple really believe Yehoshua is that cynical and unhopeful about the plight and power of his church?

Does YHWH not have the might to overcome poverty in this world?

Or has this verse perhaps been weaponized to defend wealth accumulation, and in reality, requires just an inch deeper investigation?

First, let us consider the statement itself. It is a rabbinical head nod to Deuteronomy 15:11, which starts, "For there will never cease to be poor in the land." But that is certainly not where the text starts or ends. What precedes and follows that Deuteronomic sentence is a veritable barrage of economic policy aimed at obliterating poverty within the Israelite family, and a warning that poverty is a *direct result* of disobedience to YHWH. By invoking this phrase, Yehoshua is scolding his disciples for thinking like the world (Matthew 26:10–11).

Second, let us consider the audience who receives Yehoshua's statement. Are these universal words preached to all people in all places for all time? No. Are they even words preached to the Jewish masses before a handout of free bread and fish? No. Yehoshua is staying with friends in Bethany, and a woman has just anointed his head with some extremely expensive oil. His disciples (namely Judas Iscariot, a known thief) start griping about the waste of money. Yehoshua's retort starts with "Leave her alone." Is every Christian in history to also leave "her" alone? You can see the absurdity here. Scripture *must* be read contextually. This applies to every single verse in the Bible. No one is arguing that "go sell all your possessions" applies to everyone. No one defends "Come down immediately, I must stay at your house today" as a universally applicable lunch statement for short people. No one believes "Pick up your mat and walk" applies to all non-ambulatory folk. So why does this statement about poverty get a universal pass?

When Yehoshua says the poor will always be among *you,* he is not speaking to *us* but to *them*. And who are *they*? An audience of peasant disciples stuck under corrupt Roman and Jewish rule. We now know that it is mathematically possible to create an economy where poverty simply does not exist, but because some people make a killing, others cannot even eke out a living. Where does this story take place? In a destitute village called Bethany, which means "house of the poor," "house of affliction," or "house of misery." Why? Because it lies in the shadow of Jerusalem, the national headquarters for extractionist Romans and the rapacious House of Annas. For the disciples to whom Yehoshua addresses this statement, the meaning is obvious: The poor will always be among them because the rich will always be *above* them.

Let us read the whole verse in Matthew 26:11 (emphasis added): "For you always have the poor with you, *but you will not always have me.*" If one is to believe that this verse is for all people at all times, then we are forever surrounded by poor people *and we no longer have God.* You don't get to keep only half the verse. Is not God still with us? Clearly, Yehoshua is speaking about his physical presence dwelling with a specific group of people.

Now turn to the same story in Mark 14:7 (NIV, emphasis added): "The poor you will always have with you, *and you can help them any time you want.*" Many churchgoers misinterpret Matthew 26:11 and somehow think this lets them off the hook from making a college try at eliminating poverty. But Mark 14:7 obliterates that option. Christians can and should always help the poor until there are no more poor among us.

Let us further trouble the theological fatalist by turning to Deuteronomy 15:4–5. When will there be *no poor among them*? Whenever the entire faith community submits to YHWH's economic system. Deuteronomy 15:4–5 makes it crystal clear: "There need be no poor people among you . . . if only you fully obey the Lord your God and are careful to follow all these commands I am giving you." Now flip forward to Acts 4:4. There are around five thousand Christians in the Jerusalem faith community—probably well over ten thousand when you include women and children—and Acts 4:34 says "There was not a needy person among them."

So the poor will always be among the universal *us* . . . except among faithful followers of YHWH? If we believe Yehoshua is saying the poor will always be among all people at all times, including truly Christian communities, *then these texts prove he is a liar.*

But he is not saying that the poor will be among all people at all times. There absolutely will be poor among groups of people who suffer economic injustice from the Caesars and Annases of this world, suffer personal setbacks, make poor decisions, disobey YHWH's teachings, and/or contain thieves like Judas Iscariot, but perpetual poverty is decidedly not one of Yehoshua's promises to his church.

What if Matthew 26:11 is not a fatalistic statement but a challenge to his disciples? *Really put into practice kingdom economics and see how quickly poverty can evaporate.* Perhaps there are only still poor people in our churches because our interpretation of this verse is so intolerably poor, and our economic obedience even more so.

Conclusion

Yehoshua ben Yehoseph leaves behind no economic textbook, yet his economic policy is clear: When it comes to money, he is uncomfortably radical. Money is an idol, and Christians are in the full-time idol-smashing business. What, then, is the Christian attitude toward earthly money in the mind of so heavenly a rabbi?

It is to value God's kingdom far more than our individual empire, and in doing so, see that the kingdom of heaven is worth selling all our earthly possessions to attain.

It is to pay our taxes, even to a vile and corrupt government who crucifies our family members, and in doing so, remember there is a higher authority than Caesar.

It is to renounce our possessions, and in doing so, consider the great cost Christ pays for our lives.

It is to use our wealth to show mercy, and in doing so, remember to love our enemies as the Good Samaritan did.

It is to give like the widow with her two copper coins, and in doing so, live out the notion that financial faithfulness requires radical sacrifice.

It is to give and lend to the poor without question, and in doing so, to do it secretly to honor their humanity.

It is to lead our hearts by reallocating our treasure, and in doing so, choose to love God instead of mammon.

It is to stop hoarding wealth and place our economic reliance on God, and in doing so, bank what we cannot keep in an account we cannot lose.

It is to refuse to participate in exploitation, and in doing so, create a world where the poor get richer and the rich get less rich.

It is to be honest with money, and in doing so, see that money is a character technology that tests trustworthiness.

It is to stop trying to buy our way into heaven or get more money, and in doing so, accept the gifts of persecution and God's church.

It is to give back what we have stolen, and in doing so, know that reparations are a sign on the path of salvation.

Yehoshua is interested in how we spend our money because he is interested in how we spend our lives. Every time we act in obedience, we embody God's radical giving economy in a greedy and grasping world.

Earn your money righteously; pay your taxes; tithe; do not accumulate earthly wealth; relinquish your possessions; do not charge interest or profit off the poor; bank your riches in heaven; destitute yourselves for your enemies; do not seek financial security if it changes your allegiance or misplaces your trust. We can begin to see why almost no one in history has heeded what Yehoshua ben Yehoseph has to say about money.

Yet isn't this clearly what the ideal economy—dare I say the economy of heaven—might look like?

The Political Josh

"Politics is too serious a matter to be left to the politicians."

—Charles de Gaulle

Yehoshua is not a politician like Annas the fake high priest. Yehoshua has no designs on buying himself Roman citizenship and working his way up the ranks. He has no master plan for leading an insurgency that somehow manages to defeat an ever-expanding military that has endured with iron might for centuries. Yes, he will perform one very scandalous, public political stunt near the climax of this story, but overall, he has no party platform, issues no policy briefs, courts no corporate campaign contributors.

Yet isn't it fun to fantasize about Yehoshua running for president, especially in our over-politicized age?

What political principles can we glean from the non-political rabbi whose non-political beliefs revolutionized the world of politics? What policies will spring forth from his think tank? What are the planks upon which he will stump?

I must warn you: For those of us who are looking for a politician-savior to make our lives more comfortable, Yehoshua definitely isn't our man. In fact, his politics might be downright disastrous for us.

1. Universal healthcare

I am being nothing short of facetious in including this point, but there can be no doubt that Yehoshua ben Yehoseph is in favor of free healings for all. That Yehoshua ben Yehoseph was known as a healer is an uncontested statement. It's the only thing that quite literally everyone—from disciples and followers to opposing Jews and Romans—agrees on. Whether his healings were real is a question of faith for modern believers and skeptics, but either way, Yehoshua is incontrovertibly *known* as a healer.

But unlike the hundreds if not thousands of charlatans who roam the world around him, Yehoshua does not charge for his healing services. *Gratis* medicare helps explain why he is mobbed by people whenever he enters a city. He heals constantly, out of mercy, with the understanding that healings are simply signs that he is the Messiah. Yehoshua believes that healing people—both physically and spiritually—is one of the core reasons he has been anointed (Luke 4:18). In his famous "least of these" sermon in Matthew 25:36, Yehoshua makes it very clear that Christians who do not care for their sick simply do not know him.

In Matthew 10:1, Yehoshua gives his inner twelve disciples authority to "heal every disease and every affliction," but just in case they think about charging for the service, he tells them not to even pack a purse (Luke 10:4). What does Peter say to the crippled beggar in Acts 3, so beautifully rendered in King James English? "Silver and gold have I none; but such as I have give I thee: In the name of Jesus Christ of Nazareth rise up and walk" (v. 6 KJV).

It is quite telling that the early and historical church prioritized free care for the sick above all else. In chapter 36 of the Rule of Saint Benedict, he writes, "Care of the sick must rank above and before all else so that they may be truly served as Christ." Christian monastics invented free hospitals for this very God-glorifying purpose, and only centuries later would it be consumed by the profit motive.

2. No national distinctions

Yehoshua sees nations for what they truly are—legal fictions.

As we saw in chapter 4, Yehoshua doesn't bat an eye at traveling through and staying in Samaria. He openly heals a Canaanite (Matthew 15:28) and doesn't hesitate to heal a Gadarene (Matthew 8:28) or a Roman (Matthew 8:10).

Yehoshua says his kingdom is not of this world (John 18:36), and therefore his disciples are not of this world. Paul of Tarsus picks up this theme when he says Christians are de facto citizens of another nation (Philippians 3:20) and ambassadors to this one (2 Corinthians 5:20).

If Yehoshua recognizes no sovereignty but his own, then earthly citizenship is rendered irrelevant to citizens of the kingdom of God. His disciples should act as ambassadors in foreign lands—submissive to their resident states but ultimately reporting to a far higher power (Acts 5:29). An ambassador's job is not necessarily to change the politics of the lands in which they temporarily reside but to build friendly relationships between citizens of their host nation and the king they represent.

3. No hierarchies

Perhaps the most comedic scene in the gospels occurs in Matthew 20, just days before Yehoshua's murder. He and his disciples are tramping somewhere in the vicinity of Jericho, and he tells them a parable that concludes with, "The last will be first, and the first will be last." He then tells them they're heading to Jerusalem, where he will be betrayed by the temple elite, sentenced to death, flogged, and crucified.

For some reason, Yehoshua's Aunt Salome thinks this is the perfect time to make an exceedingly impertinent request: "Say that these two sons of mine are to sit, one at your right hand and one at your left, in your kingdom" (v. 21).

That's right, the adorably moronic sons of thunder have convinced their mother to ask cousin Yehoshua to make them the vice president and prime minister of heaven and earth.

The other ten disciples are indignant, but Yehoshua gently reminds his power-grasping cousins of the parable he *just* told them. "You know that the rulers of the Gentiles lord it over them, and their great ones exercise authority over them. It shall not be so among you" (vv. 25–26).

How many times does he have to say it? *There is a massive difference between rulership and leadership*. No doubt James, John, and Salome blush with embarrassment as Yehoshua continues. "Whoever would be great among you must be your servant, and whoever would be first among you must be your slave, even as the Son of Man came not to be served but to serve" (vv. 26–28).

These aren't the first anti-hierarchical instructions he has given the seventy-odd along their travels. He tells them in Matthew 23:8 not to call themselves "rabbi" because they "have one teacher, and you are all brothers." He tells them in Matthew 23:9 to dispense with the honorific title of "father" because "you have one Father, who is in heaven." In the next verse, he says not even to bother with the term "instructor" because "you have one instructor, the Christ." He doesn't give two hoots about public reputation (Luke 6:22) and understands the embarrassing weakness of positional power compared with true authority (Matthew 28:18).

In other words, this is no divine bureaucracy. The kingdom of heaven's org chart is flat. There are no high priests like Annas who monopolize the church's treasury, backed by an army of scribe-lawyers and stave-wielding thugs. The guy in charge washes feet like he's a slave, and everyone else is to follow suit (John 13:14–15).

4. Human rights for all humans, no rights for disciples

Yehoshua gives worth to worthless children (Matthew 19:14). He gives worth to worthless women (John 8:11). He gives worth to worthless slaves (Luke 7:2). He gives worth to the worthless poor (Matthew 25:40).

He doesn't affirm their value with a series of bills or laws, with suffragette protests or a march on the capital. He does so by planting the seeds of spiritual revolution. He defies cultural norms and shows no discrimination toward these abused people groups. He treats them as equals. He ministers to their needs. He gives them his love and time.

His emancipation proclamation is Luke 4:18–19: "The Spirit of the Lord is upon me, because he has anointed me to proclaim good news to the poor. He has sent me to proclaim liberty to the captives and recovering of sight to the blind, to set at liberty those who are oppressed, to proclaim the year of the Lord's favor." Victor Hugo said, "There is nothing more powerful than an idea whose time has come," and it is Yehoshua who sets in motion the long moral arc toward justice.

Conversely, he makes it clear that he and his disciples must forfeit all their supposed "rights." Christians do not fight for their *own* freedoms but happily offer themselves up as living sacrifices (Romans 12:1). They don't resist evil but instead turn the other cheek (Matthew 5:39). They bless those who rob them (Matthew 5:40). They walk the extra mile (Matthew 5:41). Why? Because in Yehoshua's world, "Whoever loves his life loses it" (John 12:25). A seed must fall on the ground and die if it is to root and fruit (John 12:24). Coercive legislation will never transform hearts and minds. It is the inspiring and selfless actions of Yehoshua's disciples that will eventually tilt the world to right.

5. Economic equality

Don't let communists and socialists fool you: Christians believe in private property rights. Just read Psalm 24:1 (NIV): "The earth is the LORD's, and everything in it." The universe is Yehoshua's private property. Humanity's job is to steward God's property to serve the poorest people in the world (Matthew 25:31–46), not for personal gain. Any pastor who preaches anything less is just another false prosperity preacher.

Yehoshua is neither a socialist nor a rules-free marketeer. He does not favor the lording of power over others (Mark 10:42–43); therefore, he cannot champion a state-controlled nor a corporate-controlled nation.

As we have seen in chapter 8, Yehoshua's economic policies are a gut punch to those of us with possessions. If his thoughts on stewardship and generosity can be summed up in a singular stunning phrase, it is—and I say this knowing I step on a hornet's nest—"From each according to his ability, to each according to his need." Indeed, Karl Marx and those before him lifted that phrase directly from Scripture (Acts 11:29; Acts 2:45; Acts 4:35), but then wrongly assumed that a secular government could somehow force non-believers to act like Jesus. Second Corinthians 8:13–15 is clearly another inspiration for communism, but only the Holy Spirit can compel us to joyously level the playing field. When our abilities are greater than our needs, we should gladly give the surplus. When our needs are greater than our abilities, we should gratefully receive the shortfall.

But again, this equality-creating concept can *never* be enforced by a secular state, otherwise it is simply dictatorial communism. Consider the one time that forced wealth distribution is mentioned in the gospels (Luke 12:13–15 NRSVUE): "Someone in the crowd said to him, 'Teacher, tell my brother to divide the family inheritance with me.' But Jesus said to him, 'Friend, who set me to be a judge or arbitrator over you? . . . Take care! Be on your guard against all kinds of greed; for one's life does not consist in the abundance of possessions.'"

Paul echoes this idea of radical voluntary sharing in 2 Corinthians 8:8 when he says, "I am not commanding you" (NIV). No secularist government will ever succeed at using coercion and violence to make people act like Jesus. But sadly, when it comes to money, even Christians don't act like Jesus. He's far too "communist."

While everyday governments should do their best to ensure everyone gets a fair shake, the kingdom economy simply will not come into being through coercion and the threat of punishment. It can only be achieved through a spiritual change of hearts and minds. When a heart truly belongs to YHWH, it becomes progressively more generous, self-sacrificing, and voluntarily redistributive.

6. Nonviolence

"The soldiers of Christ require neither arms nor spears of iron."

—Attributed to Clement of Alexandria

While Annas and the religionists have no problem doling out the death penalty to anyone who crosses them, Yehoshua is extremely clear regarding his stance on violence, when he states that those who live by the sword will die by the sword (Matthew 26:52).

Not only does the rabbi uphold the classic King James "thou shalt not kill" commandment of Exodus 20:13, but he scythes to the very spirit that causes murder in Matthew 5:21–22: "You have heard that it was said to those of old, 'You shall not murder; and whoever murders will be liable to judgment.' But I say to you that everyone who is angry with his brother will be liable to judgment; whoever insults his brother will be liable to the council; and whoever says, 'You fool!' will be liable to the hell of fire." He continues the passage with a strong exhortation toward reconciliation.

Moreover, look at Yehoshua's life actions. While he has no problem sabotaging commerce or destroying property if it is a tool of exploitation (Mark 11:15), not once does he kill, injure, maim, or even strike another person. He doesn't carry a concealed *sicae*. He doesn't punch his way to freedom when his hometown religionists try to hurl him off a cliff in Luke 4:28–30. He doesn't chuck rocks when people try to stone him in John 8:59. He doesn't perform a preemptive strike against those who are about to kill a woman in John 8:9. Considering he doesn't even defend himself as the world-terrorizing Romans torture and crucify him, how can genuine followers of Yehoshua ever believe he sanctions war, violence, or perhaps even self-defense? Why is our immediate reaction to defend violence instead of choosing nonviolence? These are incredibly complicated questions, which is why it is so important to stay close to Yehoshua.

Who are the blessed? The peacemakers.
Who are we to love and pray for? Our enemies.
What are we to do instead of fighting? Pick up our cross and drag it after him.
What is the most terrifying verse in Scripture? "Do not resist an evil person" (Matthew 5:39 NIV).

The early church got the message loud and clear. Prior to the unholy merger of church and state under the Roman Emperor Constantine, early church leaders were nearly unanimous in refusing military service. They refused to carry weapons. They refused to commit violence under any circumstance. They refused to resist the forces of evil. For three straight centuries, they endured unfathomably brutal persecution, and they never retaliated. What is the most-quoted verse in all their writings? *"Love your enemies."*

Agape.

Your enemies.

Even Annas and his wicked sons.

Clearly, Yehoshua the politician is unelectable; his would-be party is a joke, and his policies are too pure for any nation on earth. Even if enough voters got fed up with the current system and tossed their vote his way, he would be assassinated by the rich within weeks—likely after declaring nationwide debt forgiveness (Luke 4:18). The whole idea of Yehoshua for earthly president is absurd.

Yet isn't this clearly what the ideal political system—dare I say *the politics of heaven*—might look like? This is the greatest political framework in human history. Why are we not teaching it in every politics class on the planet? Why is this not a major unit in every political science degree? Even if no one ever puts it into practice, why are we not at least teaching Yehoshua's political theory and running simulation models of how it would play out in real time?

Perhaps it is because Christianity cannot be reduced to an earthly political system or its founder to an earthly politician. As Leo Tolstoy wrote in *The Kingdom of God Is Within You*, "The Christian religion is not a legal system which, being imposed by violence, may transform men's lives. Christianity is a new and higher conception of life. A new conception of life cannot be imposed on men; it can only be freely assimilated." Yehoshua is interested in eternal spiritual governance, not breathlessly temporary government. His mandate is not to reform earthly governments, but to *replace* them all with the kingdom of God.

Unfortunately, almost no one in first-century Judea understands his message, and within days it will get him killed.

The Road to Crucifixion

The political backdrop for Yehoshua's ministry reads like a complex action thriller: murderous Roman overlords. Corrupt Hebrew vassal kings. Warring Jewish sects. A behind-the-scenes power broker. Dangerous underground resistance movements. Apocalyptic messianic figures preaching doomsday and destruction.

And it all begins with good news.

Just look at Yehoshua's very first public words recorded by Mark in 1:15: "The time is fulfilled, and the kingdom of God is at hand; repent and believe in the gospel."

The Greek word for gospel here is *euangeliō*. Good angel. Good messenger. Good message. *Euangelion* is where we get the much-maligned word *evangelical*.

Yehoshua isn't the first person to declare a gospel over Israel. It is good news when David makes Solomon king in 1 Kings 1:42. Isaiah 52:7 blesses the feet of those who bring good news and proclaim shalom. The comic Aristophanes jokes that a decrease in the price of sardines is a *euaggelia*.

Rome also had its own *euangelion*: the so-called *Pax Romana*. Roman peace. *Euangelions* were as common as grapes in the Roman Empire, with every sociopathic, narcissistic dictator and general announcing a triumph and throwing himself a military parade. Consider this inscription found on a government building in Turkey from 6 BC, in which Gaius Octavius (aka Caesar Augustus, the "revered emperor") is called a divine savior: "The birthday of the god Augustus has been for the whole world *the beginning of the gospel* concerning him."

How does Mark 1:1 begin? "*The beginning of the gospel* of Jesus, the Son of God."

You get it. *This rabbi is bound for trouble.*

In first-century Judea, a *euaggelion* is synonymous with "royal proclamation." Both Rome and Yehoshua proclaim a gospel of peace. Rome announces the Pax Romana—no more than a temporary cessation of war, brutally enforced by shedding the blood of dissidents. Yehoshua announces an eternal shalom, paid for with his own blood.

Different gospels mean different things to different people. For some, it's simply a lucky turn of events. For others, it's a triumphal announcement. For most, it's a royal proclamation. For Yehoshua, it is a universal declaration that will make humanity forget all the other gospels and call this one *the* gospel. But when you are Roman, everything is viewed through the lens of military might. When you are a temple religionist, everything is viewed through the lens of defending your position at the top of the hierarchy.

If the House of Annas and their Roman overlords think Yehoshua's religious, philosophical, and economic beliefs are troubling, they perceive his political beliefs to be nothing short of treason, punishable by excruciating torture and agonizing death.

Because all they hear is: *A revolution is on the way.*

The Political Climate

The story of Israel starts with Abraham, but the nation gets its name from Abraham's grandson, Jacob. Nicknaming runs deep in the YHWH-Yehoshua family, from Abram/Abraham and Sarai/Sarah to Simon "Rocky" bar Jonah. In Genesis 32, Jacob has an encounter with an unnamed man. After fighting all night long, they call a draw at dawn, and the man says to Jacob, "Your name shall no longer be called Jacob, but Israel, for you have striven with God and with men, and have prevailed" (v. 28).

Yisrael. "One who struggles with God."

It is the perfect name for the people of Israel. Has any nation wrestled with what it means to serve YHWH more than Israel? Has any nation suffered so greatly and for so long? Abraham is oppressed by several kings. Jacob works as an indentured servant for fourteen years. Moses and the Israelites are oppressed by Egypt for four centuries. Samson and David wage war against the Philistines. Gideon and the judges go up against Midian. Daniel is exiled by the Babylonians and retained by the Persians. Up next to conquer Israel are the Greeks under Alexander the Great and Antiochus Epiphanes IV. After the Romans will come crusades, pogroms, the Holocaust, and widespread anti-Semitism.

In Yehoshua's day, Israel is under the boot of Rome and its dictatorial Caesars. On-the-ground governance is handled by the Herodian client kings and the House of Annas. After Herod the Great's death, three peasants tried to start armed revolts—Judas in northern Galilee; slave-arsonist Simon, east of the Jordan; and Anthronges in Judea. The power vacuum requires the Syrian governor to crucify several thousand men to restore order, at which time Herod the Great's three sons divvied up the nation.

Phillip ran northeast of Galilee, Antipas ran Galilee and Perea to the south of Phillip's territory, and Archelaus ran Judea before Rome exiled him to France for doing such a terrible job. After this, Judea was ruled directly by Rome through a governor-prefect named Pontius Pilate.

These three men are always on the lookout for potential uprisings.

During the procuratorship of Antonius Felix, a mysterious prophet-like revolutionary known only as "The Egyptian" attracted a following of four- to thirty thousand dagger-wielding Sicarii, marched them from the desert to the Mount of Olives, and planned to break into Jerusalem and overrun the Roman garrison. Felix massacred four hundred and imprisoned two hundred more, but the Egyptian himself escaped.

Opponents can spring up from anywhere—the Sadducees, Pharisees, Essenes, Zealots, Sicarii, Essenes, other desert dwellers, the temple elite, downtrodden peasants, even slaves were known to revolt.

Is Yehoshua ben Yehoseph someone the Roman and Jewish elites should be watching?

He certainly has personal motives. Yehoshua was the kinsman, friend, known associate, and potential disciple of John the Baptizer, who Antipas beheaded. Perhaps he wants revenge. John's thousands of wilderness baptisms are not without political undertones, after all. Like Moses leading the people through the Red Sea and into the Sinai wilderness before conquering the Promised Land, John led thousands of people into the wilderness, brought them through the waters of the Jordan, and sent them into the Promised Land to foment a social network of radicals preparing for apocalyptic conquest. Josephus says Antipas killed John the Baptizer as a preemptive strike. Perhaps they should do the same to the one John says is the Messiah?

If Yehoshua is not an out-and-out zealot leader himself, he clearly doesn't have any qualms about recruiting them as disciples. Plus, he is from Nazareth of all places, a traditional hotbed of insurgency. Despite Rome's massive influence, the archaeological work in and around the town of less than twelve hundred suggests the people of Nazareth roundly reject Roman culture. They are strong in their Jewish identity and deeply anti-Roman by nature and nurture.

All told, Yehoshua is a "person of interest" before he even goes public.

On the Run

From the very start, Yehoshua is in trouble. He knows he is a wanted man for his association with his apocalyptic cousin. This is part of the reason he doesn't settle down, open a rabbinical school, and let the masses come to him. *A sitting duck is a dead duck.*

Within days of launching his public ministry, he is permanently on the run. But Yehoshua knows how to bob and weave like a prizefighter. He makes forays south to Judea, then retreats north every time. After John the Baptizer is murdered, he retreats north into Galilee.

Luke 9:7–9 makes it clear Yehoshua has already come to the attention of the authorities. When Herod Antipas, who executed Yehoshua's kinsman, hears that the radical rabbi has started sending his disciples to gather more recruits, he freaks out. What does his royal court think? Some say Yehoshua is a reincarnated Elijah or another prophet of old. Herod, haunted by the murder of a prophet he knew to be innocent, believes it is John the Baptizer himself who has come back from the dead (Mark 6:16). Because Yehoshua has become so well-known (Mark 6:14), Herod calls for an investigation.

So Yehoshua keeps on the move. In Mark 6, the hometown crowd tries to hurl him off a cliff. In John 7, he escapes arrest. In John 8, he escapes a stoning. He is a hunted man, hurtling toward a date with destiny.

Yehoshua is no political slouch. When even Galilee gets too hot, he heads north toward Phoenicia, darts east toward Hermon, cuts south toward Decapolis. In other words, he's staying out of Herod Antipas's territory.

John 4:1–3 suggests Yehoshua has spies in Jerusalem too. "Now when Jesus learned that the Pharisees had heard that Jesus was making and baptizing more disciples than John the Baptist . . . he left Judea and departed again for Galilee". Just to make sure no one follows him, he cuts through Samaria (John 4:4). The religionists and the Herodians don't even bother to search for him there—no Jew, after all, would dare enter Samaria.

After Yehoshua feeds the five thousand in John 6:15, he senses that the massive crowd plans to "take him by force to make him king," so he immediately withdraws to the mountains. "After this Yehoshua went about in Galilee. He would not go about in Judea, because the Jews were seeking to kill him" (John 7:1). Some Temple elites try to seize him yet again, and he decides his time has come. So what does Yehoshua do in John 10:40 in preparation for the final advance on the enemy? He retreats. More specifically, he starts the end of the story where the story began. "He went away again across the Jordan to the place where John had been baptizing at first, and there he remained." For how long, we don't know, but for what purpose, we are certain. Just as Moses crossed the Red Sea and marched his people through the desert toward the conquest of the Promised Land, this rabbi will reenact the Exodus.

He knows he can't bob and weave forever. At some point, he must come out of hiding and publicly confront the forces of evil.

Where and when should such a violent clash happen?

Yehoshua knows the perfect time and place.

The Beginning of the End

Sunday, March 29, 33 AD

Passover.

Jerusalem.

It's the perfect time and place.

Passover in Jerusalem is a religio-political powder keg. Remember, Passover celebrates the Jewish liberation from slavery in Egypt to freedom in the Promised Land. It is a decidedly un-Roman celebration if ever there was one. The memory of 4 BC lingers in the mind of Annas and the religionist elite—after the death of Herod the Great, inept Archelaus's men slaughtered three thousand pilgrims *in the temple*. Passover falls during the Festival of Unleavened Bread, a weeklong celebration of the nation's exodus from Egyptian slavery. Potentially hundreds of thousands of Jewish pilgrims pack the capital—excellent for starting riots—and it is a security nightmare for the Romans: Jews everywhere—in every nook, cranny, valley, and hilltop. Tents as far as the eye can see, smoke billowing skyward from ten thousand fires, blood pouring from the temple sacrifices like a swollen river. Moreover, the Jewish prophet Daniel predicted YHWH would show up and end the occupation in 70 x 7 years. After the centuries of abuse at the hands of the Greeks and Romans, Jewish expectation is at an all-time high.

A few weeks before Passover, Yehoshua decides it's time to head back into Judea. The disciples think it's a terrible idea, but Thomas resolutely says, "Let us also go, that we may die with him" (John 11:16). Yehoshua gathers his seventy-odd disciples, plus his family and a crowd (Luke 19:11), and begins his final pilgrimage to Jerusalem. He does so extremely slowly and publicly—no point getting arrested or assassinated before the big finale—and makes several stops along the way.

The most noteworthy is when he learns of his dear friend Lazarus's passing. Two miles outside Jerusalem in a village called Bethany, Lazarus and his two sisters, Martha and Mary, are old pals and regular hosts for the rabbi on his trips to Jerusalem (Luke 10:38). Lazarus's corpse has been decomposing in a tomb for four days. Martha scolds Yehoshua for not coming sooner and healing her ill brother but professes faith that YHWH can still heal through Yehoshua. When a weeping Mary joins her sister, Yehoshua cries, and then does what no itinerant rabbi-healer has done before: He raises the dead.

This unsurprisingly freaks out the locals. Many believe in him, but others hightail it to the Pharisees and tell them what has happened. The Pharisees run and tell the high priests. As Yehoshua predicted in his Luke 16 parable of the rich man and Lazarus, the House of Annas not only do not believe that Lazarus has risen from the dead, but they immediately hatch a plot to have Lazarus murdered because so many Jews are crossing over to Team Yehoshua (John 12:9–11).

In John 11:48, the chief priests and Pharisees call an emergency assembly of the high priestly advisory council, the synedrion. Much self-centered hand-wringing ensues: "If we let him go on like this, everyone will believe in him, and the Romans will come and take away both our place and our nation." The ice-cold high priest, Caiaphas, however, cuts to the chase, saying "It is better for you that one man should die for the people, not that the whole nation should perish" (v. 50). This may seem patriotic on the surface, but it is nothing more than a war strategy to maintain his family's exploitative sources of income.

Word evidently makes its way back to Yehoshua (perhaps through sympathizers in the synedrion like the Galilean Nicodemus or Joseph of Arimathea), and he retreats into a wilderness village called Ephraim, a dozen or so miles northeast of Jerusalem. We don't know how long he laid low, but six days before Passover he heads back to Lazarus's house. A large crowd of Jews gets wind of the arrival and comes out to see Yehoshua and gawk at Lazarus. It's just the kind of gathering the Romans don't want to see during Passover.

The march on Jerusalem begins. Despite having heard more than a hundred teachings on the kingdom of God, Yehoshua's disciples are evidently still fuzzy on what this kingdom is. This is where Aunt Salome asks if her sons can sit at their cousin's left and right hand when he takes over. We can only imagine what is going through the revolutionary minds of hot-headed Rocky, Simon the Zealot, Judas, and the Thunder Sons. *Is this the part where we stir up the Passover masses and take over the capital? Will Yehoshua bankrupt Annas and his thieving family? Are we going to get to fight alongside angels? Will our rabbi kill all the Romans with a firebolt from heaven?*

As they near Jerusalem, Luke 19:11 says that the rabbi's crowd "supposed that the kingdom of God was to appear *immediately*." Instead, Yehoshua tells them a parable about how systems of exploitation empower the powerful and weaken the weak (Luke 19, Matthew 25).

It is time for the presumed Christos-Messiah to make his grand conqueror's entrance into Jerusalem. Where does he base camp? The Mount of Olives (Matthew 19:29)—the same place from which other would-be messiah claimants had and will launch their attacks on the capital. He sends two of his disciples, likely Peter and John, to a nearby hamlet to borrow a colt. The more violent insurgents in the caravan are no doubt confused. *A colt? Why not warhorses and chariots? What is happening here?*

What is happening is that Yehoshua is trolling the powers that be by fulfilling Zechariah 9:9: "Rejoice greatly, O daughter of Zion! Shout aloud, O daughter of Jerusalem! Behold, your king is coming to you; righteous and having salvation is he, humble and mounted on a donkey, on a colt, the foal of a donkey." Not only that, but he'll be taking the same route into Jerusalem that Solomon used when he was proclaimed king (1 Kings 1:32–40).

Donkey in hand, the disciples fashion a makeshift saddle from their *himation* cloaks and help Yehoshua climb aboard. As the rabbi clip-clops down the hill from Olivet, the whole crowd of disciples decides to stir up some press.

"Hosanna!"

"Hosanna in the highest heaven!"

"Peace in heaven and glory in the highest!"

"Blessed is the King who comes in the name of the Lord!"

"Blessed is the coming kingdom of our father David!"

Them's fightin' words.

Having heard in advance of Yehoshua's visit (and always up for a good spectacle), a huge Passover crowd joins in the fun, tossing their *himations* on the ground and lobbing branches off nearby trees—rolling out the green carpet, as it were. There is a slight sense of charade to this procession, as though some of the disciples (probably the women) know it is more spiritually symbolic than it is physically militaristic. Either way, this is an unbelievably dangerous stunt Yehoshua is pulling. But he believes it is his time to die (John 12:23). If he is not YHWH, then he is unfathomably reckless, mentally ill, or suicidal. The Pharisees in the crowd try to restore order. "'Teacher, rebuke your disciples.'

Jesus answered, 'I tell you, if these were silent, the very stones would cry out'" (Luke 19:39–40).

Everyone knows what happens next. Yehoshua pulls out a machete and starts slaughtering Romans left and right. Judas slices throats with his *sicae*. Simon lobs off ears with his sword. Maggie lights the temple on fire. By nightfall, every Roman in the city is dead, and Yehoshua is triumphantly proclaimed king of Israel.

Well, not exactly.

"Jesus entered Jerusalem and went into the temple. And when he had looked around at everything, as it was already late, he went out to Bethany with the twelve" (Mark 11:11).

That's it. Because it's nearly closing time, he simply looks around the outer courts and then heads back to Mary and Martha's place.

Triumphal entry? Talk about anti-climactic. We can almost hear the crowd deflate. Not one Roman lost their head. Not one high priest got himself deposed.

The crowds disperse and Yehoshua beds down in Bethany. He'll cause a ruckus tomorrow, during office hours, when more people are watching.

Monday, March 30, 33 AD

The next morning, Yehoshua reenters Jerusalem and stomps to the temple's outer court, the court of the Gentiles. "The whole city was stirred up" (Matthew 21:10). "Who is this?" the crowds ask. Others answer, "This is Yehoshua, the prophet from Nazareth of Galilee." Yehoshua surveys the scene. The place is packed. The pilgrim-milking market is open. "In the temple he found those who were selling oxen and sheep and pigeons, and the money-changers sitting there" (John 2:14). To be clear, there is nothing illegal about this. There is nothing in the Torah that says this is a sin. If anything, this marketplace is necessary to fulfill the sacrifice mandates.

But Yehoshua sees this place for what is has become—a money-making, power-broking, Rome-colluding religionist sham. Not only must the Jewish nation pay heavy taxes to Rome and even heavier tithes to the House of Annas, but all adult male Jews in the nation must pay a temple tax (Exodus 30:12–16). Even though it isn't mentioned anywhere in the Law of Moses, the high priests insist the tax can only be paid with a Tyrian shekel, which most Jews don't have. Accordingly, the moneychangers charge them criminally high exchange rates as they trade Roman coins for Annas's monopoly money. And that's not including a commission for their rip-off banking services. Both are tantamount to usury and forbidden by God. The official reason the religionists give for rejecting Roman coins is that they contain images of pagan gods. But the truth is simpler: Roman coins are 80 percent silver, whereas the Tyrian shekel is the purest silver on the market, a whopping 94 percent. In fact, when the mint at Tyre shuts down, its operations are quietly transferred to Jerusalem and placed under the control of the temple elite. Still, the design on the coins doesn't change because they're now a trusted symbol of high-quality silver coinage. The men in charge of the Jewish temple are willfully breaking the Exodus 20:3–4, Deuteronomy 4:16–18, and Deuteronomy 5:8 prohibitions against making graven images. Annas doesn't care that the Tyrian coins proclaim Tyre is the holy city, nor that they proclaim "power of the Romans" or are stamped with the graven image of an eagle and Melqarth-Herakles. That's right: Jews must fund the temple of YHWH with graven images of the son of Baal, king of the underworld.

Not only does Annas control the mint, the exchange rate, and the commission rate, but to add insult to injury, the House of Annas makes the temple tax an *annual* tax instead of a one-time life payment, disobeying Exodus 30:15. No wonder his family is so wealthy—they have a recurring revenue model with built-in exploitation mechanisms that force the entire nation to disobey God. Instead of adult Jewish males making a small contribution to maintain the temple for one more generation, they are forced to pay more than a hundredfold straight to the pockets of Annas in exchange for nothing.

But this is not the end of Annas's frightful fleecing of the faithful Passover flock.

Jewish pilgrims from faraway Galilee or Alexandria who cannot realistically, affordably, or safely transport their unblemished sacrificial animals all the way to Jerusalem must purchase Annas-approved animals from the temple booths at wildly marked-up prices. Moreover, the temple cartel reserves the right to reject any sacrificial animal they feel is less than perfect, forcing pilgrims to buy last-minute replacements at ten to twenty times their non-Jerusalem market price. Who can afford to run such a risk? (The extortionate prices rise so high that, according to Mishnah Kerithoth 1:7, Hillel's great-grandson will later drop the price of doves by *96 percent*.) Annas and his sons make a habit of regularly rejecting outside animals, no matter how pure and perfect they may be, leaving pilgrims with no other choice but to purchase replacements at the bilking bazaars.

This temple sacrifice con is a colossal money-making machine. Annual revenue estimates range from tens to *hundreds of millions* of dollars in today's currency—the kind of gangster crime syndicate that finances 13,000-square-foot stone palaces with multiple floors and an inner courtyard.

Remember, the needs of the high priest and his family are sufficiently met by lawful, God-honoring taxes, tithes, offerings, and sacrifices. All this extra dross is pure theft, a storing up in barns instead of being rich toward God (Luke 12:18–21). This theft is a personal affront to God and his command not to turn a profit off the poor (Leviticus 25:35–37). Remember also that the Court of the Gentiles is supposed to be the place where people of all nations can come and pray to YHWH.

Instead, it is a foul-smelling, pilgrim-exploiting, half-barn-half-bank fraud.

As Yehoshua stares at the corrupt marketeers who once overcharged his soon-to-be-refugee parents when he was a baby (Luke 2:24), all four gospels report that this is where he makes his public stand.

Yehoshua braided a whip out of rushes and "drove all from the temple courts, both sheep and cattle; he scattered the coins of the money changers and overturned their tables" (John 2:15).

Please note that the nonviolent Yehoshua never lays a hand on a human being while he seizes their means of corruption, that as he performs this angry act of economic sabotage, he never sins.

"He overturned the tables of the money changers and the benches of those selling doves, and would not allow anyone to carry merchandise through the temple courts" (Mark 11:15–16 NIV). "And he told those who sold the pigeons, 'Take these things away; do not make my Father's house a house of trade'" (John 2:16).

In grinding the cartel's business to a halt during the busiest week of their fiscal year—while symbolizing the temple's total destruction like a prophet of old—Yehoshua has just made the biggest "mistake" of his life.

Why?

Because the temple booths are controlled by an ultra-wealthy, supremely powerful, and altogether shadowy Jewish elite—the aristocratic Annas ben Seth, High Priest Emeritus and the ultimate puppet master who holds the temple's purse strings in the tightest of nooses.

Not only does Annas have a monopoly on the temple court stalls (and the nation's tithes), he has four additional branches on the Mount of Olives. The infamous markets are literally called "The Booths of the Sons of Annas." Here, pilgrims have no choice but to purchase sacrificial lambs, oil, and wine at exorbitant prices from the godfather and his mafia family. It is pure exploitation of destitute pilgrims, a blatant affront to the Leviticus 25:35–37 laws that forbid turning a profit off the poor, and Yehoshua will not abide its continuance.

The House of Annas hears of the commerce-crushing commotion and rushes to the Court of the Gentiles.

Amidst the stampede of cattle and callous merchants, Yehoshua the economic saboteur stares at the high priests and their lawyers and invokes Isaiah 56:7 and Jeremiah 7:11—two texts the Sadducee high priests roundly reject—publicly proclaiming that the religionists are robbing Jews under the guise of helping them worship YHWH.

"Is it not written, 'My house shall be called a house of prayer for all the nations'? But *you* have made it a den of robbers" (Mark 11:17, emphasis added). Note that Yehoshua does not call them legalists or heretics or even religionists. The Greek word he uses for robbers is *lestai*—violent zealots, bandits hellbent on political corruption and economic robbery. I will leave it to the reader to look up the context of both Old Testament passages and realize Yehoshua's double-quotation serves as a resounding eviction notice of the House of Annas from the House of God. By adding "you" to Isaiah 56:7 and Jeremiah 7:11, Yehoshua makes these verses a declaration of war against the temple administration.

Annas is simultaneously furious and fearful. This Galilean racketeer has ground his temple thievery to a halt in the busiest week of the year. What's more, he has publicly indicted the high priestly family as thieves, murderers, and worshipers of Baal (which their jam-packed treasury of Tyrian shekels prove they are). It is a personal affront and the final straw. Mark 11:18 says the chief priests *immediately* begin looking for a way to kill Yehoshua.

With zero transactions in today's market, the massive Passover crowds flock to the rabbi, hanging on his every word as he heals the lame and blind. The high priests want to kill Yehoshua on the spot, but they are rightly terrified of the people (Luke

22:2). They send their spies to keep a close watch on the rabbi's proceedings this day.

The religionists patiently listen to Yehoshua's teachings and witness his miracles but grow furious when they hear kids shouting in the temple, "Hosanna to the Son of David!" Can you hear it echo off the walls of the courtyard, the once-bustling marketplace that is now a place of holy teaching for Galilee's greatest son?

Hosanna to the Son of David.

An extremely political phrase.

The elites confront Yehoshua. "Do you hear what these children are saying?"

Yehoshua, always ready to defend children, retorts with, "Yes; have you never read, 'Out of the mouth of infants and nursing babies you have prepared praise'?" (Matthew 21:16).

Perhaps the parents in the crowd cheer. The kids certainly do.

While the religionists lick their wounds for being publicly chastised in front of the pilgrim faithful, Yehoshua and the disciples head back to their lodgings in Bethany.

Tuesday, March 31, 33 AD

Since arriving for the festival, Yehoshua has staged a mock-military triumphal entry into the city and an act of economic terrorism. What will day three hold?

Yehoshua returns to Jerusalem in the morning for another full day of preaching in the temple courts. He presumably continues to protect the temple from doing any commerce all of Holy Week, encouraging the faithful masses and infuriating the temple aristocracy. The chief priests and their entourage storm up to Yehoshua, demanding answers: "Tell us by what authority you do these things, or who it is that gave you this authority?" (Luke 20:2).

The good rabbi answers with a question. "Tell me, was the baptism of John from heaven or from man?"

It's an excellent question. The masses believe John the Baptizer is a prophet, so if the religionists say "from man," the people will stone them on the spot. If they say "from heaven," Yehoshua can ask why they didn't believe John. The religionists answer that they don't know the answer.

Yehoshua replies, "Neither will I tell you by what authority I do these things" (v. 8).

Then, with insane levels of boldness, the Galilean peasant preacher launches into another barely veiled parable (Matthew 21:33–41):

> "There was a master of a house who planted a vineyard and put a fence around it and dug a winepress in it and built a tower and leased it to tenants, and went into another country. When the season for fruit drew near, he sent his servants to the tenants to get his fruit. And the tenants took his servants and beat one, killed another, and stoned another. Again he sent other servants, more than the first. And they did the same to them. Finally he sent his son to them, saying, 'They will respect my son.' But when the tenants saw the son, they said to themselves, 'This is the heir. Come, let us kill him and have his inheritance.' And they took him and threw him out of the vineyard and killed him. When therefore the owner of the vineyard comes, what will he do to those tenants?" They said to him, "He will put those wretches to a miserable death and let out the vineyard to other tenants who will give him the fruits in their seasons."

Yehoshua levels his gaze at the religionists (Matthew 21:42–43): "Have you never read in the Scriptures: 'The stone that the builders rejected has become the cornerstone; this was the Lord's doing, and it is marvelous in our eyes'? Therefore I tell you, the kingdom of God will be taken away from you and given to a people producing its fruits."

No, Yehoshua is not condemning all Jews and replacing them with all Gentiles. This parable has been used as a justification for persecuting Jews for more than a millennium, but its true meaning is obvious to anyone with ears to hear: The kingdom of God is the vineyard. YHWH is the vineyard's owner. The tenants are the House of Annas and all religionists before and after. The servants are those martyred doing the will of God (specifically the prophets—Matthew 23:37). The son is Yehoshua himself. What he's saying is that the religionists have not only been fruitless in their stewardship of God's kingdom but they've been actively trying to poison it.

The chief priests and their cadre—not the faithful Jewish crowd—realize *he is speaking about them* (Matthew 21:45), but they are too afraid to arrest him because the crowds are now convinced that Yehoshua is a prophet.

They have no other option. They must find grounds for an arrest.

While the Pharisees and Herodians temporarily set aside their differences and unify in their attack against Yehoshua, Annas sends wave after wave of temple elites to try to get the rabbi to say something worthy of arrest, a sound bite to cancel him, or better yet, crucify him. By whose authority do you teach? Should Jews pay taxes to Caesar? What happens at the resurrection if a woman's been married to seven brothers in a row? What is the greatest commandment?

Yehoshua rebuffs each question brilliantly, and eventually the elites stop asking him questions for fear of a mob reprisal. With no more interruptions from the aristocrats, he mocks their ridiculous outfits and positions and titles (Matthew 23:5–7), then launches a blistering counterattack. At this point, the gloves are off, and Yehoshua is no longer bobbing and weaving in and out of Galilee and Judea. He charges in with a barrage of verbal uppercuts, pronouncing seven scathing woes on the religionists, calling them blind guides, hypocrites, whitewashed tombs, children of hell, prophet-murderers, and (echoing his kinsman John in Matthew 3:7) serpents and vipers, an expression meaning *sons of Satan himself* (Matthew 23:13–39).

With this brutal oratorical assault, Yehoshua makes his intentions clear: He is here not to align himself with the religionists, but to overthrow them for all time—and it will be a fight to the death.

At the end of the day, the rabbi and his followers head back to Bethany. Note the difference in familiarity between a rabbi whose family pilgrimaged to Jerusalem every year for Passover, versus his country-bumpkin disciples who likely never have. "As he came out of the temple, one of his disciples said to him, 'Look, Teacher, what wonderful stones and what wonderful buildings!'" Yehoshua is not in any way impressed with buildings. "Do you see these great buildings? There will not be left here one stone upon another that will not be thrown down" (Mark 13:1–2).

Back on the Mount of Olives that evening, the disciples are growing desperately impatient. The two sets of brothers (Peter, Andrew, James, and John) ask Yehoshua when, exactly, everything he's been saying will come to be.

He tells them to stay tuned, stay alert, and stay awake.

Cause of Death

Wednesday, April 1, 33 AD

Two days until Passover. Yehoshua knows his actions and teachings have sealed his fate. He tells his disciples as much in Matthew 26:2: "You know that after two days the Passover is coming, and the Son of Man will be delivered up to be crucified."

Sure enough, "the chief priests and the elders of the people gathered in the palace of the high priest, whose name was Caiaphas, and plotted together in order to arrest Jesus by stealth and kill him. But they said, 'Not during the feast, lest there be an uproar among the people'" (Matthew 26:3–5).

The temple elites are desperate to off Yehoshua without causing a festival riot. They not only have to get through Passover, but also the following six days of the festival until the hundreds of thousands of pilgrims go home sometime after Thursday, April 9. There's no way Yehoshua won't make another scene before then. They have to arrest him covertly before he pulls a stunt that forces the Romans to get involved and sell the high priesthood to someone else. But how to do the deed?

There are essentially only three things that nearly all biblical and secular scholars agree on: The first is that Yehoshua ben Yehoseph was a Jewish healer who preached in Judea and Galilee. The second is that his message was something he called "the kingdom of God." And third, that this so-called kingdom—earthly, spiritual, or otherwise—eventually posed a big enough threat to the Roman Empire that they executed him for it.

Before we proceed to Yehoshua's arrest, trials, and execution, we must stop and ask a question most historians and theologians have overlooked for centuries: What capital crime did Yehoshua commit?

We know that Yehoshua is not killed for calling himself the Jewish messiah, because it is not illegal to call oneself a messiah. Indeed, all sorts of folk had called themselves a messiah and not one received so much as a rap on the wrists from the temple elite.

It is not his claim of messiahship that brings down the wrath of Annas's synedrion, so perhaps it is their belief that he claims to be YHWH himself, and is therefore a blasphemer. But this poses two major problems:

The first is that temple elites aren't legally allowed to execute anybody even if they wanted to (John 18:31). Annas knows he can't just execute Yehoshua, because it would risk Caiaphas's seat and their political dynasty. But he still needs to find a way to get the Romans to end Yehoshua's life.

The second problem is that Romans don't give two hoots about Jewish theology. They don't execute rabbis for claiming to be a god they don't even believe in. If you were to tell a polytheistic Roman that Yehoshua claims to be God, said Roman might respond, "Which one?"

No, Jewish blasphemy doesn't earn you a Roman execution. It's the physical, here-and-now, political declaratives that make the Romans pay attention. Let the temple elite administer the opioid of religion to the masses, just don't declare yourself king of the Jews. Annas understands this dynamic perfectly well.

Scripture makes it clear that Yehoshua was not killed by the Jews. He was killed by the Romans, and not for his "errant" theology.

He must have been assassinated for political reasons.

Let us put ourselves in the luxurious shoes of the high priest and his corrupt father-in-law for a moment. We have a fellow who says he is the Messiah and the Son of God. He undermines our credibility and erodes public trust. He disrupts our highly profitable businesses and makes us into a laughingstock. For several years we have been trying to concoct a basis for accusing him to the Romans (John 8:6), yet his power and following keep growing. If it were up to us, we would execute him under the guise of blasphemy. But we are under the boot of the Romans, and it is their decision. As it stands, this apocalyptic rabble-rouser is worse than his forebear John the Baptizer, and if we can't find a way to kill him, he will spark a Passover uprising that sees Rome destroy Jerusalem, raze the temple, and unseat us from our lofty place in the power structure, if not crucify us while they tear down our city's walls. Can we build a case against this rabbi that will convince our overlords to do away with him once and for all?

That is the task to which Annas and Caiaphas and their synedrion now set their sights.

Do they know that Yehoshua is named after Joshua son of Nun, the greatest warrior in Jewish history?

Do they know he has two disciples called Judas, a name made popular by Judas Maccabeus, who led the revolt against the great power before Rome?

Do they know that Yehoshua ben Yehoseph is a double bloodline king candidate with a better claim to the throne of Israel than Herod Antipas?

While Annas's ultimate case is flimsy at best, Rome doesn't require a particularly high burden of proof. The case will rest on two major points: Yehoshua's seemingly political message, and his known and presumed political associations.

1. Seemingly political message

We return to Yehoshua's first public words: "The time is fulfilled, and the kingdom of God is at hand; repent and believe in the gospel" (Mark 1:15).

People have misunderstood this message from day one. Even three to five years in, the disciples still aren't sure they know what it means.

How would Roman ears receive or understand this announcement? The time has come . . . a new empire is here . . . return to the king . . . believe in his royal proclamation.

Yehoshua is already guilty of treason.

2. Political associations

Let's set aside the fact that Yehoshua has at least two former followers of John the Baptizer, plus the potential reality that Judas Iscariot is a throat-slitting Sicarii-type and Simon is a tad overzealous.

Because we live in such over-politicized times, these tenuous political associations lead excitable authors to the likely incorrect conclusion that Yehoshua is little more than a revolutionary politician—a power-seeking demagogue bent on Roman overthrow and the establishment of a new party, kingdom, or even empire. Some even believe Yehoshua was a *leading member* of the Zealots, his mind fixated on expelling the Romans from Palestine and restoring the Mosaic Law over Israel.

I do not believe for one second that Yehoshua's purpose for preaching was to overthrow the Roman Empire. If that were the case, he would have spent far less time healing, feeding, and preaching about love. Instead, he would have focused on military exercises, combat training, and weapons making. No, Yehoshua could not have been a revolutionary politician for at least eight significant reasons:

1. He does not seek achievable power. Yehoshua had a large enough following and strong relationships with several leading Jews to have easily won himself a seat on the synedrion, an alliance with Annas to bilk the commoners, and perhaps even a seat in the Herodian court via his relationship with Herod's household manager's wife. Yet he eschews such positions of rank and privilege for life among the lowly.
2. If he were truly a Zealot, why would he tell his followers to enrich that very empire by paying taxes and tribute? Why not call for a tax strike and use the money to buy weapons?
3. If Yehoshua is such a political contrarian, why does he heal a government official's son (John 4)? Or the centurion's servant (Matthew 8)? Or recruit one of Rome's tax collectors as an inner-circle disciple? Or have dinner with a traitorous head tax collector as corrupt as Zacchaeus? Or accept financing from Herod's household?
4. He is too smart to be so stupid. Most of the revolutionaries of the time were barbarians. Yehoshua is nuanced, subtle, literate, and extremely smart. He knows the impossibility of overthrowing Roman might. Even if every person he ever preached to showed up to fight for him, he would still be outnumbered ten to one against a vastly better-trained and better-equipped Roman army.
5. This is a big one—he readily surrenders himself. Why the blazes didn't he head back to the desert from whence his whole story started? Those of you who have been to the

Mount of Olives know as well as I do how easily he could have escaped. Instead of praying in the garden of Gethsemane on the night of his arrest, he could have walked the ten minutes to Lazarus's house, borrowed a donkey, loaded it up with provisions from Mary and Martha, and made a wide berth around Jerusalem, heading south along the Dead Sea. He is not afraid of a few hundred miles of desert, having previously lived and traveled through it. From there, he could've set his course due west to fertile Egypt, settling in Cairo or catching a ship at Alexandria to spend his retirement somewhere in the Grecian islands. Instead, he stays. He believes he *must* die. He is either suicidal or insane, or he is the Savior he claims to be.

6. When Peter chops off Malchus's ear (we'll get to all the gory details in the next chapter), Yehoshua immediately heals him. This is not the behavior of a Zealot; such a man would borrow a sword and finish the job.
7. Violence is incompatible with his message. That's why he forgives his murderers while dying on the cross. Yehoshua preaches enemy love, turning the other cheek, and making the heart (in the words of John Mark Comer) "a graveyard for hate." He is willing to take all the sin and hate and violence of the world and drag it into the pit of hell in order to burst back to life in a phoenix-like fireball of love and truth and holy perfection.
8. It is not the Romans Yehoshua confronts. He does not overturn the tables of the Praetorium or the Herodian Palace. He makes it more personal, more Jewish, more pointed at the everyday exploitation endured by everyone in Israel. He rages not against Rome, but against the religionists. Politics isn't his game—righteousness is.

But more than his political message and political associations, it is Yehoshua's seemingly political actions that turn the water from hot to boiling.

The first action that courts his eventual execution is his disruptive behavior at the autumnal Feast of Tabernacles in John 7. After declining to join his brothers at the festival (perhaps he wanted to celebrate his birthday at home with his friends), Yehoshua changes his mind and sneaks into Jerusalem. Halfway through the festival he starts teaching in the temple, publicly taunting the religious establishment. When Annas and Caiaphas send officers to arrest him, Yehoshua talks his way out of arrest. On the last and busiest day of the festival, he stands up and makes a public scene, shouting at the top of his lungs. Thinking he's a demon-possessed Samaritan, they try to stone him before he gets away. Yehoshua has been on the radar of the House of Annas for at least six months. What if he plans a major disruption on the final day of the Passover festival, which is a much bigger celebration, focused entirely on liberation from corrupt power, with far greater crowds to inflame?

The second action, as a pesky rumor has it, is that just days before Passover, the Galilean rabbi raised his friend Lazarus from the dead. No doubt the friend was in on the conspiracy, and he got his sister Mary to wrap him up like a mummy while Martha packed enough food in the burial cave to last for four days. But the rumor has spread like wildfire, clearly part of the rabbi's plan to delude the mob into thinking he really is YHWH in the flesh.

Then there is his third action: His symbolic, anti-triumphal entry. The temple elite know exactly what this is. It's Yehoshua's attempt to re-enact the prophecy of Zechariah 9:9 (NIV). "Rejoice greatly, Daughter Zion! Shout, Daughter Jerusalem! See, your king comes to you, righteous and victorious, lowly and riding on a donkey, on a colt, the foal of a donkey." But there can only be one king in Israel: Rome for now, Annas at the right moment.

Yehoshua's fourth and final action is the hijacking of the temple marketplace that grinds Annas & Co. to a halt. Mark 11:18 says his symbolic destruction of the temple is *the* catalyst for his arrest. John confirms this by placing the event near the beginning of his gospel as a foreboding flash-forward (John 2:13–22). Yehoshua himself is certain that this act of economic sabotage is what will incite the chief priests to kill him (Mark 10:33). How can we be certain that disrupting the economy of Annas is the catalytic event? Because Mark uses a literary device called an *inclusio* to highlight it, sandwiching the table-overturning scene (Mark 11:15–19) within a story about the destruction of a fruitless fig tree (Mark 11:12–14 and Mark 11:20–21). Fig trees are a common symbol of Israel in Scripture (Jeremiah 8:13; Joel 1:7; Hosea 9:10, 16), and the meaning is obvious: The religionists run a decrepit institution that bears no fruit. It's time to purge the House of Annas from the House of YHWH.

What is the "evidence" the religionists take to their Roman overlords?

A presumed political message, known political associations, and openly aggressive political actions during a politically charged festival with a history of violent political outbreaks. If they have to sum it up in a sentence, they will say, "He claims to be the king of the Jews."

In other words, Annas and the Jewish religionists don't get Yehoshua killed for saying he is God. Sure, Caiaphas goes through the motions of tearing his clothes and pretending he cares about defending YHWH's honor, but Caiaphas and his family are so far out of touch with God that they can't see God's Son standing before their eyes. Yes, there are some religionists among them who really do care about blasphemy, but getting the Romans to crucify Yehoshua for political purposes fixes this problem as well. As pastor-theologian Richard John Saunders puts it, "Jesus's death and burial are two birds with one big stone rolled in front."

It is often said that "the Jews killed Jesus." No, they didn't. A small group of hyper-violent religionists misrepresented Judaism, took YHWH's name in vain, and had Yehoshua murdered by the Romans for political power and personal profit. The text says so (John 11:48, 50). Yehoshua was murdered by the Romans because the House of Annas claimed he was the "king of the Jews."

In the same way that a war waged in the name of Yehoshua by an African warlord today is easily dismissed as false, we cannot accept the idea that godly, faithful, wholehearted Jews had Yehoshua assassinated. Aristocrat Annas wasn't a YHWH-loving leader like Moses, Isaiah, or Elijah; he was a power-loving, money-grubbing, secular political elitist who had no qualms about murder. He and his barbarous gang of temple infiltrators do not represent true Judaism. They literally could not be any further from the truth of heaven.

Unfortunately, the errant belief that God-honoring Jews killed Yehoshua has caused untold anti-Semitism over the past two millennia, with Catholics torturing and murdering Jews for nearly ten centuries. But what has Yehoshua been saying about Annas and the temple elites the whole time? *Fake Jews!* Yehoshua is the greatest Jew of all time, calling out bad Jewry.

Anti-Jew Annas and his machinating minions have all the political evidence they need. And they have something else, or rather, some*one* else too: There's an inside man who's willing to betray Yehoshua for a price. The House of Annas has no problem sharing a small slice of their festival takings—just thirty pieces of silver, a mere handful of Tyrian shekels from the temple treasury—if Judas Iscariot can find an opportunity for them to arrest the rabbi *quietly*. Judas knows just the time and place.

It's time to sell out a fellow Jew to the Romans.

Thursday, April 2, 33 AD

Passover preparation day.

The House of Annas is hard at work in the temple, skinning animals and skimming millions off the backs of the hard-working masses, slaughtering sacrificial animals and filling their coffers to the brim.

Yehoshua has sent two of his inner twelve ahead to help prepare the feast (Luke 22:8). Because of his fame and his impending arrest, the whole affair is executed with espionage-like secrecy, complete with the clandestine signal of a man carrying a jug of water (Luke 22:10), a task normally reserved for the women-folk.

Sunset in Jerusalem arrives at 6:58 p.m.

It's now technically Friday by the Jewish sundown-to-sundown reckoning of a day, but we'll call it Thursday until we reach midnight in the garden of Gethsemane.

Yehoshua and his inner twelve disciples come into Jerusalem and make their way to a large furnished upper room (suggesting yet another wealthy gospel patron). Yehoshua washes their feet, eats a full sunset Seder supper, shares a bunch of legendary teachings, predicts one of the Twelve will betray him posthaste, foretells Simon Peter will disown his rabbi three times before the morning rooster crows, tells them to drink wine and break bread as a way to remember him, and sings a hymn. The song in question is probably the traditional Passover dirge of Psalms 113–118. In an ode to his former career as a *tektón,* one of the last lines triumphantly declares, "The stone that the builders rejected has become the cornerstone."

It is no coincidence that Yehoshua has chosen his death day to fall on Passover. He is the ultimate sacrificial lamb whose blood shields us from the obliterative power of YHWH's holiness. Yet the disciples still don't get it. They sense Yehoshua's climactic overthrow of the Romans is just moments away, so they pepper him with questions about the details (John 14:5; John 14:22). The disciples are still convinced this is going to be a military conflict, and they bicker about who will be the greatest among them (Luke 22:24).

The meal finished, the group takes their post-prandial stroll across the Kidron Valley to the Mount of Olives, with Simon

Peter and everyone else insisting they will never deny their master (Mark 14:29–31). Yehoshua promises that he will soon stop speaking in figures of speech (John 16:25), and the overconfident disciples immediately think they understand him.

This is not the first time Yehoshua and his disciples have taken this specific saunter. Luke 22:39 says Yehoshua left the last supper and went "as was his custom, to the Mount of Olives." The exact destination on the mount is a quiet garden called Gethsemane. John 18:2 tells us that during their festival week, they "met there often."

In other words, Judas knows the place well.

The God Josh

"We are as much afraid in the light as children in the dark."

—Lucretius as quoted by Seneca,
Moral Letters to Lucilius

Friday, April 3, 33 AD

The garden of Gethsemane is perfectly named for that which is about to take place within its environs this dark night. The name means "Garden of the Oil Press," and like the olives that surround him, Yehoshua is about to be pressed to death, drained of life under the weight of sin, so that through his spilled blood we may experience life anew.

Yehoshua issues his Farewell Discourse to the disciples, concluding with his longest recorded prayer, praying for himself, his disciples, and all his future followers (John 17:1–21).

It is dark.

It is quiet.

It is late.

Most Passover pilgrims are asleep.

It is the perfect time to arrest a rabbi.

And Yehoshua knows it.

The story is told in all four gospels, and it is fraught with terror.

Yehoshua instructs his disciples—more than eleven, as we shall see—to "Sit here while I pray."

He takes Rocky and the Thunder Sons out of earshot. He is visibly distressed. "My soul is very sorrowful, even to death; remain here, and keep watch with me" (Matthew 26:38). He withdraws a stone's throw further and kneels down to pray. We don't know what he prays or how long he prays, but the gist of it is: "Father, if you are willing, remove this cup from me. Nevertheless, not my will, but yours, be done."

In Luke 22:44, the doctor reports that Yehoshua's agony is so great that "his sweat became like great drops of blood falling down to the ground." Whether this means he is simply sweating profusely, or suffering from an extremely rare case of hematidrosis, we don't know. He eventually returns to the inner three, likely an hour or so later, and they are fast asleep. He nudges them awake. "Simon, are you asleep? Couldn't you keep watch with me even one hour? Watch and pray that you may not enter into temptation. The spirit indeed is willing, but the flesh is weak."

Yehoshua returns to his prayers and eventually returns to the three. It is so late that they can neither keep their eyes open nor form a coherent sentence (Mark 14:40). He returns for a third round of prayers, but this one is cut short by an approaching mob. Yehoshua rushes back to his disciples. "The hour has come. The Son of Man is betrayed into the hands of sinners."

Before he can finish speaking, Judas Iscariot and a mob breach (or surround) the garden. Judas has procured officers of the temple guard and a crowd supplied by Annas, Caiaphas, and the Pharisees, plus a Roman captain and his band of soldiers in case things get out of control. They have lanterns and torches and are armed with swords and clubs. Judas wends his way through the sleeping crowd of disciples. "Greetings, Rabbi!" He kisses Yehoshua on the cheek. Embodying forgiveness to the bitter end, the rabbi replies, "*Friend*, do what you came to do."

Yehoshua steps toward the crowd. "Who are you looking for?"

"Yehoshua of Nazareth," they reply.

"I am he."

John says the mob draws back, perhaps as the rest of the disciples rouse and make ready for battle.

He asks them again, "Whom do you seek?"

"Yehoshua of Nazareth."

"I told you that I am he. So, if you seek me, let these men go."

As the mob closes in, the disciples panic. "Lord, should we strike with our swords?" a disciple asks. Simon Peter doesn't wait for an answer. He draws his sword and swings at the high priest's slave, chopping off his right ear. The slave is called Malchus (a nickname meaning "the king"), and there is some speculation that this is actually a young Saul of Tarsus. Whether or not this is the case, this slave, acting as the eyes and ears of high priest, has likely heard Yehoshua speak many times in the temple courts. There is a definite sense this violent episode is historical, as it is unlikely the gospel writers would make up a story that paints them so poorly.

Peace-loving Yehoshua snaps at Simon. "Put your sword back into its place. For all who take the sword will perish by the sword. Do you think that I cannot appeal to my Father, and he will at once send me more than twelve legions of angels?" (Matthew 26:52–53).

Doctor Luke reports that Yehoshua touches Malchus's ear and heals him before addressing the mob. "Have you come out as against a robber, with swords and clubs to capture me? Day after day I sat in the temple teaching, and you did not seize me.

But all this has taken place that the Scriptures of the prophets might be fulfilled" (vv. 55–56).

The soldiers rush in and arrest Yehoshua. As the mob tries to seize the rest, the disciples scatter and flee. One young disciple, wearing nothing but his linen nightgown, escapes arrest by pulling free of his would-be captors and sprints away naked (Mark 14:52).

Yehoshua is bound and led away, abandoned by those he has loved and served.

The Five "Trials"

Trial #1

Making good on his promise to never desert his master, only Simon "Rocky" Peter and John the Thunder Son have the stones to follow their rabbi at a distance.

They trail the murderous mob in the dark for at least ten minutes, down the hill from the Mount of Olives, across the Kidron Brook, up the hill to Jerusalem, and through the gate where the not-so-triumphal entry took place.

Where are they taking our rabbi?

Peter and John wend their way through a warren of streets to the soundtrack of a hundred thousand Passover pilgrims snoring softly.

They head uphill, to the posh part of town.

The soldiers don't take Yehoshua to the Roman praetorium.

They don't take him to the Herodian palace.

They don't even take him to the Jewish temple.

Instead, they take him to a colossal two-story villa with an inner courtyard, the palace of an aristocratic Sadducee priest (Matthew 26:3)—the kind of place only the most corrupt and powerful of Jews could afford.

Yehoshua is about to meet the political mastermind who quietly engineered this murder plot.

Inside the villa, an aging terrorist in a high priest's costume emerges from the shadows. It is none other than Israel's premier power broker, the head of the most powerful crime family in Jerusalem, the father-in-law of Joseph Caiaphas, the current high priest. It is Annas himself (John 18:13). He is in his mid-fifties, but he is more lethal than ever. Like his son-in-law, Annas has zero reservations about sacrificing the life of one peasant Galilean to save the nation and his profitable place atop the echelon.

Yehoshua and Annas stare at one another by firelight.

The former believes himself to be God enfleshed; the latter believes himself to be the holy mediator between man and God.

One believes he is the fulfillment of Judaism as a living temple; the other wishes to maintain the status quo as controller of a man-made temple.

One offers direct access to God for free; the other acts as a middle-man broker for a crushing fee.

While Caiaphas assembles some like-minded priests, elders, and lawyers, Annas grills Yehoshua in hopes of extracting a useable accusation (John 18:19–23). It is the first of five corrupt "trials" Yehoshua will endure this dark night.

While Annas interrogates his nemesis, the "other disciple" (presumably John), being somehow known by Caiaphas (John 18:15), is permitted by the gate girl to come inside. Once inside, he convinces her to let Simon Peter in as well. She does, but asks, "You also are not one of this man's disciples, are you?" Simon says he is not.

Once inside, Simon sits down with the guards and warms himself by the charcoal fire they've lit in the middle of the courtyard. With the fire now lighting up his face, the girl looks at him closely and recognizes him. "This man also was with him," she tells the guards. He denies his connection for the second time: "Woman, I do not know him."

Meanwhile, Annas accosts Yehoshua with questions about his disciples and his teaching. This is not a formal trial—none of the Jewish mock trials have any legal Roman weight—and this one is best seen as a private inquisition by a mafia boss. This preacher is a major threat to the family business. Yehoshua has a huge following, including some zealot-types and who knows how many warlike Galileans. Messiahs always try to take over the temple, and Yehoshua is the most popular candidate yet. The rabbi insists he has nothing to hide. "I have spoken openly to the world. I have always taught in synagogues and in the temple, where all Jews come together. I have said nothing in secret. Why do you ask me? Ask those who have heard me what I said to them; they know what I said" (John 18:20–21).

Like every good mafia interrogator, one of the nearby temple officers illegally slaps the still-tied-up Yehoshua in the face. "Is that how you answer the high priest?"

Yehoshua knows his legal rights. "If what I said is wrong, bear witness about the wrong; but if what I said is right, why do you strike me?" (v. 23).

We do not know how long Annas interrogates Yehoshua, but it is likely the longest of his trials. If Yehoshua is arrested around midnight, it may have lasted as long as six hours. Does Annas try to cut a deal with Yehoshua, offering him a bribe to go away or join the temple hierarchy? It wouldn't be out of character. If the wildly popular rabbi says no, everything is at stake for Annas. It doesn't matter if Yehoshua plans to destroy the temple, overthrow the temple hierarchy and occupy it himself, or be the military messiah who finally overthrows Rome—any scenario sees an immediate unseating for Annas and the end of his wealth and power. The highest of priests does the math. No matter what, Yehoshua must die. It's not personal—it's just business.

Nearing dawn, Annas realizes he is getting nowhere. He sends Yehoshua to his son-in-law's synedrion, who have now assembled in Caiaphas's quarters within the mansion. It's time to get their corrupt court to charge this man with something the Romans can execute him for, while still maintaining the charade that this is all about faith and religion. It's not an easy needle to thread, but this isn't his first execution.

Down in the courtyard, Simon continues to be plagued by inquisitors all night. Around the fire, someone insists Simon is a disciple because of his northern accent. "Certainly this man also was with him, for he too is a Galilean."

Simon is empathic. "Man, I do not know what you are talking about" (Luke 22:59–60).

Trial #2

Sunrise in Jerusalem is 6:26 a.m. It is the third day of the Roman month of Aprilis, the day of Venus, which we now call Friday.

Luke 22:66 says the chief priests, their lawyers, and the aristocrats gather at the crack of dawn, thus fulfilling their religionist rule about not holding a trial in the dark, and lead Yehoshua before their synedrion. There are almost certainly fewer than seventy people present, if only because it is so early, and because only twenty-three are necessary to form a quorum in the Sanhedrin's later iteration. Moreover, Annas has probably excluded anyone and everyone who will vote against his will. The Sabbath is less than twenty-four hours away, and everyone is desperate to get this errant rabbi killed quickly so they can maintain the appearance of being ritually clean for the most profitable of festival weekends.

They cut straight to the point and ask Yehoshua if he is the Christ. Yet another messiah claimant could be very bad for business. Luke 22:67 clocks the rabbi's reply: "If I tell you, you will not believe."

An exasperated synedrion seeks testimony and/or evidence they can use to put him to death, but they can't find any. A whole host of folk break the ninth commandment by bearing false witness against Yehoshua (Exodus 20:16), but they can't find a way to make their stories match up, and it takes two male witnesses to make an ironclad Jewish case. Not only that, but they break all sorts of their own religionist rules by holding a trial during a feast week, by not voting individually but by acclamation, by not waiting a full night before carrying out a death penalty sentence, by asking the accused questions of self-incrimination, and by not allowing the accused to have legal representation. But again, these are not good and faithful Jews.

Finally, two religionists stand and falsely claim, "We heard him say, 'I will destroy this temple that is made with hands, and in three days I will build another, not made with hands'" (Mark 14:58). This likely gets the high priests to pay attention, as the temple is their golden goose. But this isn't what Yehoshua actually said. When asked by whose authority he preaches, Yehoshua said that if *they* "Destroy this temple . . . in three days I will raise it up" (John 2:19). As usual, it's just a rabbinical play on words. The temple he's referencing isn't the physical Jerusalem stone pile, but his own body.

Greatly annoyed, Caiaphas stands and addresses Yehoshua. "Well, aren't you going to answer these charges? What do you have to say for yourself?" Before a corrupt court, an innocent man need not waste his breath, so the rabbi stays silent. Plus, he knows what every religionist in the room knows—that Caiaphas has broken the law. As high priest, he is supposed to be the impartial judge, not the accusatory prosecutor.

Caiaphas presses him again. "I adjure you by the living God, tell us if are you the Christ, the Son of God" (Matthew 26:63).

It is an excellent question—two heavily load questions, actually—and no matter how Yehoshua answers, it's a win for the House of Annas. If he says he isn't the Messiah and the Son of God, they can publicly discredit him. If he says he is, they can hand him over to the Romans.

Knowing they have him—and more important, knowing his time has come—Yehoshua finally admits it publicly: "I am, and you will see the Son of Man seated at the right hand of Power, and coming with the clouds of heaven" (Mark 14:62).

There it is. The theological and political shoe drop. In one sentence, Yehoshua has declared himself God of the universe and king of Israel. The great irony is that this is what *real* Jews have been praying for forever. The House of Annas has what it needs to convince the Jews *and* the Romans.

Joseph Caiaphas tears his clothes, the formal sign of condemnation according to the religionist rulebook. Disregarding the fact that the high priest is forbidden by Mosaic law from performing this action (Leviticus 10:6; Leviticus 21:10), he launches into an oh-so-holy tirade. "He has uttered blasphemy. What further witnesses do we need? You have now heard his blasphemy from his own lips. What is your judgment?"

The sycophant synedrion replies, "He deserves death" (Matthew 26:65–66).

Annas must be proud of his son-in-law for another hit job well executed. His boy is the high priest, the only individual in the nation who can enter the Holy of Holies once each year on the Day of Atonement and offer a sacrifice to God for his own sins and the sins of the people. Sure, killing this Galilean rabbi isn't ideal, but it's nothing that the blood of a spotless lamb can't wash away.

The guards lead Yehoshua out of Caiaphas's chambers and through the courtyard on their way to the Roman governor's headquarters.

In the same courtyard, one of the slaves of the high priest, a relative of Malchus who was there for the arrest, asks Simon Peter if he wasn't just in the garden with Yehoshua. For the third time, Simon Peter denies his association with Yehoshua, and *within earshot of his rabbi, no less*. "Man, I do not know what you are talking about" (Luke 22:60). Before he can finish speaking, the morning rooster crows.

Yehoshua turns and looks straight at Simon (Luke 22:61). It hits the lead disciple like a ton of bricks. Simon Peter rushes outside and weeps.

The courtyard mob wants their pound of flesh before handing Yehoshua over to the Romans. As they take him away, they spit on him, blindfold him, slap his face, and punch him.

While Annas's temple guards abuse Yehoshua, the chief priests and their synedrion put together their plan for how to see this man successfully executed by the Romans as quickly as possible (Matthew 27:1). While Yehoshua is pummeled with hands and fists, the high priests settle on a charge that all but guarantees the death penalty. It will go down as one of the most brilliant legal moves in history.

Trial #3

It is early morning (John 18:28). The religionist mob (with Yehoshua's Thunder Son cousin John likely on the edges) heads for the gates of the Praetorium, a former Herodian palace now occupied by the governor and his soldiers. The Passover crowd is mostly still slumbering, sleeping off a heavy Passover supper and at least four cups of wine. Little does the Roman governor know that this morning's verdict will make him world famous, or rather, eternally infamous. The man in question is Prefect Pontius Pilatus, who is likely unhappy at being awoken so early on the busiest and most nuisance-filled weekend of his year. He normally lives in the cushy seaside town of Caesarea Maritima, but political necessity requires him to keep the peace in Jerusalem—the *Pax Romana*—during these tinderbox festivals. In his *Legatio ad Gaium*, Philo of Alexandria calls Pilate "a man of inflexible, stubborn and cruel disposition," and on this dark day, he will declare a man innocent and then sentence him to death.

This is not Pilate's first run-in with the House of Annas. Indeed, the two have been doing the delicate dance for seven years, jostling for power without openly antagonizing the other. The great exception to this is the Aqueduct Riots. Jerusalem needs water and Annas refuses to do his duty, so Pilate forces him to hand over temple funds to get the job done. In retaliation, Annas waits for Pilate to arrive at the aqueduct's dedication and then leaks it to the masses that it is a Roman robbery. Annas sits back and lets the people riot in the streets. Pilate had expected this double-cross and is ready with his own response—his men use clubs to beat an unspecified number of Jews to death. (This may be the clash alluded to in Luke 13:1.) No doubt Annas files a complaint with the Romans to have Pilate sacked, but so far, the governor has held on.

Still, Pilate's position as prefect is far from secure. The number two man in charge of the Roman Empire, Sejanus—potentially the friend or military mentor who got Pilate the job—has recently been executed for suspected treason, and Pilate must not only maintain the *Pax Romana* but ensure his personal commitment to the Caesar at all costs. Annas, of course, knows all of this and will wield it to great effect.

Being the good religionists that they are, Yehoshua's nominally Jewish accusers refuse to set foot inside the Gentile building. This way, they remain undefiled and can carry out their all-important priestly duties for the rest of the festival, aka their most profitable week of the fiscal year. No doubt greatly annoyed by their idiosyncratic superstitions, Pilate knows he can't meet them on the streets—it's too dangerous for him, and Annas wants to keep the whole thing quiet because he's terrified of the crowds. Instead, they meet between Pilate's outer gate and inner gate, inside a private 26- by 36-foot open-roofed courtyard that archaeologists now call the Hidden Gate. The spot is perfect: safety for Pilate, privacy for Annas, sanctity for the religionists. The House of Annas and their hangers-on flood the small space as Pilate comes out to meet them (John 18:29).

The most powerful Roman in Israel squares off against the most powerful Jew in the world. He has lost to Annas before, but Pilate has a plan this time. He will follow Roman legal procedure and then play his trump card at the last possible moment.

He begins with the Roman *interrogatio*, or statement of charges. "What charges are you bringing against this man?" (John 18:29 NIV).

They—likely Annas—reply pathetically, "If this man were not doing evil, we would not have delivered him over to you."

Pilate scoffs. He is not interested in conjecture and the arcane rules and ramblings of backward religionists. "Take him yourselves and judge him by your own law" (John 18:30–31).

But only the Romans were permitted to execute someone. So they level accusations that will appeal to a *Roman* ear: "We have found this man subverting our nation. He opposes payment of taxes to Caesar and claims to be Messiah, a king" (Luke 23:2 NIV).

Not a charge of blasphemy. Not a charge of Sabbath-breaking. A presumed political message and aggressive agitator actions. The House of Annas has entered their charge: Yehoshua claims to be the king of the Jews.

It is a brilliant, lethal charge, locked and loaded with an implicit threat aimed squarely at Pilate. If the Roman prefect lets this man go, the House of Annas will fire off a letter to Tiberius, claiming Pilate isn't faithful to Caesar. Pilate will not only lose his post but will likely lose his head just as his boss Sejanus recently did. But if Annas leaks word that Pilate has executed the most popular teacher in Israel, the crowds could lose their minds.

What a nightmare for the prefect.

Pilate stares at sleep-deprived Yehoshua's bruised face and starts Rome's official examination by asking the defendant flat-out if he is the king of the Jews.

This is an excellent question. Yehoshua can't lie—he really does believe he is the king of the Jews—but he can't simply say yes because the answer is far more nuanced than Pilate can imagine.

So Yehoshua neither confirms nor denies the accusation, essentially pleading no contest. "You have said so" (Mark 15:2).

One would think the chief prosecutor would be Caiaphas the high priest, but all three synoptic gospels say the chief *priests* bring multiple charges against Yehoshua (Mark 15:3; Matthew 27:12; Luke 23:4–5).

Yehoshua responds to none of them.

Pilate basically yells to Yehoshua, "Don't you have an answer?!"

Still nothing.

Pilate is amazed at the rabbi's composure. He brings him inside for private questioning, once again asking, "Are you the king of the Jews?"

Yehoshua answers the question with a question. "Do you say this of your own accord, or did others say it to you about me?" (John 18:34).

Pilate likely laughs. "Am I a Jew? Your own nation and the chief priests have delivered you over to me What have you done?"

Yehoshua repeats what he's been saying the whole time, assuring the Roman that he poses zero threat to their earthly political order. "My kingdom is not of this world. If my kingdom were of this world, my servants would have been fighting, that I might not be delivered over to the Jews. But my kingdom is not from the world."

Pilate likely laughs again. "So you are a king?"

"You say that I am a king. For this purpose I was born and for this purpose I have come into the world—to bear witness to the truth. Everyone who is of the truth listens to my voice."

Pilate answers cynically, "What is truth?"

The prefect returns to Annas's mob outside and announces, "I find no guilt in him" (John 18:35–38).

But the crowd is insistent and presses the political angle: "He stirs up the people, teaching throughout all Judea, from Galilee even to this place" (Luke 23:5).

Pilate's ears perk up when he hears the word *Galilee*. This fellow is Galilean? Perfect. Galilee is the jurisdiction of Herod Antipas, and the half-Jew client king is in town as we speak. Let him deal. The temple guards cannot be happy with the decision, but it pleases Pilate, who hates Antipas. The religionists have no choice but to once again drag Yehoshua across town.

Trial #4

Herod Antipas the Tetrarch-Fox is delighted to see the famous rabbi. He's been wanting to meet him for a long time and is hoping to see a miracle (Luke 23:8). But today he is sorely disappointed. He plies Yehoshua at length, but the exhausted rabbi refuses to answer. Not content with a second of silence, the chief priests and their lawyers vehemently hurl their baseless accusations at the sleep-deprived defendant (Luke 23:10).

As with Yehoshua's kinsman John the Baptizer before him, Herod's admiration quickly turns to contempt. But he decides not to behead Yehoshua, because the rabbi clearly hasn't committed any crime (Luke 23:15). Plus, Antipas doesn't need the political headache of killing two desert apocalypse preacher-cousins. If the Galilean will not play court magician, Antipas will make him play court jester. He tells his soldiers to dress up the rabbi in kingly clothing (Luke 23:11) and send him back to Pilate.

Trial #5

Pilate thinks this royal dress-up gag is hilarious. In fact, the two former enemies actually bond over the joke and later become friends (Luke 23:12). Still, this Galilean rabbi is clearly not guilty of anything warranting Roman execution. Pilate calls together the chief priests and their posse (Luke 23:13). Mark 15:10 notes that Pilate "perceived that it was out of envy that the chief priests had delivered him up."

"You brought me this man as one who was misleading the people. And after examining him before you, behold, I did not find this man guilty of any of your charges against him. Neither did Herod, for he sent him back to us. Look, nothing deserving death has been done by him. I will therefore punish and release him" (Luke 23:14–16).

Pilate thinks this is a fair deal for both parties. Annas will get the guilty verdict he so desires, Yehoshua will get a stern warning to cool it, and Pilate will be seen as a faithful Roman while simultaneously avoiding an Annas- or Yehoshua-led riot. *Pax Romana* resolved.

To sweeten the deal, Pilate offers them a prisoner exchange, but not because he is scared of these Jewish religionists—if anything, he is trolling them, trying to get them to give up their obvious persecution of an innocent man. The prefect has a hardened criminal in his dungeon, a notorious insurrectionist who committed murder in one of many recent uprisings (Matthew 27:16; Mark 15:7). Surely these God-loving Jews will take the innocent preacher over the proven murderer. The criminal's name, according to some ancient manuscripts of Matthew 27:16–17, is . . . wait for it . . . Yehoshua Barabbas.

Pilate asks the crowd, "Which one do you want me to release to you: Jesus Barabbas, or Jesus who is called the Messiah?" (Matthew 27:17 NIV).

Note the wordplay here. Yehoshua Bar-abbas means "Son of the father," and our Yehoshua claims to be the heavenly father's son. Will the religionists choose death or life, violence or nonviolence, flesh or spirit? Will it be an armed insurgent or an unarmed messiah?

The chief priests whip their sycophants into a frenzy (Mark 15:11). "Barabbas!" they shout.

Pilate begins to deftly move into position for the final kill.

Instead of passing judgment, he throws it open to the House of Annas. "Then what shall I do with the man you call the King of the Jews?"

They shout back: "Crucify him."

"Why? What evil has he done?" (Mark 15:12–15).

They scream him down—justice and evidence have never mattered in this case. "If you release this man, you are not Caesar's friend. Everyone who makes himself a king opposes Caesar" (John 19:12).

Annas's implicit threat has now been vocalized. Murder this Jew, or we will report you to Caesar and you will lose your job if not your head.

It may seem as though Annas has Pilate on the ropes, but this is exactly where Pilate wants Annas. The prefect plunks down on his judgment seat and parades Yehoshua before the mob of high priests, lawyers, aristocrats, temple guards, religionists, and supporters, taunting them. "Behold your King!"

The crowd shouts, "Away with him, away with him, crucify him!"

"Shall I crucify your King?"

The *chief priests alone* answer: "We have no king but Caesar" (John 19:15).

And there we have the truth of the matter. This is not an assembly of faithful Jews, but rather a mob of political expedients whose allegiance is not to YHWH but to power itself. The House of Annas is not faithful to the God of heaven but to the *Pax Romana*. They have denied their nation, denied the messianic hope, and denied the ultimate authority of the Jewish nation—YHWH himself (Judges 8:23; 1 Samuel 8:7).

Does a crowd of faithful Passover pilgrims really want a corruption-ending, temple-mocking, body-healing, food-providing revolutionary fellow Jew to be tortured and murdered by the Romans? No. This is a crowd of paid actors, rounded up and controlled by the House of Annas, less than a hundred of the most zealous beneficiaries who profit greatly from their unearned place in the corrupt political hierarchy.

Pilate realizes he has the start of a proper Passover riot on his hands—the very thing Yehoshua has been accused of inciting. He comes to the same conclusion as Annas's son-in-law Caiaphas: Better to let one Jew die than to have a whole city in an uproar. So rather than enforcing holy justice and cracking down on the riotous crowd—and certainly not wanting to gain a reputation as a sympathizer against Caesar—he plays his trump card.

The prefect calls for a bowl of water and publicly washes his hands. "I am innocent of this man's blood; see to it yourselves."

The crowd answers, "his blood be on us and on our children!" (Matthew 27:24–25).

Checkmate.

Pilate wins.

The House of Annas has issued the charges, declined the lesser punishment offer, rejected the prisoner trade, chosen the final penalty, pledged their allegiance to the *Pax Romana*, and promised to deal with the fallout. Pilate finally has the upper hand on the highest of priests. Now Annas owes him. Pilate will grant Annas's request and kill this Galilean, but if the rabbi's followers rise up in protest, Pilate knows the temple administration will deal with it. Unlike with the aqueduct fiasco, the House of Annas will support Rome against the disciples of Yehoshua to their dying day.

Does Pilate feel bad that this Galilean is just a chess piece in the priest and prefect's game?

Does Pilate have any clue that he and Annas are chess pieces in Yehoshua's infinitely bigger game?

Having finally extracted loyalty from Annas, Pilate turns the rabbi over to the Roman soldiers to be flogged and crucified. Yehoshua ben Yehoseph will be murdered as a public and private political nuisance.

Crucifixion

Author's note: The following section is extremely graphic. Readers with weak stomachs should finish this paragraph and then skip ahead. I include what follows with a determined purpose; to sugarcoat or gloss over the crucifixion is to cheapen and dishonor Yehoshua's vast sacrifice. We must not for a moment allow ourselves to romanticize the cross. While most Christian books gloss over the naked facts, the sheer brutality of crucifixion cannot be overlooked. We can get a sense of this truth by realizing that symbols of the cross appear nowhere in ancient Christian art for the first three centuries after Yehoshua's murder. The early church simply could not bring themselves to face this horrific instrument of torture, as it was still in use against members of their own communities. The cross was the looming threat over all their lives, and when we see a cross, we should quake as they did.

Rome practices the vile art of capital punishment in many forms. Paul of Tarsus will be decapitated. Nero will burn Christians to death. Some are hurled from the eighty-foot-high Tarpeian Rock. Others are forced into the arena to compete as gladiators, or to play a role in savage war reenactments, or to be eaten by wild beasts for the entertainment of the bloodthirsty masses. Seneca will be forced to drink hemlock, while others will slit their wrists in warm baths. A few are tied in a sack with a snake or an ape and thrown in the Tiber River. But the *summum supplicium*—the supreme penalty—is crucifixion.

As a prelude to crucifixion, Pilate sends Yehoshua for a flogging. Deuteronomy 25:3 set a legal limit of forty lashes, with additional religionist rules ensuring one less (just to be safe), delivered in three sets of thirteen unlucky blows. But the Romans obey no such law and set no limit on their whippings, which are reserved exclusively for non-Romans.

The scourge in question is a *flagrum* or *flagellum*, made of two or three ox-hide straps attached to a wooden handle. The leather thongs are knotted with bone, tooth, or shards of zinc or iron or bronze; perfect for flaying chunks of flesh from the bodies of its victims. Victims experienced disfiguring lacerations, the loss of eyes, and the exposure of veins, muscles, sinews, or even bone. Josephus proudly notes in *Wars* Book 2, 21:5, that he had a handful of Galilean rebels whipped until their entrails were visible. Multiple Roman historians report that flagellation victims occasionally died of shock and copious blood loss, though the idea is to beat them to within an inch of their life, leaving them with just enough strength to carry their own cross before crucifixion finishes them off.

Yehoshua is stripped naked and either tied to a low post (so the flesh on his back is loose and will easily rip) or strung taut from a high pillar (so the tight flesh will split upon contact). Roman floggings were not limited to the bare back but could range from the neck and shoulders to the lower back and buttocks to the soles of the victim's feet. While none of the four gospel writers go into detail, we may assume Yehoshua takes an above-average beating—in moments, he will be unable to carry his cross, and the flagrum's only consolation was that it shortened the agony of crucifixion by inducing death sooner, as will soon be the case for Yehoshua.

Yehoshua is unchained from the dreaded pole. He has not slept all night, his face is swollen from earlier punches, and the flesh of his back now hangs in shreds. It is around 9 a.m. (Mark 15:25), and the whole garrison comes out of their barracks to bid farewell to their latest victim. They dress him up in a scarlet-purple robe, set a crown made of twisted thorns on his head, and put a staff in his right hand. Upwards of six hundred Romans kneel and salute, taunting "Hail, King of the Jews!" They rise and spit on him, slapping his face and pounding him on the head with the staff. Roman mockery is well documented in history, and Yehoshua is just one of an untold number of victims to endure this shame and abuse. Once they've had their fun, they take off the royal robe, put his own clothes back on him, and lead him out to be crucified with two other criminals—political revolutionaries in some translations.

But Yehoshua is too weak to carry his cross for long. As they leave the city gates, the Romans force a North African passerby coming in from the countryside to carry the cross behind the struggling rabbi. The man is Simon from Cyrene, and he has two sons, Alexander and Rufus, though the text doesn't necessarily say they are with him (Mark 15:21). A large crowd follows Yehoshua and Simon and the Romans, including "many grief-stricken women."

Their destination is one of the few Aramaic words that break into our English Bibles: Golgotha. It means "place of the skull," either for the shape of a human skull on the cliffside just outside the city walls, or for the number of human remains scattered in the vicinity. When they reach the place, Yehoshua is offered (likely by the women) a mix of wine and myrrh, meant to help deaden the agony of crucifixion. It is by no means a sedative, but more of a mild analgesic. But after tasting it, *Yehoshua refuses to take the painkiller.*

The soldiers then crucify Yehoshua with the two other criminals—not likely mere thieves if they're receiving the death penalty—placing one on each side of the rabbi (John 19:18).

Crucifixion most likely started with the Assyrians and Babylonians and was used by the Persians since the sixth century BC. Alexander the Great readily seized upon the innovative torture in the fourth century, and it is the Phoenicians who introduced it to the Romans in the third century BC. Romans crucify their enemies in one of four ways, but the gospel writers do not specify the method used on Yehoshua.

The first and most primitive option is the *crux simplex*, a straight pole without a crossbeam. The victim is either impaled upon the pole (as in Ezra 6:11), or they are nailed to it with their arms stretched above their head. A single spike is driven through crossed wrists into the stake, with a second spike driven through crossed ankles. The single-pole method is how Jehovah's Witnesses believe Yehoshua was crucified.

But more often than not, a crossbeam is used, as in the T-shaped *crux commissa*. In this instance, the victim's arms are nailed to the crossbeam, or their arms and elbows are draped and tied over the beam. If a cross is not available, a victim can be affixed to a tree trunk with his arms nailed to the branches. Having a crossbeam prolongs the victim's suffering compared with having the hands nailed above the head, the latter of which can induce death by suffocation in less than an hour. Many early church fathers believe this is how Yehoshua is crucified.

The *crux decussata* is X-shaped. The Roman numeral X is our ten, and their *decussis* coin was worth ten of the next smaller coin. Now known as a saltire or St. Andrew's cross, the victim is nailed and tied in a spread-eagled position.

The *crux immissa* has a horizontal crossbeam, called a *patibulum,* affixed to an upright pole (called a *stipe*) in the shape of a lower-case t. This is the shape that will become the macabre symbol of Christianity. *Immissa* means "inserted"—in this case, connoting how the *patibulum* inserts into the vertical *stipe* by way of a mortise and tenon joint. There are two variations on this cross, namely, the *crux sublimis* (the tall cross) and the *crux humilis,* which could stand the victim just a few inches above eye level. A wooden *sedulum* can be affixed halfway down the cross to act as a makeshift seat, and in later times a second block of wood, called a *suppedaneum,* would very rarely be added under the feet.

These are not the only ways to crucify a victim. The Romans executed so many thousands during the Siege of Jerusalem that they took it upon themselves to concoct new methods and bodily arrangements. Josephus writes in *The Jewish War,* "The soldiers, out of the wrath and hatred they bore the Jews, nailed those they caught, one after one way and another after another, to the crosses, by way of jest." Seneca wrote to his friend Marcia (*Moral*

Essays), "I see instruments of torture, not indeed of a single kind, but differently contrived by different peoples; some hang their victims with head toward the ground, some impale their private parts, others stretch out their arms on a fork-shaped gibbet; I see cords, I see scourges, and for each separate limb and each joint there is a separate engine of torture." In other cases, they simply drive the stake "straight through a man until it protrudes from his throat."

Based on the length of time Yehoshua suffers, let us presume that he is not crucified on a *simplex*. Knowing Andrew's future request to be killed in a different shape as his rabbi, we can also rule out the saltire. This leaves us with an upright pole and a horizontal crossbeam. The low capital-T cross is the preferred shape in Palestine in the first century, but we cannot say for sure that it was not a high T.

Yehoshua is stripped naked—the entire purpose of this public execution is to induce as much shame and humiliation as possible—and his arms are stretched along the crossbeam as he lies in the dirt, his open wounds making blood-mud on the ground. Some victims have their arms tied, while others are nailed through the hands or wrists. John says his cousin is indeed nailed to the cross; crucifixion spikes that have been found are roughly six inches in length with a square shaft. Each hammer blow would send shockwaves of agony through Yehoshua's nervous system.

Once both of his arms are firmly nailed to the wood, the crossbeam and victim are hoisted onto the *stipe*. Four or fewer soldiers can perform the maneuver on a low cross, with forks and ladders used for taller crosses. Once the cross is in place, the victim's feet are wrenched into extension as a spike is driven through the feet, twisting the knees into extreme flexion.

From here, it is simply a waiting game. Death can come from heart failure, sepsis, dehydration, blood loss, and a host of other painful conditions including acidosis or hypovolemic shock. If

Yehoshua's arms are extended upward behind him, death is induced by slow asphyxiation. As the whole weight of the body is supported by outstretched arms, the chest presses down on the lungs, making every breath a nightmare.

This is by no means the end of the victim's torment. Soldiers were free to do what they wanted with the victim, such as cutting off an ear or tongue or spearing out an eye. Josephus reports how one set of soldiers under the Greek king Antiochus IV hung a victim's strangled child around his neck.

In addition to harassment from soldiers, crucifixion victims also have to endure nature. Any manner of insects can feed on or burrow into open wounds. Birds of prey can swoop in for a quick peck of flesh. The slow process of dying can take as long as four days—fewer, if the earlier scourging is particularly severe. The entire process of crucifixion is unbelievably painful; it is where we get the word *excruciating*.

But there is a spiritual component as well. Crucifixion is tantamount to hanging from a tree, which both Old and New Testament writers view as being cursed by God (Deuteronomy 21:22–23; Galatians 3:13). As Yehoshua tries to find the least painful position on this horrific "tree," we must remember that this entire act is voluntary. He believes he must be murdered to take the punishment of all human sin on his shoulders. This horrendously slow murder is nothing less than self-sacrificial agape in action.

With the crucifixion underway, soldiers can affix a *titulus* atop the cross, listing the name of the criminal and his crime. This is easier done on a low T than a high T, but it can be done in either case with the help of a ladder. Sometimes they simply hung it around the convict's neck. Sticking with Herod Antipas's dress-up king joke, Pilate orders a sign to be posted on the cross in Aramaic (the common tongue), Latin (the official Roman), and the international Greek: *Iēsous Nazōraios Basileus Ioudaiōn*. He wants all the Passover pilgrims to know this offender and his offense: *Yehoshua of Nazareth, King of the Jews*.

His crime is unquestionably political.

Ever the nit-picking religionists, the chief priests unbelievably ask Pilate to edit his sign: "Do not write, 'The King of the Jews,' but rather, 'This man said, I am King of the Jews'" (John 19:21).

Pilate has had enough from the House of Annas this day, and replies, "What I have written I have written."

We cannot comprehend the public humiliation of this sort of death. Golgotha is a well-trafficked area, close to the city, perhaps even at an intersection or crossroads, and each cross serves as a warning and a deterrent against disobedience and uprising at this Passover feast. Moreover, the naked victims are disfigured, bloody, looking inhuman enough to treat with contempt despite their sorry state. No wonder they called it the slave's death. We cannot imagine the level of PTSD and psychological torture the average Jerusalemite endured at the regular sight of dying bodies twisting in pain, lungs gasping, throats howling. No wonder they never spoke of crucifixion in public.

Rome massacred millions upon millions during its centuries-long reign of terror; it is impossible to know exactly how many victims met their end by crucifixion. General Varus crucified two thousand Jews in 4 BC. The Spartacus revolt of 73 BC saw upwards of six thousand crucified along the Appian Way in a *single day*. Adult male political "terrorists" weren't the only ones murdered in this horrific fashion. In 66 AD, the Roman governor Florus whipped and crucified 3,600 victims, including women, children, and infants. Four years later, during the Siege of 70 AD, the starving poor who tried to escape Jerusalem were crucified at a rate of five hundred per day until the Romans *ran out of wood*.

Crucifixion was nothing short of state terrorism.

The Romans crucified tens if not hundreds of thousands of victims over more than half a millennia. Guess how many crucified skeletons we have recovered in the Middle East to date?

One. The first-century specimen was found in 1968 in northeast Jerusalem. The burial site contains the bones of thirty-five people in all, including three children who starved to death, a mother and infant who died in childbirth, a teenager roasted alive on a rack, and a preschooler pierced with an arrow. The crucified man was found in a wealthy family tomb, and the name on the ossuary identifies the victim as Yehohanan ben Hagkol—John son of Hagkol. He is no older than age twenty-eight, stands just under five-feet-six (average height at the time), and there is a 7.5-inch spike through the heel bone. The spike was driven into the olive wood so hard that it bent and could not be removed, thus leaving us with proof of crucifixion at the same time and place as Yehoshua. Young John's crucifixion varies from the image we have of Yehoshua's. John's ankles were hammered into the sides of the wooden pole, and his hands and elbows were draped over the beam and tied instead of nailed.

Why only one skeleton out of potentially hundreds of thousands? Perhaps because it was rare to bury the body of a crucifixion victim. Normally, victims were denied even this last dignity, instead being thrown in rivers or trash heaps or shallow graves, serving as carrion for birds and meat for dogs and worms. In other words, there was almost never a body left to bury. Very rarely, a family member or relative would petition the court to retrieve the corpse, but it was dangerous to do so as it would immediately identify you as a friend of the criminal. Normally only people in positions of power made such requests. For example, Josephus manages to save the life of an old acquaintance who is in the middle of being crucified during the Siege of Jerusalem.

As readers, we can envision many serene Jesus statues we have seen carved on church walls, but what does the crucified Yehoshua look like?

He is completely naked, genitals exposed, on a high-traffic thoroughfare filled with the sounds of mockery from Jews and

Romans alike. He is presumably cursed by God, sunburned and parched by Middle Eastern heat and the afternoon sun, wounded and bruised from head to foot, his head and back bleeding from countless festering mud-caked cuts, his eyes and ears plagued by flies he cannot swat away. If he is the average victim of the time, he hangs on a T-shaped crossbeam that is just a few inches above eye level. He is wracked with pain. He rocks his cross to heave out every breath, the whip wounds scraping open against the cross's grain with each inhalation. At the foot of the cross is a slowly expanding pool of blood, sweat, urine, and feces. Vultures circle above and wild dogs linger nearby, ready to strip the meat from his bones when the crowd goes home.

May we forever shudder at the sight of a cross.

It is midmorning, and now that Yehoshua is dangling in the air, the Roman soldiers turn their attention to his clothing. What is Yehoshua's net worth on the day of his execution? Nothing but the clothes off his bloody back.

The Romans divide his outer *himation* cloak into four pieces, then cast lots to see who gets to keep his cheap one-piece *chiton* tunic.

As people go about their morning business, some recognize the rabbi and hurl insults in passing. "Aha! You who would destroy the temple and rebuild it in three days, save yourself, and come down from the cross!"

Annas, Caiaphas, the aristocrats, and their lawyers, even though it is Passover weekend and they've been up all night, cannot help but venture out of the temple to taunt their dying enemy (Mark 15:31; Matthew 27:41–43): "He saved others; he cannot save himself." "Let the Messiah, the King of Israel, come down now from the cross that we may see and believe." The great irony is that the two "robbers" being crucified with Yehoshua are called *lestai* (Matthew 27:44), the exact same thing Yehoshua called Annas and Caiaphas when he purged the temple. The gospel writers leave readers to wonder if the Romans didn't execute the wrong pair of thieves on April 3, 33 AD.

Inspired by the House of Annas, the Roman soldiers pile on the indignities, offering Yehoshua sour wine and saying, "If you are the King of the Jews, save yourself!" Even one of the two criminals rails against this so-called Savior.

So who of the disciples are left to witness this scene? Of the tens of thousands who ate Yehoshua's bread, of the hundreds who acquired his healing, of the seventy-odd disciples who accepted his teaching, who remains at the foot of the cross?

All four gospel writers admit the truth: It is the female disciples who stay faithful and courageous to the end.

Matthew says, "Many women were there, looking on from a distance, who had followed Jesus from Galilee, ministering to him" (27:55).

Mark says that some women were watching from a distance. "When he was in Galilee, they followed him and ministered to him, and there were also many other women who came up with him to Jerusalem" (15:41).

Luke says that "the women who had followed him from Galilee stood at a distance watching these things" (23:49).

John names Yehoshua's mother Mary, Yehoshua's aunt Salome, Maggie, and Aunt Mary the mother of Yehoshua's disciple Little James (John 19:25). Notice John's wonderful literary juxtaposition: the four plundering soldiers versus the four prayerful women.

In total, the full count of named witnesses numbers just five: Mary the mother of Yehoshua, Maggie, Aunt Mary the mother of Little James, Aunt Salome mother of the Thunder Sons, and "the disciple who Yehoshua loved," cousin John, who has likely been awake all night, staying close to his rabbi for the duration of this horrific affair.

Where are all the cocksure young men now? Eleven of the inner twelve disciples are entirely absent from the story, yet nearly a third of their mothers show up.

While the other female disciples hang back at a distance, the four closest women and John stand near the cross, within earshot of Yehoshua's weakening voice. It is at this moment that Yehoshua touchingly commits his mother Mary to his cousin John's care, suggesting that her husband Joseph has indeed passed away and Yehoshua has been caring for her. The rabbi's cousin reports in John 19:27 that "from that hour the disciple took her to his own home."

It is surreal to stop and consider the reality that crucifixion victims continue to speak while being crucified; even more so if it happens near eye level. We have seven recorded sentences from Yehoshua's hours on the cross, and it is not hard to imagine that he doesn't say much more than that over the six hours his lungs slowly drain of oxygen. They are words of forgiveness (Luke 23:34), salvation (Luke 23:43), provision (John 19:26), petition (John 19:28), trust (Mark 15:34), faith (Luke 23:46), and triumph (John 19:30).

At around noon, all three synoptic gospels report "there was darkness over the whole land" for three hours. The Passover full moon rules out the possibility of an eclipse, so we may guess an exceedingly black, God-sent storm system passes over Judea. This is Yehoshua's dark night of the soul. At around 3 p.m., he cries out in a loud voice, "*Eloi, Eloi, lema sabachthani*?"

"My God, my God, why have you forsaken me?"

This is decidedly *not* a desperate cry of despair. Yehoshua is not expressing deep feelings of abandonment toward YHWH. He is not questioning his faith. In fact, he is doing the exact opposite.

Because this phrase is a verbatim quoting of the first line of Psalm 22.

Rabbis often quoted just the first line of a text (or even the first word, in the case of the *Shema*), and sharp disciples immediately seized the inference. For those of us unfamiliar with the unbelievable beauty of Psalm 22, here are a few stanzas written by Yehoshua's ancestor almost exactly a millennia earlier:

> "My God, my God, why have you forsaken me?
> Why are you so far from saving me,
> from my words of groaning?
> O my God, I cry by day, but you do not answer,
> and by night, but I find no rest.
>
> My strength is dried up like a potsherd,
> and my tongue sticks to my jaws;
> you lay me in the dust of death.
> For dogs encompass me,
> a company of evildoers encircles me;
> they have pierced my hands and my feet—
> I can count all my bones—
> they stare and gloat over me;
> they divide my garments among them,
> and for my clothing they cast lots.
>
> All the prosperous of the earth eat and worship;
> before him shall bow all who go down to the dust,
> even the one who could not keep himself alive.
> Posterity shall serve him;
> it shall be told of the Lord to the coming generation;
> they shall come and proclaim his righteousness to a
> people yet unborn,
> that he has done it."
>
> (vv. 1, 15–18, 29–31).

These are the thoughts that run through the mind of a dying Yehoshua. He knows his situation is dire, yet his is a prayer of complete and total surrender, truth, and faith that YHWH will fulfill his promise.

Yehoshua has voluntarily undergone this entire horrific ordeal because he believes it is necessary to save humanity from sin and death. Without offering up his life as a substitute atonement sacrifice for human sin, people like Maggie and Rocky and you and I will be obliterated by the radiant perfection of YHWH himself. While Yehoshua's bodily death is a political assassination, the spiritual implications reverberate beyond existence itself.

It is afternoon.

Yehoshua calls out for a drink, gasping out just two words: "I thirst."

He does not do this because he suddenly now needs a shot of painkiller after multiple hours of heinous torture. No, he is in complete control of this execution, and he speaks these words to fulfill the prophecy of Psalm 69:21. Someone (not likely a Roman soldier) soaks a sponge in sour wine, impales it on a hyssop branch, and holds it to Yehoshua's parched lips. After receiving the wine, Yehoshua summons the last of his strength and again cries out in a loud voice, "Father, into your hands I commit my spirit!" (Luke 23:46), another bold declaration of unshakeable faith in YHWH—and rather intimately, part of the bedtime prayer that Jewish children pray to their Father in heaven.

Yehoshua then speaks—or more likely whispers—his last words: "It is finished." This can mean several things: The task is completed. The purpose is fulfilled. The debt is paid.

At approximately 3 p.m. on Friday, April 3, 3 AD, after three and a half decades of life and no more than six hours on the cross, Yehoshua bows his head and breathes his last breath.

Meanwhile, the religionists are busy fretting about Sabbath preparation. It's against their rules and regs to leave a Jewish corpse on a cross over Sabbath—especially a High Sabbath during a Holy Week—so they pester Pilate to hurry along the demise of the three political criminals so they can have them down before sunset (John 19:31).

Roman soldiers are forbidden to leave a crucifixion victim unattended lest their friends help them down and squirrel them to safety. But when time is pressing, or there are hundreds or thousands of people to murder in a short period of time, expedience is required. This can be achieved in one of several ways. For a low cross, a soldier can smash the victim in the skull or chest with a hammer. For a high cross, they can pierce them once or several times in the heart or lungs with a spear. Another option is to build a smoking fire at the foot of the cross and asphyxiate the criminal to death. A fourth option is a *crucifragium*—to shatter the tibia or fibula, or both. With both legs broken, a crucifictee can no longer push themselves up for air and will die of suffocation in a matter of minutes.

Like a good mafia don, Annas gets his people to ask Pilate to break Yehoshua's legs (John 19:31). The soldiers proceed, sledging the legs of the revolutionaries on Yehoshua's left and right (John 19:32). But when they come to the tortured rabbi, they realize he is already dead. Just to be safe, a soldier plunges a spear into the limp corpse. John watches as blood and fluid pour from his cousin's side (John 19:34).

The crowds who have watched the spectacle return home, but the female disciples remain, unwilling to take their eyes off this ghastly portrait.

Evening is coming. Will Yehoshua's body be yet another of the tens of thousands that will be thrown to the dogs and vultures? Who among the remaining is willing and able to expose themselves as a follower of the would-be king of the Jews?

His name is Joseph. He is from the nearby Judean town of Arimathea. He's a member of Annas's synedrion, but he follows Yehoshua in secret because he is afraid of the temple elites. Setting aside these fears, he goes to the praetorium and asks permission to take custody of the body. Pilate is surprised to hear Yehoshua is already dead. After confirming with a centurion, Pilate assents to Joseph's request.

Joseph purchases a linen shroud (Mark 15:46), then returns to Golgotha and does the difficult work of un-spiking the corpse from the cross. As he does so, another secret disciple approaches. Joseph's courage has evidently inspired his own, and it is the Galilean Nicodemus—and fellow member of the synedrion—who helps with the burial process. He brings with him seventy-five pounds of myrrh and aloe, and together they wrap the body in the linen shroud with the spices according to Jewish burial custom.

It is nearly sunset and Shabbat is about to begin. They need to get the body in the ground quickly. There is a garden near Golgotha. It contains a rock-cut sepulcher—a communal tomb or burial vault. Once a body decomposes, the bones are moved to a stone ossuary box as a final resting place. (Caiaphas's was discovered in 1990.) In other words, this is just a temporary resting place for Yehoshua. Joseph and Nicodemus carry the wrapped body into the tomb. Joseph uses a large rock to plug the entrance, ensuring no birds or dogs will taste Galilean flesh this night.

Across the garden, Maggie and Aunt Mary mother of Little James have watched the whole thing. Not satisfied by the hasty preparations made by the men-folk, they return to wherever they are staying to prepare their own mix of spices and ointments for the body. The Law of Moses requires them to rest on the Sabbath, and no doubt they will spend every moment of it in mourning, but they will be back first thing Sunday morning.

Saturday, April 4, 33 AD

Despite all their protestations and posturing about their so-called care for the Sabbath, the Pharisees and the House of Annas now decide to *break the great Passover Sabbath* and get the Romans to do some work for them. "The next day, that is, after the day of Preparation, the chief priests and the Pharisees gathered before Pilate and said, 'Sir, we remember how that impostor said, while he was still alive, "After three days I will rise." Therefore order the tomb to be made secure until the third day, lest his disciples go and steal him away and tell the people, "He has risen from the dead," and the last fraud will be worse than the first.' Pilate said to them, 'You have a guard of soldiers. Go, make it as secure as you can.' So they went and made the tomb secure by sealing the stone and setting a guard" (Matthew 27:62–66).

Annas and his men—who don't even believe in resurrection or the afterlife—have proven once and for all that they are not faithful Jews who obey YHWH's holy law, but are simply hypocrite imposters, usurpers of the high priest's throne.

Resurrection

Sunday, April 5, 33 AD

We are now solidly out of the pages of provable history and into the realm of sublime faith. The gospel writers all go into great detail, and for good reason: Without faith, what we are about to read is well and truly unbelievable.

Sunrise in Jerusalem on April 5 is 6:23 a.m. John 20:1 says it is still dark when Maggie; Aunt Mary, mother of Little James; Herod's manager's wife, Joanna; Yehoshua's aunt Salome; and at least one other woman make their way to the garden tomb with their spices, their minds set on making this a burial fit for a king. They discuss their one logistical challenge: who they can find to roll the stone away for them at this early hour (Mark 16:3).

The breaking sunrise answers their question, revealing what they could not see in the dark: The stone has been rolled away from the entrance. Maggie assumes that religionists, Romans, or robbers have stolen the rabbi's body. There is no thought that perhaps Yehoshua is alive. After all, she was one of the few who watched him die.

Maggie rushes away to find a mourning Simon Peter and John. When she locates them, she breathlessly reports, "They have taken the Lord out of the tomb, and we do not know where they have laid him" (John 20:2). Not a single one of Yehoshua's seventy-odd disciples is expecting a resurrection, including these two. Simon Peter and John sprint for the garden tomb.

Back in the garden, the older women see a holy messenger dressed in white. "Do not be afraid, for I know that you seek Jesus who was crucified. He is not here, for he has risen, as he said. Come, see the place where he lay" (Matthew 28:5–6). The women enter the tomb. They cannot find Yehoshua's body, but they see a young man seated to the right, wearing not a tunic nor cloak but an upper-class *stolé*—a long white robe. The two men in their white robes shine radiantly in the early morning sun. The women are terrified and lower their gaze, but the seated man echoes the assurance of the first. "Do not be alarmed. You seek Jesus of Nazareth, who was crucified. He has risen; he is not here. See the place where they laid him. But go, tell his disciples and Peter that he is going before you to Galilee. There you will see him, just as he told you" (Mark 16:6–7).

It all floods back to the women. *Yehoshua has been telling us this the whole time. The Son of Man had to be delivered into the hands of sinful men and be crucified . . . and on the third day . . . rise.*

The older women, trembling and bewildered, flee the tomb and are so terrified that they tell no one. But as they stumble out of the garden, it dawns on them. Their terror mixes with joy, and they head into the city to find the apostles and the seventy-odd disciples.

Meanwhile, Simon and John have left Maggie in their dust. Young John cannot help but report in his gospel that he outruns Simon and beats him to the tomb (John 20:4). As he looks into the open tomb, he sees Joseph of Arimathea's freshly purchased linen burial cloths lying there, but he can't bring himself to go in. Simon arrives and goes straight in. He sees the linens, along with a separate, folded face cloth. John musters the courage and enters the tomb, and finally understands what his cousin-rabbi has been on about for the past three to five years. John had failed to grasp the resurrection until this very moment. Simon, for his part, is simply puzzled about what has happened.

The older women find the weeping and grieving apostles and disciples and spill the beans, but their story is so farfetched that, like Thomas later, *no one* believes them at first. Because no one—not Simon, not John, not the apostles, not the seventy-odd disciples—is expecting a resurrection this day.

Maggie arrives back at the tomb as Simon and John exit it to return to their lodgings. They clearly haven't found any answers either. She stands outside the tomb and weeps. As she weeps, she looks into the tomb and sees the two holy messengers in white, now seated at the head and foot of where Yehoshua's body had been laid. John 20:13–17 describes the rest:

When they ask why she is weeping, she tells them, "They have taken away my Lord, and I do not know where they have laid him."

She hears a noise and turns around. Through the garden foliage and mist and early morning light, she sees a man. She assumes he is the gardener. He also asks her why she is weeping.

She turns away, sniffling. "Sir, if you have carried him away, tell me where you have laid him, and I will take him away."

Yehoshua likely steps closer and into more light, and says just one word to her: "Miryam."

She instantly recognizes his voice, wheels on him, and exclaims in Aramaic, "Rabboni!"

Maggie throws her arms around her teacher and won't let go. Yehoshua says to her warmly, "Do not cling to me, for I have not yet ascended to the Father; but go to my brothers and say to them, 'I am ascending to my Father and your Father, to my God and your God.'"

Maggie departs to find the others.

The older women, meanwhile, have had zero luck convincing the apostles and the seventy-odd. They depart the disciples and head on their way, either to their Passover lodgings or back to the garden. Wherever they are heading, Yehoshua meets them along the way. "Greetings!" he says.

The older women come up to him and grab hold of his feet and worship him. "Do not be afraid," he instructs them. "Go and tell my brothers to go to Galilee, and there they will see me" (Matthew 28:10). Once again, Yehoshua is retreating into the wilderness.

Meanwhile (there are a shocking number of *meanwhiles* on this day), Maggie finds the apostles and seventy-odd still mourning and weeping over the loss of their rabbi. It has not occurred to even one disciple that Yehoshua could come back from the dead.

"I have seen the Lord!" she blurts, and then delivers Yehoshua's message.

Still, none of them believe the news, especially not from a woman formerly occupied by seven demons.

Would we believe her?

Simon Peter steps out to get some air.

An Explanation for "Resurrection"

What, exactly, happened in the early hours of Sunday, April 5, 33 AD? While no one knows for certain, there are a number of possibilities:

1. The first is simply that Yehoshua died on the cross, his body ignominiously tossed to the vultures and dogs like nearly every other crucifixion victim in history. Joseph of Arimathea is a made-up character, there is no tomb, there is no Sunday morning appearance, there is no ascension. End of story.
2. The second possibility is that Yehoshua's body was placed in a tomb but was stolen during Shabbat. Either the Romans re-buried it elsewhere to avoid the start of

yet another messianic cult, the Jewish elite squirreled it away for similar reasons, grave robbers stole it as a relic (though keep in mind the absurd notion that any grave robber would go through the effort of unwrapping a naked body and carefully folding and leaving the expensive head linen), or Yehoshua's disciples moved it to a more appropriate burial ground or stole it to pretend he had resurrected. Since the Sadducees don't believe in resurrection, this is the story that Annas and his administration immediately begin to circulate (Matthew 28:12–15).

3. Another possibility is that the women visited the wrong tomb. Either they were confused in the early morning light or they misremembered the location.
4. Perhaps Yehoshua *didn't* die but somehow survived his scourging, crucifixion, and spearing. His deep unconsciousness or coma slipped by the watchful eye of experienced Roman crucifiers. In the garden or tomb, he either auto-resuscitates or is resuscitated by Joseph, Nicodemus, the women, or other disciples. After recovering over the weekend, he is somehow in good enough shape to walk by Sunday.
5. One possibility maintained by Muslims: Yehoshua was never crucified, and the Romans mistakenly arrested and executed someone like Judas Iscariot instead.
6. Perhaps Yehoshua had an identical twin. Mother Mary had been in on the scheme since the moment Joseph threw her out for having an affair, perhaps with the Roman soldier Tiberius Pantera. Having been raised by a single mother in ridicule and poverty, Yehoshua became even more hardline on divorce than Shammai. Conspiring with her kinswoman Elizabeth, Mary raised Yehoshua to create a Judean uprising with his kinsman's help. When John fell to Antipas, Mary soldiered on. If or

when Yehoshua died, she was ready to substitute her secret second son upon the death of her first to win herself a place in iconographical history forever.

7. Perhaps one of Yehoshua's cousins or brothers substituted as messiah and continued to perpetuate the family fraud. James and Jude are too recognizable among the early church, but with the right haircut, clothing, voice, and message, Joses or Simon might pass for their big brother.
8. Another possibility is that Yehoshua didn't come back from the dead, but that his disciples experienced a classic case of cognitive dissonance and started to see very real visions or apparitions of their master. So road-weary from their ministry travels, so tired from the last few days of political drama, so worked into a PTSD tizzy from witnessing the torture of their would-be messiah, they all simply cracked.
9. And then there is the most astonishing suggestion of all. It is the one put forward by Mark, Matthew, Luke, John, and the untold number of eyewitnesses who informed their testimonies, and it is far and away the least likely of all possible scenarios: That Yehoshua ben Yehoseph resurrected.

From the dead.

Not "heartbeat stopped for a few minutes" dead.

Dead as in, multiple-days-in-the-ground, rigor-mortis dead.

Did Yehoshua really die and come back from the dead? We cannot say so with historical and scientific certainty. The first person who sees him alive is a woman—and a formerly demon-possessed woman at that. Her testimony is not admissible in a first-century court of law. Does this help or hinder the author's attempt to convince us that Yehoshua was seen alive after his crucifixion? Or is it too brutally honest to be false?

Later that Sunday afternoon, two of the seventy-odd disciples are walking to the village of Emmaus, about seven miles northwest of Jerusalem, deep in deliberation about everything that has just happened. One of the disciples is named Cleopas (maybe the father of Little James), and the other unnamed disciple might be his wife, Aunt Mary, but it could also be Luke the gospel writer himself, as he records the scene in chapter 24 with such precise detail.

As the two disciples are in vigorous dialogue about what on earth has just happened, Yehoshua sidles up and walks with them. For some reason, they do not recognize him—because of his clothing, his disfigurement, their deep distraction, we do not know—even when he asks, "What is this conversation that you are holding with each other as you walk?"

The two disciples halt, heartbroken at the memory of the horrible saga.

Cleopas is blunt in his reply. "Are you the only visitor to Jerusalem who does not know the things that have happened there in these days?"

Yehoshua plays dumb and asks yet another question. "What things?"

The disciples catch the new guy up. "Concerning Yehoshua of Nazareth, a man who was a prophet mighty in deed and word before God and all the people, and how our chief priests and rulers delivered him up to be condemned to death, and crucified him. But we had hoped that he was the one to redeem Israel." Note the defeatist tone without the slightest hope of resurrection. Yehoshua was just another prophet like his kinsman John the Baptizer.

"It is now the third day since these things happened. Moreover, some women of our company amazed us. They were at the tomb early in the morning, and when they did not find his body, they came back saying that they had even seen a vision of angels, who said that he was alive. Some of those who were with us went to the tomb and found it just as the women had said, but him they did not see."

Yehoshua chides his disciples. "O foolish ones, and slow of heart to believe all that the prophets have spoken! Was it not necessary that the Christ should suffer these things and enter into his glory?" He then takes them back to Torah 101, beginning with Moses and the prophets, interpreting the entire story of Scripture through the lens of himself.

As the two disciples near Emmaus village, the rabbi looks as though he is going to continue north. The disciples strongly urge him to stay with them, as it's getting toward evening. He accepts their offer of hospitality. When they sit down to eat, Yehoshua grabs the bread and blesses it. Then he breaks it and gives it to them, just like at the Last Supper. Suddenly, the two disciples recognize their rabbi.

No doubt with a smile, Yehoshua swiftly disappears from the house.

The two disciples turn on each other. "Did not our hearts burn within us while he talked to us on the road, while he opened to us the Scriptures?"

First he breaks the Word, then he breaks the bread. Despite the late hour this Sunday night, the two disciples rush back to Jerusalem.

Meanwhile, the apostles (minus Thomas) and the seventy-odd disciples have locked themselves in a room in Jerusalem for fear that the temple elite will come for them next. The two disciples enter, and the crowd exclaims that they now believe in the resurrection because a man has seen it: "The Lord has risen indeed, and has appeared to Simon!"

The details of Yehoshua's appearance are recorded by none of the four gospel writers, but it happens at some point between the afternoon and early supper. The two disciples then recount what just happened on their little road trip *but the group doesn't believe them.* Everyone spends the next while in confused conversation as they tuck into supper. *How can our rabbi appear to Simon near Jerusalem and to Cleopas seven miles away?*

Then, toward the end of their hotly debated, anxiety-laden meal, Yehoshua appears in the middle of the crowd and speaks the word they need to hear. "Shalom to you!"

Cheeky monkey.

The whole lot are startled and terrified, thinking they're collectively seeing a ghost. Yehoshua tries to offer comfort and assurance. "Why are you troubled, and why do doubts arise in your hearts? See my hands and my feet, that it is I myself. Touch me, and see. For a spirit does not have flesh and bones as you see that I have."

He shows them his wounded hands and feet.

And they still don't believe. But at least they're now "filled with joy and wonder." He chides them for their unbelief and hardness of heart, specifically for not believing the myriad women to whom he first appeared.

Yehoshua, having previously dashed without dining in Emmaus, now asks if there's anything to eat.

They give him a piece of broiled fish. He starts to eat it. They watch carefully. After all, ghosts can't hold fish down. But this man does. As he tucks into tilapia, he brings them up to speed. "These are my words that I spoke to you while I was still with you, that everything written about me in the Law of Moses and the Prophets and the Psalms must be fulfilled." He unpacks the details and unlocks their minds to understand the Scriptures through the lens of himself.

Yehoshua eventually departs. Within hours, the disciples tell Thomas the Twin that they have seen their Lord, and he is just as doubtful as they were prior to seeing Yehoshua in the flesh: "Unless I see in his hands the mark of the nails, and place my finger into the mark of the nails, and place my hand into his side, I will never believe."

There are no sightings of Yehoshua for a whole week. On the following Sunday, the disciples are once again locked inside (potentially in the same Jerusalem flat as before), but this time Twin Tom is in tow. Yehoshua appears with his trademark "Shalom to you!" and turns to Thomas. "Put your finger here, and see my hands; and put out your hand, and place it in my side. Do not disbelieve, but believe." So-called "Doubting" Thomas is the first to say what none of the others have yet voiced: "My Lord and my God!"

With the Festival of Unleavened Bread well over, the company of seventy-odd disciples follows Yehoshua's instructions to the women and journeys the sixty-odd miles to Galilee. Heading north—away from Jerusalem, the Romans, and Annas's seat of power—it is probably beginning to dawn on the more militant members of the group that Yehoshua really and truly has no interest in a political overthrow.

Upon arrival, Simon says he's going for a night fish (so he can sell them fresh at the morning market, likely to replenish his funds after an expensive, multi-week stay in the tourist-trap capital). Twin Tom, Nathanael, the Thunder Sons, and two others join him on the Sea/Lake of Galilee/Tiberias. They are back to where their story started, but like Bilbo Baggins, they are utterly changed. It is the hero's journey writ to perfection, except they are not the heroes of their story.

Just as dawn breaks, Yehoshua stands on the shoreline. It is his third appearance to (at least some of) the inner twelve. He hollers to ask if they've caught anything. A hundred yards offshore, they assume he's a would-be customer and relate the bad news that they've caught zilch all night.

Just as he did when he first called them, Yehoshua tells them to throw their empty nets on the other side of the boat. They do so and trap a school so large they can't haul it in. Simon Peter doesn't care. "It is the Lord!" He puts on his clothes and throws himself into the sea.

When the seven arrive on the beach, breakfast is already cooking. Bread, plus fish on charcoal—the same fuel source by which Simon Peter warmed himself while denying his rabbi three times. After they finish eating, Yehoshua takes a moment to walk on the beach with the lead disciple who deserted him, calling him *not* by his nickname. "Simon, son of John, do you love me more than these?" It is unclear whether he is referring to the other disciples or to the fish that represent Simon's successful career.

Simon replies, "Yes, Lord; you know that I love you."

"Feed my lambs."

Simon doesn't say anything, possibly because he has started crying.

Yehoshua repeats the question. "Simon, son of John, do you love me?"

"Yes, Lord; you know that I love you."

"Tend my sheep."

Is Simon now weeping? The rabbi repeats his question a third time. "Simon, son of John, do you love me?"

The third ask grieves Simon. "Lord, you know everything; you know that I love you."

"Feed my sheep."

Yehoshua then raises the stakes for Simon Peter, forcing him not only to relinquish his dream of destroying the Roman imperium, but preparing him for martyrdom. "Truly, truly, I say to you, when you were young, you used to dress yourself and walk wherever you wanted, but when you are old, you will stretch out your hands, and another will dress you and carry you where you do not want to go. Follow me."

Simon realizes that ever-faithful John is following Yehoshua (just as he did on the night of the crucifixion), once again eavesdropping on an important conversation. "Lord, what about him?" Simon asks.

Yehoshua tells him it's none of his business. "As for you, follow me!"

Yehoshua continues to appear for forty days and proves to them in various ways that he actually is alive. He also keeps talking about his favorite subject: the kingdom of God (Acts 1:3).

Word spreads quietly, with the biggest crowd being just five hundred people. The disciples and potentially others go to the mountain where Yehoshua had told them to meet him. They see him coming up the hill. Matthew 28:17 notes that "they worshiped him, but some doubted."

Yehoshua climbs up to them and issues his great commission: "All authority in heaven and on earth has been given to me. Go therefore and make disciples of all nations, baptizing them in the name of the Father and of the Son and of the Holy Spirit, teaching them to observe all that I have commanded you. And behold, I am with you always, to the end of the age."

Thousands of books have been rightfully written on this commission, so we will make note of just three things. First, Yehoshua assumes God is a trinity. Second, the word for *nations* here is *ethnē*—not nation-states, but every tribe, nation, people, and tongue. Samaritans included. Our third note is that, contrary to popular belief, these aren't actually Yehoshua's final words.

He still has one more festival to attend.

Ascension

Toward the end of the forty days, Yehoshua and the disciples—still all faithful Jews—head back south to Jerusalem for the Jewish feast of Pentecost. Now the rabbi stays with them (Acts 1:4), potentially in the same upper room where they had the last supper before his crucifixion. We don't know where he meets up with his brother James (1 Corinthians 15:7), whether in their home region of Galilee or in Jerusalem, but the reunion is the catalyst that leads James to finally believe his kid brother Yesh is, indeed, YHWH.

While eating yet again, Yehoshua tells the disciples not to leave Jerusalem for a while. "Wait for the promise of the Father, which you heard from me; for John baptized with water, but you will be baptized with the Holy Spirit not many days from now. Stay here in the city until the Holy Spirit comes and fills you with power from heaven."

After supper, he takes them on their usual post-prandial saunter across the Kidron Brook and up the Mount of Olives, past the garden of Gethsemane, all the way to Bethany.

Still fuzzy on whether Yehoshua is going to slay the Romans and make himself king in Jerusalem, some say, "Lord, will you at this time restore the kingdom to Israel?"

He tells them the timing is up to YHWH alone but reassures them, "You will receive power when the Holy Spirit has come upon you, you will be my witnesses"—the word here is *martyrs*—"in Jerusalem and in all Judea and Samaria, and to the end of the earth."

Yehoshua lifts his hands and blesses them, his final words excruciatingly unrecorded by all four gospel writers. As he finishes speaking, he is lifted up and a cloud takes him out of sight (Acts 1:9).

The disciples stare at the sky. Two men in white robes (are they the same pair from the empty tomb?) address them. "Men of Galilee, why do you stand looking into heaven? This Jesus, who was taken up from you into heaven, will come in the same way as you saw him go into heaven."

A question remains for the reader: Where in the world did Yehoshua go? The answer is found in John 14:2–3, where Yehoshua speaks about the ultimate temple. "In my Father's house are many rooms. If it were not so, would I have told you that I go to prepare a place for you? And if I go and prepare a place for you, I will come again and will take you to myself, that where I am you may be also."

In other words, Yehoshua is back to work as a *tektón*.

The disciples return to Jerusalem from the Mount of Olives. They devote themselves to prayer and continue to bless God in the Jewish temple.

But mostly, they wait.

Conclusion

"Sometimes the questions are complicated and the answers are simple."

—Attributed to Dr. Seuss

Who in the world is Yehoshua ben Yehoseph?

This is the most important question in the Bible, and in all of human history, and it is the question Yehoshua poses to Simon Peter in Mark 8:29: "Who do you say that I am?"

Some first-century Jews think he is John the Baptist reincarnated, others Elijah reincarnated, still others that he is a prophet. Simon thinks he is the Messiah. C. S. Lewis of *Narnia* fame believes there are three options: that Josh is either a liar, a lunatic, or the Lord. I discern ten possible categories for Yehoshua ben Yehoseph:

1. *He is a dangerous fiction.*

   In this scenario, Yehoshua is not a real person but a concocted legend. He is made up by an insidious group of profoundly brilliant writers to deceive the world into helping the poor, rejecting harmful discrimination, and loving their enemies.
2. *He is an inspirational myth.*

   In this case, Yehoshua is a historical human who is badly misinterpreted by his gospel recorders.
3. *He is a lunatic cult leader.*

   A strongish case can be made that Yehoshua was either mentally ill or suffered a serious breakdown as an adult and that he ran a fringe apocalyptic cult that attracted people of the same bent. He may very well have been a suicidal lunatic, a savant since childhood with notions of grandeur and godhood, who read the Torah and imagined himself its fulfillment.

Think about it cynically for a moment: At the beginning of his story, he hears an audible voice and sees the skies ripped open (Mark 1:10). He has a Joshua Tree-style desert trip where he doesn't eat for more than a month and has a hallucination of Satan tempting him to commit suicide (Mark 1:12–13). He believes he has been sent by God to announce a new kingdom (Luke 4:43). His own family believes he is out of his mind and tries to take custody of him (Mark 3:21). Many Jews think he is "demon-possessed and insane" (John 10:20). He believes he has come to give his life "as a ransom for many" (Matthew 20:28). He tells his disciples he's about to hand them a God-granted kingdom and that they will sit on thrones and judge the twelve tribes of Israel (Luke 22:30). He is so crippled with narcissism that he believes he is "the way and the truth and the life" (John 14:6). His so-called triumphal entry to Jerusalem and overthrowing temple tables at the start of ultra-tense Passover are undeniably inciting acts that would court a Roman execution. He's so conflicted about the whole thing that he starts sweating heavily in anticipation of his arrest. Craziest of all, he believes his execution is a martyrdom that will somehow save the entire world from sin and death. If Yehoshua appeared today, would we not lock him in an asylum or pump him full of pills? What is to say Yehoshua isn't a madman?

4. *He is a failed Messiah claimant.*

In this case, we have a story of Shakespearean tragedy. Yehoshua believes he is an earthly messiah, a spiritual deliverer of the Israelite nation, and he fails.

Or perhaps he is not a failed Messiah, but just *a* messiah. There is also a small but slowly growing wing within Judaism to creatively classify Yehoshua not as a failed Messiah, but as a *forerunner* messiah in the first of two phases, leading to the ultimate Messiah in the future. The term *mashiach* originally applied to kings, priests, and even non-Jewish saviors. All were rescuers of the Jewish nation-state to some extent. Perhaps Yehoshua was just one in a long line of *mashiachs,* just another *Christos* who tried to move the liberation ball a little further down the field. In this scenario, Yehoshua is not Jesus the Christ, but Jesus *a* Christ.

5. *He is a political zealot.*

Another Galilean rebel, a warlord bent on violent conquest, he firmly believes he is a double-bloodline-king candidate and the rightful heir to the Jewish throne. His goal is to establish a family dynasty that will rule for all time. His disciples will feast at the king's table and sit on thrones and judge the twelve tribes of Israel (Luke 22:29–30). Yehoshua's first step is to break the economy of the House of Annas, inciting a Passover riot that leads to the capture of the temple. Once they possess the colossal wealth and weaponry of the national treasury, they will expel Pilate and the Romans.

If this is the plan, Yehoshua is the leader of yet another failed guerrilla insurgency, just one of many millions who crashed into the Roman Empire and shattered against its mighty breakers.

6. *He is a great rabbi.*

In this instance, Yehoshua is simply an exceedingly good rabbi. He is greater than the House of Shammai because he runs roughshod over their literalism and abolishes religionism. He is greater than the House of Hillel because he makes women equal at the table of humanity.

He is greater than the House of Annas for exposing the high priest's entire aristocratic family as anti-Jewish war criminals. Above all three and all others, he is the major global popularizer of Judaism to the Gentile world. If billions of people have heard the stories of the Old Testament, it is because he inspired a new one.

7. *He is a Jewish national hero.*

   Here Yehoshua is a Moses-style liberator, one who is both political *and* spiritual. Though his valiant attempt to restore Israel's independence has failed, he becomes an immortal martyr like Spartacus.

8. *He is a liberal philosophical sage.*

   Yehoshua in our eighth iteration is a Hellenistic Greek-style philosopher. His godhood/Son of Man/Messiah/Christos claims are concoctions of his chroniclers, and the remnants of his true philosophy is whatever little remains in the god-ified text. He lives like Epicurus, with a bit of Diogenes thrown in, and dies a philosophical hero like Socrates.

9. *He is history's highest moral being.*

   Yehoshua's penultimate possibility is as a prophet of God at least on the level of Buddha. He is not God made flesh, but rather, the Torah made flesh. He is not God the Son, but definitely a son of God. He is an avatar, a living Bible, a near-perfect *Homo sapiens* specimen if ever there were one, an embodiment of truth and love and life itself.

10. *He is God himself.*

    In the final permutation, Yehoshua ben Yehoseph is not his name. His real name is Yehoshua *ben YHWH*. This is the scenario put forward by the gospel writers, apostles, and other eyewitnesses. Moreover, as we shall soon see, it is sealed and witnessed in their blood.

What can we know for a *historical* fact? Simply that a man named Yehoshua ben Yehoseph from Nazareth taught about the kingdom of God and was known as a healer; that he was crucified by the will of the Jewish House of Annas and the Roman prefect Pontius Pilate solely for political reasons; that his disciples had experiences that led them to the life-threatening belief that Yehoshua had resurrected; that this story has endured and spread for nearly two thousand years and counting.

Yehoshua's influence affects untold facets of our lives, from women's rights to democracy to human rights to child protection to the abolition of slavery to hospitals and universities. If the goal is global shalom, Yehoshua ben Yehoseph is the greatest rabbi, philosopher, political thinker, and economist to ever live. The question we must now ask our society is: *Do we need more or less of him*?

Do you and I need more or less of Yehoshua in our lives?

There is no proving Yehoshua is YHWH, just as there is no way of proving he is not. When Yehoshua asks Simon Peter in John 6:67 if he wants to abandon his rabbi, Simon answers his rabbi's question with another question: "To whom shall we go? You have the words of eternal life." Indeed, this is the unbearable question most humans never face: If not Yehoshua, *who*?

Were Yehoshua and his disciples telling the truth? Were they deceived? Were they deceivers? I have known several pathological liars in my day, but I have never met one who would voluntarily subject themselves to the tortures of the flagrum and crucifix to defend a lie.

If Yehoshua is not God, he certainly *thinks* he is. Remember, Yehoshua's suffering and death are *entirely voluntary*. He believes he must become the embodiment of self-sacrifice. He believes he must endure infinite suffering so we can know endless shalom. If He is a liar, why does he agonize in the garden of Gethsemane instead of making his getaway? There can be no other option: If He is not God, he is suicidally deranged. If he is not God, his followers are equally so. Why? Because *dozens* of eyewitnesses allow themselves to be tortured and murdered for this same belief.

What does it mean to genuinely be a Christian and not just say one is a Christian? It is to faithfully believe that the historical Yehoshua ben Yehoseph is the human incarnation of YHWH himself, and to actively surrender to the word, will, and way of this king and his kingdom. It is a huge leap, which is why Yehoshua says the gate is small, the way is narrow, and few find it (Matthew 7:14). But let me tell you, those who do genuinely discover this king and his kingdom tend to lead exceedingly interesting lives.

If a churchgoer sees the resurrection as anything short of preposterous, you can rest assured they have been warming a pew for far too long. Resurrection is humanly impossible. Only God could resurrect someone from the dead. If the resurrection really did happen, and a churchgoer truly comprehended and believed it, it would have profound implications for their life. If someone really believed that Yehoshua resurrected and was YHWH incarnate, then they would gladly dedicate their entire lives to Yehoshua—all of their work, time, and money included—to seek the kingdom of God above absolutely everything else.

This, history shows, is exactly what Yehoshua's closest disciples did.

After the death of Yehoshua, the eleven remaining disciples gather in the upper room of a rented house in Jerusalem and devote themselves to prayer in the lead-up to the Jewish festival of Pentecost. They aren't the only ones present. Luke mentions that the women and Mary the mother of Yehoshua, and his brothers, are also there. So we have Mary, James, Joses, Jude, and Simon, plus probably Maggie, Aunt Mary the mom of Little James, Aunt Salome the mother of the Thunder Sons, gospel patrons Joanna and Susanna, and many more.

Yehoshua had a mere seventy disciples in life, but evidently the crucifixion and resurrection caused quite a stir because Acts 1:15 says their numbers have now nearly doubled to 120. They choose a replacement for Judas Iscariot, selecting a seasoned disciple who's been around longer than most of the inner twelve (Acts 1:21–26).

They gather around 9 a.m. on the day of Jewish Pentecost (Acts 2:15). The sound of a windstorm fills the room. Divided tongues that seem to be like fire rest on each of them. They are filled with *agiou pneumatos*—sacred wind, the Holy Spirit—and start speaking in different languages.

Down in the festival-packed streets of Jerusalem, a crowd of Jewish pilgrims from all over the ancient world gather in the street, confused by the loud noise and hearing their mother tongues from the mouths of Galileans. Some in the crowd think they've gotten drunk. Simon gets up with the eleven and gives a barn burner of a sermon that cuts to the quick. Many ask what they should do, and he says, "Repent and be baptized every one of you in the name of Jesus Christ for the forgiveness of your sins, and you will receive the gift of the Holy Spirit" (Acts 2:38). Three *thousand* people take him up on the offer and get baptized either in the Kidron, the twelve temple mikvehs, by the Holy Spirit, or some mix thereof.

While the Annas Sadducees find themselves increasingly isolated from the Pharisees in their persecution of followers of the Way (Acts 5:17), the Christian faith family continues to grow. In Acts 2:47, Luke reports that "the Lord added to their number day by day those who were being saved." By Acts 4:4, they are up to five thousand men—so likely well over ten thousand disciples—causing the power-broking High Priest Annas to rally his entire family to launch an investigation (Acts 4:6). Unlike most Jews then and most churchgoers today, the disciples know exactly who is responsible for their rabbi's crucifixion. Peter and John *publicly blame Annas and his family* for murdering Yehoshua (Acts 4:6–10). In fury, Annas has them imprisoned (Acts 5:17). When Peter miraculously escapes from prison and is back preaching in the temple by sunrise (Acts 5:17–21), the high priest has him flogged (Acts 5:40).

It has a diametrically opposite effect to the intended one. "And the word of God continued to increase, and the number of the disciples multiplied greatly in Jerusalem, and a *great many of the priests* became obedient to the faith" (Acts 6:7).

Three years after Yehoshua's murder, tensions with the temple elite reach a boiling point. Caiaphas is deposed in 36 AD and replaced by Annas's son Jonathan, who hauls a disciple named Stephen before his monkey court (Acts 7:1). Stephen also blames the house that Annas built for murdering Yehoshua (Acts 7:52), earning himself a public stoning to the death, making him Christianity's first martyr—and breaking Rome's capital punishment laws in the process.

Immediately following Stephen's grisly murder, a "great persecution" breaks out with the written blessing of the House of Annas (Acts 9:1–2). True to his word, Annas will deal with the fallout from Pilate's decision; for nearly thirty years, the House of Annas will attempt to suppress the church of Christ; it is nothing short of an organized purge to wipe out the disciples of Yehoshua (Acts 9:14; Acts 9:21; Acts 26:10; Acts 26:12). This has the opposite effect: While the twelve apostles hold down the fort in the capital, the rest of the Jerusalem church scatters throughout Judea and Samaria, taking their faith with them. Soon, so many Samaritans come to faith that Jewish Peter and John pay a visit to join in the preaching action. Back in Jerusalem, the murder of Stephen and the exodus of Christians causes such an uproar that Jonathan is deposed within a year, replaced by Annas's son Theophilus.

The church spreads like wildfire as thousands of missionaries re-settle abroad. While Philip is leading Ethiopian court officials to faith in the south near Gaza, Saul of Tarsus is chasing down converts all the way north to what is now Syria, putting them to death on the authority of the high priests (Acts 25:26). An Italian centurion starts a house church in Acts 10. By Acts 11, there are followers of the Way in what are now Lebanon and Syria and the island of Cyprus.

What becomes of the religionists? Unbelievably, some of the Pharisees have a radical change of heart and become followers of the Way (Acts 15:5). We can only imagine the relief these leaders must have felt in throwing off the crushing burden of man-made laws and stepping under Yehoshua's light yoke (Matthew 11:30). For the first time in their lives, they burst out of the temple's stiflingly religious air and into the fresh winds of the Holy Spirit. In Matthew 13:52, Yehoshua accurately predicted that religionists who became his disciples would become especially useful: One of these redeemed religionists becomes *the biggest popularizer of Christianity in human history* (Acts 23:6).

The shadowy Annas, meanwhile, continues to use his power-hungry sons to dominate Jewish religious life, robbing the poor for profit and persecuting the church for pleasure. Caiaphas is deposed in late 36/early 37 AD and is replaced by Annas's son Jonathan. Jonathan doesn't live long—when the Sicarii start covertly stabbing people to death in broad daylight, Jonathan ben Annas is the very first to fall under their blade (Josephus, *Jewish War* 2.254–257).

Judas Iscariot kills himself, but according to Matthew 27:3, he hangs himself right after confessing to betraying innocent blood, while according to Luke in Acts 1:18, Judas fell headlong and "burst open in the middle and all his bowels gushed out." How do we reconcile these seemingly conflicting accounts? Was Matthew speaking more generally of a death of dishonor with allusions to a traitor in 2 Samuel 17:23? Or did Luke the doctor simply record the more gory detail that Judas hanged himself and the tree branch snapped, or that his once-dangling corpse wasn't discovered until partially decomposed in the hot Judean sun? Or did a swaying Judas hasten death by turning the *sicae* on himself? We don't know much beyond the fact that he died ignominiously.

Though Iscariot's character is opportunistic and he is a known thief, if we give him the benefit of the doubt, it seems as though he commits suicide out of pure regret (Matthew 27:4). What triggers this guilt? Seeing Yehoshua condemned to death (Matthew 27:3). Perhaps Iscariot wanted to trigger the kingdom of God, thinking it would lead to an earthly overthrow of the Roman Empire. Perhaps when he realizes this isn't the case, he is so overwhelmed that he indicted a man he knows to be innocent, that he sacrifices himself in penance.

After his death, even the high priests cannot bring themselves to dump the thirty shekels back in their temple treasury (Matthew 27:6). Instead, they go out and buy a field on Judas's behalf to use as a graveyard. Accordingly, the locals nickname the field *Akeldama*, the "field of blood" (Acts 1:19). The chief priests tell the public they're going to use it as a burial place for foreigners (Matthew 27:7)—but history tells a different story. Archaeological work in Akeldema has revealed the cemetery isn't full of penniless travelers, but rather some of the most expensive and luxurious tombs in town. Judas's tomb hasn't been found, but Annas's family tomb has been tentatively identified in Akeldama, decorated just like the Temple Mount, located precisely where Josephus records it is (*Jewish War* 5:505–6). Joseph Caiaphas's rock-cut tomb is just farther south, making Akeldama well and truly the field of blood money.

Greedy to the bitter end, Annas dies in his early sixties around 40 AD, and when the gospel writers pen their testimonies shortly thereafter, they all place the blame where it belongs: squarely on him and his house of sin. Matthew, Mark, Luke, and John consistently differentiate between the scribes, elders, Pharisees, Sadducees, Herodians, Synedrion, and *the chief priests*. Who is the only group mentioned in every single conspiratorial action during Passion Week? Annas and Caiaphas, the chief priests.

The Greek word here is *archiereus,* the arch-priest. In the Bible, it's translated sixty-four times as "chief priests" and fifty-three times as "high priest." They are one and the same. When the gospel writers use the word *archiereus*, they are talking about Annas, Caiaphas, and their thieving aristocratic household. As the Jewish gospel writers make clear, it is not "the Jews" who killed Yehoshua. Cleopas blames the high priests (Luke 24:20). Peter blames the high priests (Acts 4:6–10). Stephen blames the high priests (Acts 7:52). Pilate blames the high priests (John 18:35). When Yehoshua heads up to Jerusalem with his disciples, he doesn't predict that the Pharisees, Sadducees, or Herodians will betray him to the Romans—it is the chief priests and their lawyers who are guilty (Mark 10:33). In total, the House of Annas is indicted eighty-four times in the gospels, officially going down in history as the anti-Jewish, anti-Israel, anti-YHWH mafia family that instigates Yehoshua's torture and murder for personal profit. The House of Annas's statement in Matthew 27:25 comes true: Yehoshua's blood really is on them and their children.

In 43 AD, Herod Agrippa appoints Annas's son Mathias to the high priesthood, and Christian persecution is renewed with vigor. Wanting to cut the church off at the head, they arrange the murder of Yehoshua's cousin-disciple James (Acts 12:2). Salome and Zebedee have lost a beloved boy; John the gospel writer has lost his big brother. One son of thunder has fallen, but the other will live to tell the tale, writing several books in the New Testament.

Seeing how much the murder of James pleases the religionists, Herod then moves to kill Simon Peter for them, arresting him during the Feast of Unleavened Bread just like his rabbi a few years earlier (Acts 12:3). Their plan is to publicly execute him with as many people watching as possible—right after Passover, just like Yehoshua (Acts 12:4). To make sure he doesn't escape from jail again, they chain him between two soldiers. On the night before Peter is to be executed, he miraculously escapes (Acts 12:6–19). Like his rabbi, Peter departs and lays low for a while. Herod executes his guards for losing their prisoner and deposes Mathias as high priest.

This, however, is not the end of the House of Annas and its reign of terror. During every bloody persecution of the Jerusalem church, a son of Annas is high priest at the time. Annas's son Ananus picks up his father's murderous mantle and sinks the family to new lows. Josephus describes Ananus in *The Antiquities of the Jews* as "a bold man in his temper, and very insolent" and Eusebius's writings speaks of his "exceeding bold and reckless disposition." Like his father, he is "a great hoarder up of money . . . a shrewd man in speaking and persuading the people, and had already gotten the mastery of those that opposed his designs."

After being made high priest at the turn of 62–63 AD, Ananus uses a changeover in Roman prefects to illegally assemble a monkey court and falsely accuse a man of breaking Jewish law despite the fact that the accused is so righteous he is respected by all seven sects of Judaism. Who is the man Ananus has beaten to death with rocks on trumped-up charges? It is none other than the great and good man in charge of the Jerusalem church—Yehoshua's brother James the Just.

Rival religionists immediately complain to King Agrippa—not for murdering James and several other innocent Christians, but for ignoring their traditions of due process. While James is replaced by Yehoshua's cousin Simeon (Little James's brother), Ananus is deposed within just three months of taking office.

The Romans, for their part, hate the Christians—Tacitus calls them "notoriously depraved" in his *Annals,* part of a "deadly superstition." After the mentally ill Nero burns two-thirds of Rome to the ground in July 64 AD to clear space for a new palace, he blames the fire on the Christians and sentences them to death for "hating the human race." Some are crucified. Some are thrown to the wild animals in the arena. Others are immolated as living torches at his parties. Nero will haunt the pages of Christendom for centuries as the early church's Hitler.

Like his father, Ananus never lets a deposition stop him from grasping earthly power. He gets his men to start beating priests and stealing their tithes, which he then uses to bribe people in positions of power. Josephus reports that while some of the victimized priests starved to death, Ananus "increased in glory everyday, and . . . obtained the favor and esteem of the citizens in a signal manner, for he was a great hoarder of money" (*Antiquities* 20:9:205–207).

Ananus gets his nephew appointed as high priest in 65 AD, but after a new high priest is selected in 66 AD and his temple is robbed of massive quantities of hoarded silver, Ananus rallies the Pharisees and Sadducees to murder the Zealots in the name of YHWH during the Great Revolt of Judea that temporarily expels the Romans.

Once Ananus achieves his father's dream of (co-)ruling an ever-so-shaky Judean government as a general, he then lays siege to *his own temple*. A rumor spreads that he has secretly aligned with the Roman General Vespasian to reclaim it.

Josephus reports in *The Jewish War* that in the late winter of 68, the Zealots hire mercenary forces to obliterate Ananus's army, and he meets a violent end in the massacre. He is so hated by his hunters that they refuse to bury his naked body, leaving it cursed by God and "meat for dogs and other beasts."

In the power vacuum that follows, Ananus's religionist faction continues their money-grabbing, power-broking, rule-pushing ways as Jerusalem descends into chaos and civil war, with Jew murdering Jew in the streets while the future Emperor Titus besieges their city. For the Jews who don't starve to death after the Zealots burn all the food warehouses, and who avoid being slashed to pieces by the Sicarii, the worst is yet to come. When Titus finally breaches Jerusalem's walls in 70 AD, he murders hundreds of thousands of Jews, all but extincts the Sadducees, burns down Annas's palace, destroys the House of Annas once and for all, and razes their corrupted temple to the ground, never to be rebuilt to this day.

But wasn't that Yehoshua's ultimate point in purging the temple? His plan was to replace the temple with his own body (1 Corinthians 3:16) so that people could directly commune with God without a middleman like Annas. Though we may have lost the pronunciation of YHWH in the destruction of the physical temple, we know God's name in the resurrected Son.

Yehoshua's message that this spiritual kingdom is for everyone eventually gets through the thick skulls of his disciples, and they do press out of Judea and into Samaria. Philip in particular has great success, what we would call a revival or great awakening—even among sorcerers. Philip's ministry is so powerful that Peter and John rush to join the action in "preaching the gospel to many villages of the Samaritans" (Acts 8:25). By Acts 9:31, there are churches all over Samaria.

The church is driven by radical love, embodying the highest form of all Greek loves: Agape your enemies. Even Annas and his wicked sons. Be willing to die for your Annas.

The disciples of Yehoshua continue to multiply. The church in metropolitan Antioch (modern-day Turkey) is packed with prophets and teachers, and even *black people* and *lifelong friends of Herod* get seats at the table (Acts 13:1). The Antioch church is such a smashing success that Saul of Tarsus—now Paul of Yehoshua—visits for a whole year and discovers the disciples have been given a nickname by non-believers: *Christians.*

The church of Yehoshua continues to break boundaries. The first church plant in Europe is started by women and hosted in a woman's house (Acts 16:13–15). Women continue to host churches (Colossians 4:15; Romans 16:3–5) and play leading roles in the blossoming Christian movement (Romans 16:12; Philippians 4:3). Remember the North African who carried Yehoshua's cross? Mark 15:21 likely mentions Simon's sons Alexander and Rufus because they were known persons to the early Christians. In fact, a Rufus is mentioned in Romans 16:13, suggesting at least half the next generation came to faith.

Where does tradition send the rest of the inner twelve? Simon "Rocky" Peter pushes north, through Syria and Turkey, to Greece and Italy. The Greek-named Andrew and Philip go to the Scythians. Simon the zealous hits up Cyrene, Mauritania, and Libya. Little

James walks to Spain. Doubt-relieved Thomas boldly heads east to Parthia (modern Iran) and may have made it as far as India. Tradition says Jude and Bartholomew minister in Armenia. Matthew-Levi may have gone as far as the Caspian Sea. Matthias (Iscariot's replacement) goes to Macedonia. Paul, now calling himself an apostle, is the madman missionary among the masses, evangelizing and discipling believers in Arabia, Cyprus, Rhodes, Crete, Ephesus, Athens, Corinth, Thessalonica, Philippi, Malta, Sicily, Rome, and dozens more places. All of these men pay for it with their lives, but in doing so, the Christian church goes viral, international, universal.

With their lives, they announce the good news that all people—regardless of ethnicity, sex, or murderous political affiliation—can be made right with YHWH through Yehoshua. Their message echoes through the generations, all the way down to those of us who proudly proclaim it to this day. By living out their *euangelion*, it becomes clear that Christianity is not a moral position, a rabbinical innovation, an economic structure, a philosophical system, a political party, or even a new religion. It is a living relationship with a person named Yehoshua ben Yehoseph.

In other words, it is a faithful friendship with a God named Josh.

Acknowledgments

"The end of my labors has come. All I have written appears to be as so much straw after the things that have been revealed to me."

—Thomas Aquinas, three months before dying

My thanks extends first to Andy McGuire and the whole Bethany House team for providing a welcoming home for this series.

Marketing manager Stephanie Smith, for your patience, endurance, and long-suffering as we homed in on a book cover that pleased us all, to say nothing of your marketing skills! Becca Schriner, publicist extraordinaire, for going above and beyond to get the word out about Jesus, including your heartfelt your prayers.

A special thanks to Sharon Hodge for your heartfelt encouragement and exceptional editorial skill. My thanks also to copy editor Amanda Clawson for her hundreds of fixes. An extra thanks to Cheryl Mowat, Joel Torrens, and my Las Vegas mama, Rhonda Baker, for valiant proofreading efforts at the eleventh hour.

My theological advisors on this book: Richard John Saunders, Ray Paul, Michael VanEgmond, Stu Thompson, and Christopher

Frost. Thank you all for your time and generous feedback, all of which made this book far better. All the remaining heresies are mine alone.

Michelle, my love, life, and muse. Even after fourteen years of marriage, being wed to you remains a breathtaking joy. In all honesty, I am fairly certain I could have written much of my first four books without you, but certainly not this one. Thank you for not letting me become *too* distracted by our beautiful baby Concord, and for nursing both of us as we simultaneously moved houses and battled twin cases of COVID-19 during my final week of editing. Thank you for your initial feedback on my early drafts, and for your unfailing support of the calling I cannot seem to shake.

Dave McSporran, for being my most generous and joyful encourager, patron, and friend. I am so grateful for your active love in championing my work.

Gord and Karen Brock, for lovingly beating the Bible into my thick childhood skull. You hid his word in my heart, and it made the writing of this book light-years easier.

Ari and Lea Uotila, for holding down the home fort and keeping the accounting books in order.

Thanks also to Matthew Leaker for his kind research support.

If there could only be one website on the internet, I would unquestionably keep Biblehub.com and delete the rest. GotQuestions.org and BibleGateway.com are close seconds. On the app side, I'm grateful to the noncommercial creators of TextEdit and OpenOffice, who generously support writers with their open-source software.

And last, Yehoshua ben Yehoseph, the Jesus of history and the Christ of faith. To me, you are one and the same. Have mercy on me, a sinner, and favor on me, a son.

Soli Deo Gloria.

Bibliography

"The greatest part of a writer's time is spent in reading. In order to write, a man will turn over half a library to make one book."

—Samuel Johnson

Writing a book about Jesus is, more often than not, an economically silly thing to do. After all, there are more than one-hundred-thousand biographies about Jesus in English alone, with more than a hundred published since we narrowly avoided triggering Armageddon at midnight on Y2K. That's a lot of competition for shelf space and reader attention. And can any book about Jesus prove more enlightening than the four accounts penned by Matthew, Mark, Luke, and John? Surely not. So why bother? Because Jesus the Christ, of Nazareth in Galilee, continues to prove himself the most interesting man alive.

One can neither list nor recommend everything one reads to write a book on the life of Jesus. Indeed, I have consumed many sad, misguided, heretical, and embarrassingly manipulative books in the making of this one, but I would like to take this space to make a few recommendations for the curious few who wish to dive deeper. I do not agree with everything in every book on this list, as I'm sure most readers will not agree with everything in this one. May the Spirit guide us into all truth.

Jesus and the Eyewitnesses by Richard Bauckham—dense, academic, and wonderfully vital.

What Every Christian Needs to Know About the Jewishness of Jesus by Rabbi Evan Moffic—an excellent introduction to the world of rabbidom.

What Did Jesus Look Like? by Joan E. Taylor—a beautifully produced book that really helped me envision Jesus for the first time.

The Final Days of Jesus by Andreas Köstenberger and Justin Taylor—I had already written my chapter on the Passion Week before discovering this beautiful little book and was pleased to not only see some of my conclusions verified, but several of my mistakes corrected.

The Case for Jesus: The Biblical and Historical Evidence for Christ by Brant Pitre—well worth your time, as is *Jesus Is the Question by* Martin B. Copenhaver.

I had already written much of my material on the House of Annas prior to discovering *The Final Days of Jesus* by Mark D. Smith and was delighted to discover I'm not the only one who realizes this story is a *massively* overlooked piece of biblical history. I hope pastors will join me in reintroducing Annas to their churches, if only to start long-overdue conversations about biblically faithful financial stewardship and far better Christian-Jewish relations. For those who are as fascinated as I am with the role of the mafia family in the murder of Yehoshua, be sure to check out Mark's book, along with the journal article *The Hatred of the House of Annas* by Paul Gaechter.

It goes without saying that subscriptions to *Christianity Today* and *Christian History* should be mandatory reading for every Christian.

But more than any other book, I simply combed the four gospels again and again and again. Unlike the life of Alexander the Great, which relies on texts written three or more centuries after his death, the gospel texts are the collected testimony of eyewitnesses published within one living generation. They are unparalleled in antiquity, and it is incredible what comes to the surface when you reread Mark forty or fifty times while wearing a different lens each time.

As the author of four previously published books and nearly seven hundred articles, I have a very specific writing process: I spend weeks, months, or even years researching a topic, deciding what I want to say, and then outlining my outline's outline. This book did not follow the standard course. Instead of telling Jesus what I wanted him to say, I simply listened to the text to see where it wanted to lead me. I surrendered myself to the Word, and I felt that it took me on an adventure to places I never knew existed. I cannot tell you how many times my eyes widened with surprise or my heart thumped loudly as I discovered something so new and fresh after nearly two decades in the Word. Looking back on it now, I feel as though this book wrote itself. Indeed, if you read the more than one thousand Scripture references contained in these pages, it appears I contributed nothing at all!

Like the legendary Roman concrete of the Pantheon that continues to harden after more than twenty centuries, the case for the gospels grows stronger with each passing decade. We will continue to discover new insights in these old words until the end of humankind, for it really does appear to be a living and breathing book. Another hundred-thousand books will be written about Josh in the centuries to come, and still we will have only just scratched the surface. Mine is not the first word on Jesus, nor will it be the last. He is the author of life, the alpha and omega, the beginning and end, and every bit of *logos* in between. I hope *A God Named Josh* drives you to Scripture and the singular God-man it is about. If it does not, I have failed.

Jared Brock is an award-winning biographer and PBS documentarian. His writing has appeared in *Christianity Today*, *Relevant*, *USA Today*, *Smithsonian*, *The Guardian*, and *TIME*.

www.jaredbrock.com
twitter.com/jaredbrock
facebook.com/jaredAbrock